HABERMAS

An independently minded champion of 'the project of modernity' in a supposedly post-modern age, Jürgen Habermas (1929–) is one of the most widely influential thinkers of our times. *Habermas: The Key Concepts* is an easy-to-use A–Z guide to a body of work that spans philosophy, sociology, politics, law and cultural theory. Explore the writings of Habermas on:

- Capitalism
- Genetics
- Law
- Neo-conservatism
- Universal pragmatics

Fully cross-referenced with extensive suggestions for further reading, this is an essential reference guide to one of the most important social theorists of the contemporary era.

Andrew Edgar is Senior Lecturer in Philosophy at Cardiff University. He is the author of *The Philosophy of Habermas* (Acumen, 2005) and *Cultural Theory: The Key Concepts* (with Peter Sedgwick, Routledge, 1999).

YOU MAY ALSO BE INTERESTED IN THE
FOLLOWING ROUTLEDGE STUDENT
REFERENCE TITLES:

Fifty Key Contemporary Thinkers
John Lechte

Cultural Theory: the Key Thinkers
Andrew Edgar and Peter Sedgwick

Cultural Theory: the Key Concepts
Edited by Andrew Edgar and Peter Sedgwick

Communication, Culture and Media Studies: the Key Concepts
Third Edition
John Hartley

The Routledge Companion to Postmodernism
Second Edition
Edited by Stuart Sim

HABERMAS

The Key Concepts

Andrew Edgar

Routledge
Taylor & Francis Group

LONDON AND NEW YORK

First published 2006
by Routledge
2 Park Square, Milton Park, Abingdon, Oxon OX14 4RN

Simultaneously published in the USA and Canada
by Routledge
270 Madison Avenue, New York, NY 10016

Routledge is an imprint of the Taylor & Francis Group

© 2006 Andrew Edgar

Typeset in Bembo by Taylor & Francis Books Ltd
Printed and bound in Great Britain by TJ International Ltd, Padstow, Cornwall

British Library Cataloguing in Publication Data
A catalogue record for this book is available from the British Library

Library of Congress Cataloging-in-Publication Data
Edgar, Andrew.
  Habermas : the key concepts / Andrew Edgar.
    p. cm.
  Includes bibliographical references and index.
  ISBN 0-415-30378-8 (hardback) – ISBN 0-415-30379-6 (pbk.) 1. Habermas, Jürgen, 2.
Sociology. I. Title.

  HM479.H32E34 2006
  301.092–dc22
                                        2005025529

        ISBN10 0–415–30378–8   ISBN13 9–780–415–30378–1 (hbk)
        ISBN10 0–415–30379–6   ISBN13 9–780–415–30379–8 (pbk)

Taylor & Francis Group is the Academic Division of T&F Informa plc.

For Antonia, and her best friends Katie and Lorna.

CONTENTS

List of Key Concepts	viii
List of names	x
Preface	xiii
Introduction	xiv
KEY CONCEPTS	1
Bibliography	168
Index	179

LIST OF KEY CONCEPTS

action
administrative power
analytic philosophy

capitalism
cognitive interests
colonisation of the lifeworld
communicative action
communicative power
communicative reason
consciousness, philosophy of
crisis
critical theory

decisionism
democracy
differentiation
discourse
discourse ethics
double structure of language

emancipation

formal pragmatics, (*see* universal
   pragmatics)
Frankfurt School

genetic structuralism
genetics

hermeneutics
historical materialism

ideal speech situation
ideology
ideology critique
illocutionary force
instrumental action
instrumental reason
interaction

labour
language
law
legitimation
lifeworld

Marxism
meaning
modernism and
   post-modernism
money

neo-conservatism
non-symbolic steering media

performative contradiction
positivism
post-conventional morality
post-modernism
   (*see* modernism and
   post-modernism)
post-metaphysical thinking
post-structuralism
power

pragmatism
principle of organisation
psychoanalysis
public sphere

rationalisation of the lifeworld
reconstructive science
reification

scientism
social evolution
social integration
speech act
strategic action

subject, philosophy of the
  (see consciousness,
  philosophy of)
system
systematically distorted
  communication
system integration
systems theory

transcendental argument
truth
truthfulness

universal pragmatics

validity claim

LIST OF NAMES

Theodor W. Adorno (1903–69): philosopher, sociologist and musicologist, closely associated with the **Frankfurt School**. Habermas became Adorno's research assistant in 1956.

Karl-Otto Apel (1922–): Habermas's long-time friend and collaborator. Habermas and Apel worked together on the theory of **cognitive interests** and on **discourse ethics**.

J. L. Austin (1911–60): English **analytic philosopher** who first proposed the idea of **speech acts**.

Walter Benjamin (1892–1940): German literary theorist and philosopher, associated with the **Frankfurt School**.

Ernst Bloch (1885–1977): German neo-**Marxist**, and author of *Spirit of Utopia* (1918) and *Principle of Hope* (1959).

Jacques Derrida (1930–2004): French philosopher, and originator of deconstruction. A key target in Habermas's concerns over **post-structuralism**.

Emile Durkheim (1858–1917): founding figure in French sociology, and contributor to the functionalist tradition. Author of *The Division of Labour in Society* (1893) and *The Elements of the Religious Life* (1912).

Michel Foucault (1926–84): French historian and philosopher, closely associated with **post-structuralism**.

Hans-Georg Gadamer (1900–2002): German **hermeneutician**. Author of *Truth and Method* (1960) with whom Habermas debated the status of hermeneutics as a science in the late 1960s.

G. W. F. Hegel (1770–1831): philosopher and key figure in the development of German Idealism. A significant influence on **Marx**, on the **Frankfurt School** and the young Habermas.

Martin Heidegger (1889–1976): German philosopher and author of *Time and Being* (1927). Both were an influence on the young Habermas, and a major target of criticism.

Edmund Husserl (1859–1938): German founder of the phenomenological approach in philosophy. Coined the term **lifeworld**.

Max Horkheimer (1895–1973): neo-**Marxist** philosopher, and long-term director of the research institute that was the institutional basis of the **Frankfurt School**.

Immanuel Kant (1724–1802): German philosopher, author of the *Critique of Pure Reason* (1781). The most influential philosopher of the modern period. Habermas draws extensively on Kant's **transcendental** approach to philosophy in his earlier work, and in his **discourse ethics**.

Lawrence Kohlberg (1927–87): psychologist and theorist of the development of the ability to make moral decisions in human being. A significant source for Habermas's theories of personal development and **social evolution**.

Niklaus Luhmann (1927–98): leading German social theorist who developed a complex **systems theory** approach to sociology. Habermas and Luhmann sustained a debate on the status of systems theory in sociology from the 1970s until Luhmann's death.

Jean-François Lyotard (1924–98): French philosopher, closely associated with **post-modernism**.

Karl Marx (1818–83): German philosopher and social theorist, whose works form the basis of various schools of **Marxist** philosophy and sociology.

Talcott Parsons (1902–79): American social theorist, responsible for developing functionalism and **systems theory**. Habermas draws on his work extensively in *The Theory of Communicative Action*.

Jean Piaget (1896–1980): cognitive psychologist, who developed a **genetic structuralist** theory of the development of human cognitive abilities. A significant source for Habermas's theories of personal development and **social evolution**.

Charles Sanders Peirce (1839–1914): American philosopher, responsible for the early development of **pragmatism**.

John Rawls (1921–2002): American political philosopher and leading defender of liberalism. Author of *A Theory of Justice* (1972). In the 1990s, Habermas entered into dialogue with Rawls over the nature of a liberal society.

Richard Rorty (1931–): American philosopher and proponent of neo-**pragmatism**.

Alfred Schutz (1899–1959): Austrian-born social theorist, whose work introduced the concept of the **lifeworld** into sociology.

John Searle (1932–): American **analytic philosopher** of language, who significantly developed Austin's theory of **speech acts**.

Max Weber (1864–1920): founding figure in the development of German sociology. Author of *The Protestant Ethic and the Spirit of Capitalism* (1904–5). His theory of rationalisation is a major influence on Habermas's mature work.

Ludwig Wittgenstein (1889–1951): Austrian-born **analytic philosopher** of language. His later work is particularly influential on Habermas's theory of **communicative action**.

PREFACE

My intention has been to offer a series of short essays that will help to introduce some of the most important ideas and theories of Jürgen Habermas. I have aimed to make each entry as self-contained as possible, at the cost of a certain repetition between entries. However, where I review an idea repeatedly, I have tried to approach it in a slightly different manner on each occasion and to offer different illustrations. As entries cannot be wholly self-contained, I have cross-referenced entries by using bold type, where appropriate and typically on the first occurrence of a key term in the entry.

In writing this book I have inevitably incurred a series of debts. First, my thanks to the staff at Routledge for their encouragement, patience and occasional hard prod, and especially to Andrea Hartill and David Avital. My colleagues at Cardiff have all continued to provide a stimulating intellectual atmosphere and working environment, but special thanks must go to Chris Norris for relieving me of some of my teaching at a crucial stage in the completion of the manuscript. Finally, my biggest debt, as ever, is to my family. Without their love and support, even if they didn't know I was writing the book, it would never have been finished.

INTRODUCTION

Jürgen Habermas was born in 1929, near Dusseldorf in Germany. He grew up during the Nazi period, and he describes the events linked to the end of the war, and not least the trial of the Nazi leaders for war crimes, as fundamental to shaping his political views (Habermas 1992a: 77). He was educated at Gottingen and Bonn, before becoming in 1956 the research assistant of Theodor Adorno at the University of Frankfurt. This established Habermas's link to the **Frankfurt School** and his place in the latest stages of the development of neo-**Marxism**. His subsequent career has taken him to various German and American universities, ultimately returning to Frankfurt, where he is now professor emeritus.

He has become without doubt the most influential and widely cited German philosopher and social theorist of his generation. In an intellectual environment dominated by **post-modernists**, his work has remained independent, if controversial, as a defence of what he calls the 'project of modernity', and thus the Enlightenment pursuit of **truth** and justice, in service of the goal of political **emancipation** (1983b; 1988a). Apart from offering a grand social theory that is grounded in a re-reading and integration of the German, French and American traditions of sociology (1984a; 1987), his prolific output covers the philosophy of **language** (1970a; 1970b; 1979a; 1999a), cognitive and developmental psychology (1979a: 69–94), Marxist accounts of the state and history (1976b; 1979a: 95–129), ethics (1990; 1993a) and **law** (1996), as well as including a continuing stream of commentaries on the contemporary political developments in Europe and Germany (1981a; 1989b). Most recently he has entered into debates on the supposed 'war on terrorism' (Borradori 2003), and the moral problems of **genetics** (Habermas 2003b). Throughout his career his work has been characterised by a willingness to engage with his critics, and frequently to modify or even radically change his positions in the light of their comments.

The first of Habermas's writings to come to the attention of the English reading public concerned his attempt to provide an account of an emancipatory social science (or **critical theory**) that is grounded in accounts of **labour**, communication (or **interaction**) and **power** as the three sources of human action and knowledge (1971a). Labour leads to natural science and technology; communication leads to the **hermeneutic** disciplines of history and the cultural and social sciences; and political power raises issues of the emancipation of humanity from oppression. This work was accompanied by a series of essays on education, and on the increasingly technocratic nature of modern society (1971b), which began to articulate Habermas's concerns over the misuse of **positivist**, or natural scientific, models in the social sciences and crucially in social policy (1976c; 1976d).

In the 1970s and 1980s, Habermas began to develop the theory of **communicative action** and **universal** (or **formal**) **pragmatics** that is now the basis of all his theorising. Humans are presented as fundamentally communicative beings. Habermas analyses the way in which ordinary people use their communicative skills to create and maintain social relationships. He suggests that in making any utterances (be they statements, questions, accusations or whatever), the speaker raises four **validity claims** – that is to say that there are four levels at which the speaker can be challenged by any listener. First, the speaker can be challenged as to the **meaningfulness** of what he or she says. Second, the **truth** of the utterance can be questioned. Any utterance will assume certain facts about the world, and these assumptions may be mistaken. Third, the speaker's right to say what he or she says (or to speak at all) may be challenged (for example, one may question a person's authority to make a particular assertion, or his or her right to make a request or issue an order). Finally, the sincerity of the speaker may be questioned (so that the speaker may be accused of lying, being ironic or teasing, for example). From this model, Habermas suggests that, as underpinning actual conversations and discussions, there is the presupposition of an **ideal speech situation**, in which every participant in a conversation is free to challenge what is said by any other speaker. In practice, real conversation falls short of this ideal (and is thus **systematically distorted**, not least by the differentials of power between conversationalists (1970a)). Habermas subsequently drops or at least heavily modifies this terminology and some of the theoretical assumptions that it presupposes.

A lasting consequence of this model of communication is the development of a **discourse ethics**. If any utterance can be challenged,

INTRODUCTION

then ethics must focus on the processes that people use to justify what they are doing, through challenges and rational responses, of underlying moral values and principles. This crucially entails that all competent language users should be free to enter the debate. Exclusion, for whatever reason, is a mark of injustice.

The English translation of Habermas's *The Theory of Communicative Action* between 1984 and 1987 spurred new interest in his earliest work (from the 1960s) on the **'public sphere'** (1989a) which, oddly, had not been translated previously. The public sphere is the realm of social life in which public opinion is formed. It emerges, historically, amongst the eighteenth-century bourgeoisie, not least in the development of journals and a free press. The public sphere thus aspires to form a general will and thus inform and control the activities of the state. Conflict is ideally resolved through open and free communication.

Communicative rationality, for Habermas, is therefore this process of problem solving and conflict resolution through open discussion. In contemporary society, this rationality is threatened. In order to analyse this threat, Habermas distinguishes between **lifeworld** and **system**, as two complementary accounts of social existence. The lifeworld is the social world as it is constructed and maintained through the taken-for-granted social skills and stocks of knowledge of its members. The lifeworld is therefore maintained through ordinary people communicating with each other, and thereby establishing a shared understanding of the world as meaningful place. Other people's actions can be responded to because they make sense – they are part of the process of communication. The lifeworld carries the traditions of the community and is the source of individual socialisation. In contrast, 'system' refers to society when it confronts the individual as a meaningless, seemingly natural force. Social systems are governed by **instrumental rationality** (not communicative rationality). The rules of social systems are determined by the need for efficiency in realising given objectives. For Habermas, the most important social systems are those that distribute power and **money** about the society. The workings of such systems still depend upon the social skills of individual agents (derived from the lifeworld), and the relationship between lifeworld and system can be beneficial. The rationality of systems thinking can be used to question and revise the taken-for-granted practices of the lifeworld (and indeed, the difference between a modern society and a traditional one is that this rational self-reflection is part of modern life). However, the system can also **'colonise'** the lifeworld. In colonisation, the rules of the system displace communicative rationality, so that social agents can no longer question (or even understand) the rules that govern their actions.

In his most recent work, Habermas has turned to the problem of law. While the law has been a concern that has run throughout his work, *Between Facts and Norms* (1994) presented a sustained and systematic attempt to explain the place of law in modern society, and to generate a critical model that would again facilitate practical intervention in social life. In effect, his study of law can be seen as the application of the theory of communicative action.

Further reading: McCarthy 1978; Held 1980; Thompson and Held 1982; Bernstein 1985: White 1988; Outhwaite 1994; Wiggershaus 1994; White 1995; Dews 1998; Passerin d'Entréves and Benhabib 1996; Edgar 2005; Finlayson 2005

HABERMAS

The Key Concepts

ACTION

The intentional and meaningful activity of a person. Habermas, following the sociologist Max Weber, distinguishes 'action' from 'behaviour' (Habermas 2001c: 4–6). Behaviour is the involuntary or causally determined activity of the person, such as a reflex response to an external stimulus (for example, flinching) or the on-going processes of the body (for example, heartbeat), as opposed to the activities that the person intends to perform, and that will have some **meaning** for them and the people around them. Weber gives the example of a bicycle accident. The accident itself is unintentional, and therefore mere behaviour. The responses to the accident, such as accusations of carelessness, apologies, threats and so on, are action (Habermas 1984a: 279). It is action (and not behaviour) that sociology studies. Hence, Habermas's understanding of action is better encapsulated in the phrase 'social action'. Precisely because action is meaningful, it presupposes that the person who performs the action is a social being typically in so far as they will share a language with other people, and in addition that most actions are carried out in response to other persons. Habermas therefore offers a typology of different social actions, including most importantly the distinction between **communicative** and **strategic action** (Habermas 1979a: 208–10).

ADMINISTRATIVE POWER

The power of the state to enact and enforce law. 'Administrative power' is a concept introduced by Habermas in his more recent work on **law**, in order to explore the relationship between public opinion (which he calls **communicative power**) and the formulation and enactment of laws by the state (Habermas 1996: 463–90). Administrative power encapsulates the real controlling force that the actions of the state, in the creation and enforcement of laws, as well as in the promulgation of specific social, welfare and other government policies, will have upon the lives and actions of its citizens. Habermas's concern is that the administrative structures of state tend to run according to their own intrinsic momentum. Within the state administration, the law is treated instrumentally, which is to say that the law is regarded as a means to the realisation of ends that are strictly external to law itself. Legal theory focuses upon the most consistent formulation and effective enforcement of the law, while the values and ends that it is supposed to protect are taken for granted. In summary, decisions and innovations in the law are made primarily so as to be consistent with the existing structure of the law. This focus on internal consistency tends to inhibit any capacity to acknowledge the real values and opinions of ordinary citizens, and thus to meet people's real needs. In Habermas's technical terminology, the state is a **system** (and **power** is the **non-symbolic medium** through which it is guided and organised). As such, it is at odds with the **lifeworld** through which ordinary people give meaning to their world and formulate their opinions and values. In his later writings on law Habermas sets himself the task of exploring how social institutions in the lifeworld can be reformed, in order to impose pressure upon the administrative and legal systems, and thus to transform the public opinion that is formulated within the lifeworld into a communicative power that will influence the administrative power of the state. In a just society, the administrative power of the state will thus be grounded in the opinions, values and interests of citizens who are subject to administrative power.

ANALYTIC PHILOSOPHY

The approach to philosophy favoured in English-speaking countries. While it may be broadly characterised by a dominant interest in logic and **language**, it is perhaps more clearly characterised in terms of its contrast to what is known as Continental philosophy (that is, the philosophical schools that have been dominant in France, Germany and Italy in the twentieth century). Indeed, it is here that analytic philosophy's significance lies for Habermas's work. Habermas was educated very much in the traditions of German – and thus Continental – philosophy, and in particular in the work of Martin Heidegger and subsequently the neo-**Marxism** of the **Frankfurt School** (see Habermas 1992a). Habermas might then have been expected to remain within this tradition. His openness to ideas and approaches from analytic philosophy, alongside his willingness to combine the analytic and Continental traditions, became a hallmark of his thinking.

In terms of their development, the analytic and Continental traditions split after Immanuel Kant, which is to say that both traditions draw significantly on Kant and his predecessors, such as Descartes, the British empiricists (Locke, Hume and Berkeley) and the rationalists (Leibniz and Spinoza). Within Germany, the immediate response to

Kant was provided by Idealists, such as Fichte, Schelling, Hegel and the young Hegelians, who understood philosophy as a pursuit of absolute truth (see Habermas 1971a: 1–63, and 1988a: 1–82). While German Idealism, and especially Hegel, had an influence on English-language philosophy in the nineteenth century, and indeed into the twentieth century (with philosophers such as F. H. Bradley and R. G. Collingwood), analytic philosophy may in large part be characterised by its opposition to Hegel. Grand projects that strove to uncover absolute truth through pure thought are dismissed as more or less nonsensical metaphysics (see **post-metaphysical thinking**). In part this may be seen as a recognition of the role that the natural sciences had come to play, with increasing importance, in generating reliable knowledge. The analytic philosopher therefore seeks to restrict the aspirations of philosophy. Its task becomes one of analysing the foundations of scientific method, logic and mathematics, and the nature of language. The first great analytic philosopher is Gottlob Frege (1848–1925), and his investigations into the nature of meaning become paradigm examples of the approach of analytic philosophy. The early work of Bertrand Russell (1872–1970) on mathematics, language and logic becomes an archetype of analytic discipline, relying as it does on an analytical and logical rigour derived from Leibniz and a recognition of the importance of empirical evidence and experience derived from the British empiricists.

Habermas's engagement with **positivism** may be seen as an early attempt to establish a dialogue between the Continental and analytic traditions (Habermas 1976c and 1976d). The key issue in the so-called 'positivist dispute' was the applicability of the positivist understanding of natural science to the social sciences. While Habermas was opposed to positivist interpretations of social science, he was more sympathetic than many of the older generation of German philosophers (such as Herbert Marcuse). Positivism, or at least its more pure analytic version, logical positivism, was a product of the early years of the twentieth century. It is, however, the analytic philosophers who come to prominence after the second world war who are most relevant to Habermas. In particular, the work of such people as the later Wittgenstein and J. L. Austin on the philosophy of language is all important. This work brings about a transformation (a 'linguistic-turn') in analytic philosophy, as the fundamental importance of everyday language in constituting our understanding of the world and ourselves is recognised. It is to this philosophy that Habermas turns in order to remedy the weaknesses he sees in both Continental philosophy and social theory (Habermas 1988b: 117–43).

Crucially it is Austin's theory of **speech acts** (and its later development by John Searle) that is fundamental to Habermas's **universal pragmatics**. In the theory of speech acts, Austin recognises that language is not just or even primarily used to convey information. This had been an assumption of earlier analytic philosophers like Frege and Russell. Austin argues that we use language to perform actions. By uttering the appropriate words in the appropriate situation I can give orders or make promises, I can baptise infants and marry couples. Such a philosophy of language has important implications for social theory, for it suggests the role that language use might play in creating and maintaining social relationships.

In his mature work, Habermas refers as readily to a range of analytic philosophers, such as Strawson, Grice and Davidson, as he does to Continental philosophers. Most recently he has perhaps consolidated this fusion of analytic and Continental traditions through his engagement with the work of the American philosopher Robert Brandom (Habermas 2003a: 131–73).

Further reading: Martinich and Sosa 2001

CAPITALISM

A form of society, characterised typically by industrialisation and crucially by the use of market exchange to organise the distribution of goods and services. It is thus the form taken by contemporary first-world nations, and the economic form that is today globally dominant. A fundamental concern that runs throughout Habermas's work, from the 1950s to the present, is the generation of an adequate account of contemporary capitalism.

In an early essay, 'Between Philosophy and Science: Marxism as Critique', Habermas identifies four key features of contemporary capitalism (1976a: 195–8). In the twentieth century the role of the state has expanded through its intervention in the economy, and in its provision of social welfare; while there is still economic inequality, a relatively high standard of living is enjoyed by the majority of the population, and not just by the dominant classes; the revolutionary politics of the nineteenth century has been largely replaced by party politics due to the expansion of democracy and the right to vote, so that there is no longer a clearly identifiable revolutionary class; capitalism's understanding of itself, especially in the post-war period, is one that is generated largely through its opposition to other political systems, and in particular to Soviet-style Communism. In sum, contemporary capitalism is more stable than nineteenth-century capitalism. A managed economy no longer suffers the catastrophic lurches between boom and bust that characterised the nineteenth-century free market, and the relative material affluence of the majority of the population secures their continued commitment to the capitalist system.

Habermas explored the social history of capitalism in one of his first books, *The Structural Transformation of the Public Sphere* (1989a), at least in terms of the development of political debate and the formation of political ideologies. In the mid-1960s his primary concern was with the role that science and technology play in contemporary capitalism, not merely in driving its economic expansion, but also in so far as models of natural scientific and technological thinking shape social planning, and begin to invade the everyday social activities and exchanges of ordinary people (see **scientism**) (1971b). *Legitimation Crisis* (1976b) is the first book-length study in which Habermas attempts to build a comprehensive model of contemporary capitalism. Here he moves away from the broadly neo-**Marxist** grounding of his early work, in order to use Niklaus Luhmann's **systems theory** as a key resource in making sense of, and criticising, capitalism. On one level, the study proceeds by treating capitalism as a social **system**, composed of four sub-systems: the economy; the administrative system of the state, that has the task of organising and stabilising the society as a whole; and the **legitimation** and cultural systems which, through educational and cultural institutions, generate meanings and values for members of the society. While Marxist models of society tended to see economic **crises** (such as loss of productivity or profitability, or mass unemployment) as having a direct and immediately destabilising impact upon the rest of society, Habermas's argument is that, in contemporary capitalism, a crisis within one sub-system can be at least partially absorbed by other sub-systems. Thus, for example, an economic crisis can now be prevented through the state's direct intervention in the economy, as both a producer and a consumer of goods and services. However, the state in turn requires support from the citizenry, which is to say that it requires legitimation. A failing economy may then still serve to undermine that support. The legitimation system therefore has, for Habermas, the increasingly difficult task of motivating citizens to support the state, and to give meaning to their lives. The reason that this task of legitimation is becoming increasingly difficult, Habermas believes, is that better-educated and thus better-informed and more sophisticated citizens will require rational justifications for the state's and the economy's actions, and will not be easily bought off with more material wealth, let alone mere political propaganda or rhetoric. The continuing history of youthful and popular protests against capitalism, from the students' movement of 1968, through ecological and nuclear disarmament protests in the 1970s and 1980s, to the mass protests at G8 summits and the anti-Gulf War protests in the 1990s and in the first decade of the new century, alongside a gradual decline in the proportion of the European population voting, and widespread public apathy and cynicism about organised politics, all bear witness to Habermas's point.

Thus, while he abandoned something of the simpler Marxist models of capitalism, Habermas continued to see capitalism as a social formation that is ridden by crises, and as being unstable in the long term. The very improvements that it offers to people's lives, in terms of better education, greater political emancipation and long-term material security, may provide the grounds for a widespread questioning of the values of capitalism and the continuing political and material inequalities that it sustains.

Habermas builds upon this analysis in *The Theory of Communicative Action* (Habermas 1984a and 1987). While *Legitimation Crisis* began to explore the relationship between what Habermas calls the **system** and the **lifeworld**, which is to say between society experienced as a meaningless, almost natural force that constrains and directs the individual's actions, and society as a meaningful cultural realm, Habermas was ultimately unhappy with the analysis given. *The Theory of Communicative Action* makes the relationship between system and lifeworld central to its analysis and criticism of contemporary capitalism. Habermas borrows and develops two themes from the sociologist Max Weber: loss of meaning, and loss of freedom.

He is thus arguing, first, as he had done in *Legitimation Crisis*, that contemporary capitalism struggles to provide the cultural resources through which life in capitalism could be made meaningful and worthwhile. Here Habermas develops Weber's notion of the 'disenchantment' brought about by the increasing instrumental rationality of contemporary capitalism. Weber was arguing that the rational organisation of capitalism drains the meaning (and, translated literally, the magic) from social life (Weber 1946a: 148). Put in terms of system and lifeworld, it is the argument that the economic and especially the administrative systems, that work instrumentally and at best inhibit and at worst actively discourage the discussion of values, intrude into the organisation of our everyday lives, draining out of them the meaning that the lifeworld should provide. Thus for example, as a teacher, I must increasingly relate to my students as fee-paying and state-sponsored clients. The economic and administrative imperatives placed on a university mean that I have less time to spend with my students, but more precisely described goals and targets that I must fulfil in relationship to them. Thus, I increasingly cease to treat them as people with whom I can debate issues of philosophy and social theory. We cease to have time to explore the meaning of what it is to do philosophy. Instead, I treat them more instrumentally, to be manipulated and spoon-fed, in order to ensure that pre-given and unquestionable goals and targets are met. So, Habermas's contention is that in more and more of our social interaction we respond to each other instrumentally, anticipating each other's reactions and attempting to manipulate or exploit each other's behaviour as we would predict and manipulate the behaviour of a drinks vending machine. This is, at least in part, what Habermas has in mind by his notion of the **colonisation of the lifeworld**.

If this is the heart of the loss of meaning, then the loss of freedom is developed by Habermas from Weber's notion of the 'iron cage of bureaucracy' (Weber 1976: 181), or more graphically from Franz Kafka's images of modern life in *The Castle* or *The Trial*. Social systems, such as the administrative systems of government or commercial enterprises, develop, not necessarily in terms of the needs of their clients, but rather in terms of their own inherent logic. They thus come to confront the ordinary member of society as social forces that cannot be challenged, and that increasingly constrain their behaviour within certain, rigidly defined channels. For example, in order to apply for social security, and even in order to apply for a job, I must present myself in a certain way. This is not just a matter of dressing properly or having an appropriate accent; I must also have a national insurance number (and thus already be recognised within the state's administration), perhaps a formal record of my previous employment, income and social security payments.

While Habermas does then identify a series of pathologies that characterise contemporary society, including the failure of the culture system to generate sufficient meaning, the loss of guiding norms or values in society, and the problems at the level of individual psychology and personal development (Habermas 1987, p. 143), he does not paint as bleak a picture of contemporary capitalism as did the **Frankfurt School** thinker Theodor Adorno, who spoke of a 'totally administered society'. Habermas refuses to accept that the capacity of ordinary people to debate and challenge can be wholly suppressed, and so he does continue to look for an emerging sources critical potential, and suggests that it may be found in the green movement and the identity politics of feminists, people of colour, and gay and lesbian groups (Habermas 1987: 391–6). In his most recent work in legal theory, he takes this further, by exploring the critical potential that exists in the formulation and application of **laws** in constitutional democracies.

COGNITIVE INTERESTS

These are the preconditions that make knowledge possible. Cognitive (or knowledge-constitutive) interests are the conditions for survival of the human species that stimulate human beings to generate knowledge about the physical world, about the social world and about the exercise of political power. In order to flourish, it is in the interest of human beings to be able to control and reshape their physical environment, to communicate with each other and thereby to maintain society, and to live free of political oppression. In the pursuit of each of these interests, humans will inquire into, and thus generate knowledge about, the natural world, society and politics. This knowledge will in turn be linked to certain forms of action: the use of technology to control nature; improved communication and understanding; and political **emancipation** of the oppressed. The three interests thus serve to make possible and to shape the natural sciences, the social sciences and the emancipatory politics of **critical theory**.

Habermas formulated his theory of cognitive interests in the 1960s, and this represented his major contribution to the philosophy of science and the theory of knowledge (or epistemology) in that period. The theory is introduced in Habermas's inaugural address at Frankfurt University (1971a: 301–49), and given its fullest exposition in *Knowledge and Human Interests* (1971a). Self-critical comments on the theory are offered in the 'Postscript' to *Knowledge and Human Interests* (1971a: 351–86), the 'Introduction' to *Theory and Practice* (1976a: 1–40), and in one of his substantial responses to his critics (1982).

Habermas's argument is important because it challenges a presupposition that was widespread in many schools of philosophy in the first half of the twentieth century: that for a knowledge claim to be sound it had to be 'pure' in some sense, untainted by biases. At one level this is perfectly acceptable. A Nazi eugenic 'science', motivated by anti-Semitism and a belief in the superiority of the Aryan race, will not produce sound knowledge. The **positivists** thus argued that science should be cleansed of 'the sewage of emotionality' (Habermas 1976a: 265) and all contaminating value-orientations (such as anti-Semitism). For many philosophers of science, their task is then to articulate the rules or methods that good scientific inquiry should follow, on the assumption that such rules would serve to exclude all that contaminating sewage. Habermas is none the less sceptical about the idea of 'pure' knowledge, or 'pure' theory. While happy to reject any appeal to particular interests (such as the interest in the victory of the Aryan race), in the theory of cognitive interests he looks for what can be called 'anthropologically deep-seated' interests, which is to say interests that are common to all humans, simply by virtue of their being human. Habermas's point, then, is that there is no such thing as absolutely 'pure' knowledge. What we regard as knowledge is not some perfect, untainted vision of how the world is, but rather a response to that world that is shaped by what we, as human beings, need to know and are capable of understanding. So, there can only be knowledge that is relevant to humans and that humans will find important and be motivated to pursue.

Habermas's inspiration here is the eighteenth-century German philosopher Immanuel Kant. Kant's **transcendental** approach to questions of knowledge asked after the conditions that must be in place in order for us to have knowledge – what is it that makes it possible for a human being to have knowledge of the world? Kant's answer appealed to the way in which the human mind processes the experiences that it receives from the senses. Habermas's more histor-ical (or 'quasi-transcendental') approach looks to the development of human beings as a biological and cultural species. That is to say that, in proposing his three cognitive interests, Habermas is suggesting that these are the three pre-conditions that have made humans beings capable of surviving, flourishing and developing, meeting both their physical and cultural needs as their civilisations become more com-plex and productive. If human beings had not been able to formulate knowledge in terms of the three interests, then they would have at best stagnated in a culturally undeveloped state or at worst would have become extinct (either because they could not meet their material needs by controlling the natural environment, or could not have sufficiently organised their social lives to overcome conflict and coordinate large-scale collective activities). Let us look at the three interests in turn.

The purposive-technological interest in the control and manipula-tion of the physical environment is the basis of the natural sciences. It is itself grounded in the human being's ability to **labour**. Here Habermas identifies Karl Marx as one of two thinkers who began to recognise this cognitive interest, precisely because Marx made labour the core characteristic of human beings – their ability to transform their environment, guided not by natural instinct, like a bee or a beaver, but rather by reflection and planning. Thus Marx could comment that the worst of architects is better than the best of bees, for however shabby or ugly the architect's building may be, it was built in the architect's mind first (Marx 1976: 284). The architect thought about it, and it could have been different. Here, then, we begin to see the relationship between labour and knowledge. As humans labour, transforming their environment, they are not simply putting plans into action, but also beginning to recognise weaknesses in those plans, and thus perhaps what needs to be known in order to realise better plans. They learn by transforming the environment. But Marx is just the first thinker to whom Habermas appeals. It is the second thinker who makes the link clearer still, and that thinker is the American **pragmatist** Charles Sanders Peirce. Peirce recognises that knowledge in the natural sciences develops only through the practical engagement of the scientist with the real world. Scientists do experiments, and if the experiment does not turn out as expected, then they must rethink their theory. Technologists put the ideas of scientists into practice in making tools, houses, cathedrals, steam engines, nuclear power stations and whatever else. Again, it is only in this application of science, transforming the environment, that science will develop. If the cathedral falls down, one learns something about the distribution of loads in a building; if the nuclear power station contaminates the immediate environment, one learns much about the dangers of radiation. Frequently, but not always, one learns the hard way that one's knowledge is not yet adequate. Peirce is making one more important point. Natural science is not an activity that is wholly separate from the practices of ordinary lay people. Rather, it has its roots in the practices of farmers, carpenters and car mechanics, and in the practice of anyone who solves an everyday practical problem (mending a bicycle puncture, sewing up a torn item of clothing). The natural sciences are thus a refined and disciplined version of the everyday capacity that humans have to labour.

Whereas this is all very well for the natural sciences, Habermas argues that the social sciences have a quite different grounding, and this is in the cognitive interest in communication. Here, what matters is not the human ability to labour, but rather the human ability to use **language**. Habermas turns here to historians and hermeneuticians for guidance. **Hermeneutics** is the study of meanings – the science of interpretation. As such, hermeneuticians are interested in the way in which meaning is contained, not just in texts, such as books and manuscripts (although this was their original concern) but also in objects (such as houses, temples, works of art) and indeed in social actions, and in the way in which those meanings may be recovered. Historians are thus hermeneuticians, whether they realise it or not, precisely in so far as they are attempting to make sense of the texts, objects and actions that past generations have left to us. The methods of the natural sciences will be of no use to them. Not only is history unrepeatable, so that there can be nothing like a laboratory experiment (the Battle of Waterloo cannot be re-run without the German troops arriving to help out Wellington, in order to see if Napoleon would have re-conquered Europe), but historical and social events are also quite different sorts of object than those studied by the natural sciences. Natural scientists presuppose that they are studying objects that exist independently of them as observers, and that are subject to regular causal laws. The natural scientist does not ask what an atom means, what motivation it might have or why it is there. He or she simply looks at the causal relationships in which it is involved (and so what caused it, and what it might cause). In contrast, the historian or hermeneutician studies an object that acts, not because it is causally determined, but because there is some meaning in its action. If a historian asks about Caesar's crossing of the Rubicon, she does not ask what caused Caesar to act, but rather what did he think that he would achieve, and how did his contemporaries understand and evaluate that act. Taking this question a little further, in order to understand Caesar's actions it is necessary to understand how he makes sense of the (cultural) world around him.

We must go further still. The object of study in history is not something wholly separate from the historian, for, like the historian, the object of study is another human being. Social or hermeneutic scientists, including historians, sociologists and cultural anthropologists, are thus involved in processes of communication with the people and societies that they study. Imagine that you are talking to a stranger. Perhaps one of the problems that you have to overcome, before you can really start talking to each other, is to make sense of each other's preconceptions about the world, about what is going on and why you are meeting. This will get the danger of various misunderstandings and confusions out of the way. In effect, the historian is doing something similar. The historian asks what Caesar's preconceptions are – what he takes for granted, and what he thinks he is trying to achieve. Like the natural scientist, the historian is then using his or her mundane social abilities, although here it is an everyday ability to communicate and to use language that is important as opposed to technical skills, but again this ability may be heightened and refined by academic discipline. When the social scientist attempts to understand a geographically or historically distant culture, or even problematic groups within their own society, they are doing something that is grounded in their ability not merely to communicate with others, but crucially also to repair broken down communication – such as misunderstandings and conflicts – within their own culture.

This gives us two types of science: a natural science grounded in our ability to labour, and a social or cultural science grounded in our ability to use language. For Habermas it is important that these two are not confused, and much of the point of his argument in *Knowledge and Human Interests* is to attack positivist claims that all scientific inquiry should be based upon the model of the natural sciences (see **scientism**). Such an approach is not only mistaken as a theory of science, it is also politically dangerous, as it reduces human beings to objects that can be manipulated like molecules or light waves. It encourages social engineering, as opposed to a democratic politics that recognises the importance of public agreement and understanding of government policies.

The two sciences are not the end of the story. The third cognitive interest, in emancipation, is slightly more problematic. It might be argued that the first two interests actually exhaust the possible forms that science can take. There are natural sciences and there are social sciences, and that is it. None the less, Habermas suggests that there is a third form of science, one that responds to a particular and historical feature of the social world – that all known societies have been characterised by political inequalities and oppression. This observation in itself would not seem to be sufficient to give rise to a third form of science. The exercise of power can presumably be dealt with by the social sciences. Upon observing an exercise of power, from the threats of the school bully, through the charge of the riot police, to the decisions of the board of a multi-national company, the hermeneutician can inquire why these people act as they do: how can they understand the world in such a way that they see their own actions to be acceptable?

Habermas now makes a bold move, albeit one that has its origins in the Marxist theory of **ideology**. He suggests that the exercise of power may often be such that its victims (and at times even its beneficiaries) are unaware of it. Further, if the exercise of power is invisible to the participants, then it will also be invisible to the hermeneutician. So, if this mysterious form of power exists, then it will indeed require a different form of social science to identify and expose it. Habermas may begin to justify these claims first by noting that a group does not typically manage to exercise control over another through the mere threat of violence (as might the bully and even the riot police). Rather, the group exercises power because it is perceived to have some right to do so. Its power is **legitimate**. The company board may thus decide to make a thousand employees redundant because the company has a legally acceptable contract with the employees that gives it that right. In all these cases the exercise of power is quite overt, and would pose no problems for a hermeneutician.

Nevertheless, we may next be asked to imagine a culture in which everyone believes that there are two types of people in the world. One group is composed of those who are naturally free, the other group is composed of natural slaves. (The Greek philosopher Aristotle argued something along these lines.) Conversely, we might imagine a culture that teaches that one group is naturally stronger and more intelligent than another, and indeed if the weaker group wasted its energies on educating itself excessively, or even working excessively, then it would damage its reproductive powers. (Here we have something of nineteenth-century beliefs about the natural inferiority of women.) The hermeneutician may still argue that they are able to penetrate these mistaken cultural beliefs. Habermas's reply, however, is two-fold. On the one hand, he might acknowledge that the hermeneutician could identify such beliefs in the past, but might still ask whether or not they could tell that they are not themselves infected by a contemporary version of such beliefs. Might contemporary social and cultural scientists be labouring under misapprehensions similar to those of the ancient Greeks or the Victorians? On the other hand, Habermas can point to the significant role that the appeal to nature plays in both these examples. The misapprehensions work by making cultural phenomena appear to be natural. If something is natural, then it cannot be changed, and there is no point in debating it or in imagining the world to be different.

It follows from these arguments that the purpose of an emancipatory science is to free humanity from such misapprehensions – which is to say to free it from self-imposed illusions, that serve to hamper its autonomy. Habermas finds two models of such an emancipatory science. One is **psychoanalysis**. The psychoanalyst treats neurotic symptoms that superficially appear to be natural, such as paralyses, physical pains, or blackouts. The analysis is successful if it traces these symptoms back, not to physical causes (as might a medicine that is grounded in the technological cognitive interest), but to traumatic and yet none the less meaningful events in the patient's history. The patient will have repressed the memory of the events, because he or she cannot cope with it consciously, only for their unconscious self to have expressed this memory in the neurotic symptoms. Thus, the analyst is finding meaning in a seemingly natural event. The other source of inspiration for Habermas, as already noted, is Marx's notion of **ideology critique**. The argument here is that the belief systems of class-divided societies work in such a way as to conceal inequalities, and to place them beyond meaningful discussion and challenge.

To illustrate something of this notion of ideology critique, it may be noted that this is precisely where the political danger of the positivist confusion of natural science and social science lies. If the social world is approached as a natural object, and is assumed to be such that it can be causally manipulated, and indeed if all alternatives to natural science (such as hermeneutics and psychoanalysis) are dismissed as nonsense, then the democratic emancipation of society may be inhibited. For example, if it is assumed that the market is a natural phenomenon, one would be unable to suggest that markets could be abandoned and fairer ways could be found to organise production and distribution. Such a suggestion would be as nonsensical as that of doing away with gravity.

The task of ideology critique is therefore to expose the real meaning – in terms of the political interests being served – that is concealed by the apparently meaningless or inevitable ideological appearance of society, just as the task of the psychoanalyst is to expose the meaningful but traumatic experience that is being concealed by the apparently natural symptoms of the patient. The emancipatory sciences may therefore be understood as a necessary fusion of the natural and hermeneutic sciences. If power is typically exercised under the veil of a 'second nature', then it will remain invisible to both natural scientists and hermeneuticians. The natural scientists will take the veil for granted, and the hermeneuticians will lack the critical resources necessary to go beyond the taken-for-granted meanings that human beings recognise on an everyday level. Only an emancipatory science that is sensitive to the limitations and failures of communication and language use, and that is prepared to suggest that such failures are not due to mere accidents or incompetence on the part of the language users, but are rather rooted in inequality and oppression, will have the resources necessary to expose illegitimate exercises of power.

Further reading: Ahlers 1970; Huch 1970; Wellmer 1970; Dallmayr 1972a, 1972b; Giddens 1982; Ottmann 1982; Honneth 1991; Powers 1993

COLONISATION OF THE LIFEWORLD

The process by which individual freedom is undermined in more complex societies, as large-scale social processes become increasingly autonomous and restrict the actions of those who are subject to them. In Habermas's terminology, this is the process by which society as a '**system**' intrudes into society as a '**lifeworld**'. Habermas develops the notion in *The Theory of Communicative Action* (1984a and 1987), not least in response to the inadequacies he sees in the account of the relation of system and lifeworld that is presented in *Legitimation Crisis* (1976b).

Colonisation may be seen as an undesirable consequence of the growth in complexity of societies, and the problems that the organisation and stabilisation of those societies present. Habermas suggests that a small-scale society can be organised largely through the everyday social competences of the people who live in it, and all importantly through their ability to communicate meaningfully with each other. If I personally know, at least as an acquaintance, everyone whom I am likely to meet, then I can generally get things done by negotiating with these people. I will know who has the particular skills or resources that I might need; I will know how to bargain with them or otherwise convince them to give me access to those resources; I will be able to make amends if things go wrong. Here I would be using the sorts of communicative competences that Habermas sought to analyse within the programme of **universal pragmatics**.

Problems begin to emerge as populations get larger, and as the sorts of projects with which I want to be involved get ever more complex. I might be able to use my communicative competence to get my canoe repaired or to enlist help in my fishing expedition, but it is not all that I am going to need to help me land a rocket on the moon. Complex scientific projects (and indeed political projects, such as the building of empires or the institution and maintenance of a national health-care system) will require the coordination of the actions of people who do not know each other, and indeed may never meet.

Resources will have to be brought together over large spaces, and at different times. In Habermas's terminology, such complex projects will 'overburden' the communicative resources of the population, and so some form of 'relief mechanism' must be found (1987: 181).

Relief mechanisms rely upon the use of instrumental, rather than communicative, action. That is to say that, in order to coordinate large-scale projects, people cease relating to each other purely as communicatively competent human beings, and instead treat each other as means to an end. While in communicative action I negotiate with my potential collaborator, answering her doubts and queries, and justifying my belief in the worth of the project, in instrumental (or more precisely **strategic**) action, I consider the other person purely in terms of his or her more or less predictable responses to certain stimuli. This is to say that I know that if I perform some particular action, then they will respond in a predictable way. In effect, I treat their **action**, which no doubt has good reasons motivating it, as mere behaviour (just as I know that, given the appropriate movement of my legs, I can raise the horse I am riding from a trot to a canter). I need not care about the reasons that these people have for acting in the way that they do, providing that they act as I expect. The apparent inhumanity of this image may be mitigated a little by considering it in more detail.

What Habermas is considering by his appeal to instrumental action is the role of systems, and the difference between **social integration** and **system integration**, within complex societies. Social integration, as a way of organising and ordering society, is achieved through communicative competence. Societies become systematically integrated as soon as there are commonly recognised cues, through which people can organise their action without resorting to communication. Habermas identifies two all important cues: **money** and **power**. They are examples of what he calls **non-symbolic steering media**. To explain this, we might consider a simple market place. I go along, wanting to buy my week's groceries. I look through the various stalls, and examine the produce available. All importantly, I also look at the price. I will buy the goods that strike me as being of the best (monetary) value. When I make my purchases, I need only point to or hold up the vegetables I want, proffer sufficient money, and wait for my change. I need not exchange a word with the stall-holders. I need not care why they became stallholders or whether or not they enjoy their work. Similarly, they need not care why I want so many kiwi fruits, providing that I pay up. The stallholders and I have each coordinated our actions through responses to the cue that monetary value gives us, and we have acted predictably. But, notice also that my purchases have not just succeeded in coordinating my actions with the stallholders. If the stallholders did not grow their own vegetables, then I have coordinated my actions with farmers who I will never meet (and who may live many thousands of miles from me, and speak a language that, in any case, I do not understand).

Precisely in the way that money facilitates the smooth running of the economy as a system, then it can coordinate (through the links that it establishes between diverse markets for labour, raw materials and manufactured goods) highly complex projects, including moon landings. That the moon landing was a programme organised and financed by the state makes little difference. Raw materials, components and the services of scientists and technicians still had to be acquired through markets and paid for at the going rate. Power works similarly, in so far as those who have legitimate power can both compel others to behave in a certain way (be this in the form of pharaohs commanding slaves to build pyramids, or judges condemning convicted criminals to periods of imprisonment), and can delegate power to others, so that subordinates can themselves control others (as captains command lieutenants, and lieutenants command sergeants) (Habermas 1987: 268–70). Again, communication is not required, providing the chain of power goes unquestioned, and the subordinate obeys the order as expected.

To this point, the account of the relationship between system and lifeworld appears to be beneficial. The lifeworld allows for rich and meaningful relationships with a few other people, while the system, in generally giving us the resources to make sense of our lives, makes it possible for us massively to simplify our understanding of the situations we are in, and thereby allows us to participate in much more complex social activities. The problem of the colonisation of the lifeworld occurs as the system ceases to be simply a means to an end, and thus something that can ultimately be checked by the lifeworld, and instead becomes a means in itself.

Action within a system is governed by a set of rules that is relatively simple compared to the rules that govern communicative action. While my communication with a friend can cover many topics, and establish all sorts of different relationships between us, my social relationship to my boss is largely constrained by the conventions and explicit rules of my contract. The fact that my boss might also be my friend is beside the point. The power that governs my relationship to my boss, as my boss, simplifies our interaction. This entails that systems, be they economic systems or political systems, such as administrations or government agencies, are organised in terms of the relatively simple rules that govern interaction between people within them. The rules governing the system will have a high degree of consistency, which is to say that they will be largely coherent with each other, and will generate relatively few conflicting instructions to the people who are following them. So, the system has its own logic. It does things in a certain way, and in accord with certain broad principles. Precisely because they are large and complex, long-standing systems will have a certain inertia built into them. It will not be easy to change the way in which they do things. This, in effect, is where the problems begin. Once complex societies are organised through systems, the autonomous logic of those systems will begin to direct what is possible and how anything is achieved within that society.

We might consider the following example. A government decides that the standards of education within its schools are declining. Too many children from marginal groups are leaving school with no adequate qualifications. That something must be done is clearly an admirable resolution. Given that schools are part of the society's political system, whatever is done must be done through the existing administrative structures. Structures might be modified in places, but the whole structure cannot be redesigned from scratch. The government therefore asks heads of schools to monitor the performance of certain target groups of pupils. While more resources will be put in to support the teaching of these groups, the instrumental thinking of the system already demands that those resources are seen to be used effectively and efficiently. Hence the monitoring of performance. But there are already problems.

First, teaching should be a prime example of communicative action, in which the pupil is encouraged to question ideas, and to justify her own arguments through appeals to reason. The classroom is thus the site of a rich and complex social interaction, full of subtle meanings and nuances. Unfortunately, the monitoring mechanisms of administrations typically require highly simplified data. As befits a system that is largely organised through the non-symbolic medium of power, the symbolic, qualitatively rich, or meaningful experience of the classroom must, somehow, be translated into simplified, and typically quantified data. Already, the possibility of disputing the government's original programme has been compromised. One is confronted by quantitative data, designed for instrumental assessment, not meaningful experiences that could contribute to discussion (see **discourse**).

Second, while the original government policy sought to improve educational standards, the monitoring system introduced into schools is that to which teachers will respond. Their immediate task is to get a good report. Because they have been treated instrumentally (in so far as the monitoring system is coercing them to change their teaching methods), their teaching is therefore in danger of itself becoming instrumental. The original communicative interaction between teacher and pupil is replaced by the teacher manipulating the pupil in order to obtain good results for the monitoring process. Discussion is replaced by spoon-feeding. Complex tasks that require time and energy are replaced by relatively simply tasks that are guaranteed to generate the sorts of results the monitoring requires.

Here, then, is Habermas's point. The use of systems in a modern society is necessary, and indeed to a degree highly beneficial. But, as economic systems and administrative systems intrude more and more into everyday life (for example, as the state increasingly regulates private and public activities, and as economic values are placed upon all activities), so the instrumentalism inherent in systematic activity begins to erode the communicative skills that are grounded in, and that serve to maintain, the lifeworld. Good intentions may be perverted by the system, and the possibility of challenging the system, through communicative rather than instrumental reason, is inhibited.

Further reading: Ingram 1987; White 1987; Brand 1990; Honneth and Joas 1991; Hahn 2000: 1–172; Heath 2001

COMMUNICATIVE ACTION

Meaningful interaction between persons. This is a major topic of much of Habermas's mature work, and not least *The Theory of Communicative Action* (1984a and 1987). An account of communicative action is initially discussed in essays such as 'What is Universal Pragmatics?' (1979a: 1–68), and the 1971 'Gauss' lectures (2001c: 1–104).

For Habermas, communicative action entails the establishing or maintaining of a social relationship between two or more individuals. As such actions are meaningful, they will involve some sort of appeal to ordinary language. At its simplest, this would be action that is couched in ordinary language, and so is saying something or writing something. More subtly the action might be a gesture that carried meaning (such as a raised fist or a blown kiss). In that all such action is an attempt to establish communication between two or more people, if it fails one or other of the people involved will resort to more language to make sense of (that is, to find the **meaning** in) what is going on (for example, by asking explicitly, 'Have I offended you?', or by spending the rest of the day wondering whether you are in love).

It may also be noted from these examples that communicative acts do not just communicate information between people. For Habermas, a problem with many earlier philosophical theories of language and communication was that they focused exclusively on this function of communication, so in developing a 'theory of communicative action' he wants a theory that can take account of the fact that we do various different things when we communicate (see **universal pragmatics**). Communicative action can be a way of doing something in the world, such as threatening, ordering or promising (see **speech act**). Habermas therefore identifies three functions that communicative action could perform. Certainly it can be used to convey information. It can also be used to establish social relationships with others (for example, through a simple promise, or by a registrar uttering the words 'I declare you man and wife', or a priest saying 'I baptise you in the name of the Lord ... '). Finally, it can be used to express one's own opinions and feelings (both straightforwardly, by saying 'I'm tired' or through exaggerated gestures of yawning and stretching, or more subtly by writing a poem or painting a picture, or even by using Welsh rather than English to say anything at all, and thereby expressing one's sense of self-identity and communal belonging).

This analysis can be taken a little further. At its most basic, when I act communicatively I presuppose that others will understand what I am doing. First, they will share the same language as I do. They are, for example, fellow Welsh speakers. Second, they understand the external world in much the same way as I do. So, when I tell them that it's a nice morning ('Mae'n hyfryd y bore ma'), they will recognise that the sun is shining and that it is warm. Third, we will share the same social norms and conventions (so that when I go on and address them with the informal 'you', they will not take offence at my over-familiarity). Finally, they will understand my self-expression, and follow me when I tell a joke or use irony. The problem is that such common understanding cannot be guaranteed. Communication can then break down. In order to repair such misunderstandings and confusions, I will turn to more ordinary language and meaningful action. For example, I repeat myself in English; I open the curtains with a flourish to let the sunlight in; I apologise and continue formally; I explain that I was only joking. Communicative action thus embraces both what Habermas calls 'consensual action', where the common assumptions are taken for granted, and 'action orientated to reaching an understanding', where I try to establish that common ground (Habermas 1979a: 209).

Communicative action is distinguished from **strategic action** in that the latter does not presuppose the need to establish any shared understandings. In strategic action, one person can simply seek to manipulate another, without the second person necessarily understanding what is going on, or consenting to it.

Further reading: Honneth and Joas 1991

COMMUNICATIVE POWER

The influence that citizens may exert upon a state, through the rational discussion of their interests, values and identities in the **public sphere**. The term is introduced by Habermas in his later work on **law**. In particular it is used to explore the relationship between the opinions of the people, as those who are subject to the law, and the official processes through which laws are created and enacted. In a just society, the people who are subject to the law must also be those who create that law. The law must therefore be grounded in public opinion. Habermas's argument is that public institutions, such as community and educational groups, churches, voluntary organisations and the mass media can ideally act as channels (or as a 'sluice' (Habermas 1998a: 250)) through which public opinion is transformed into communicative power, that in turn is transformed by the state administration into **administrative power**, so that it can be realised as enforceable laws that will constrain and direct the actions of citizens (1996: 463–90).

COMMUNICATIVE REASON

The approach to the rational resolution of problems over truth and moral goodness that is defended by Habermas. It is characterised by free and open discussion by all relevant persons, with a final decision being dependent on the strength of better argument, and never upon any form of coercion.

While a concept of communicative reason is more or less explicitly present in Habermas's early works, such as *The Structural Transformation of the Public Sphere* ([1962] 1989a), and *Knowledge and Human Interests* (1971a), it is not fully articulated until the mature work of the 1970s and 1980s, and in particular in *The Theory of Communicative Action* (1984a and 1987). In the account of the development and decline of the European **public sphere**, Habermas already stresses the role that public discussion plays in legitimating decisions made by political bodies, and presents the progress of democratic politics, not just in terms of the extension of the right to vote, but rather in terms of the increasing involvement of broader sections of society in the debate and criticism of policies of governments and political parties (1992c: 57–88). More theoretically, in *Knowledge and Human Interests*, Habermas links communicative reason to the **cognitive interest** that human beings have in mutual understanding and communication (Habermas 1971a: 155–8). That is to say that Habermas argues that, in order to survive and flourish, human beings must be able both to control their natural environment (through science and technology), and communicate effectively, so as to organise themselves in viable and complex social groups. Communicative reason is thus complementary to the **instrumental reason** that is employed in the natural sciences (and problems occur when instrumental reason alone is used in the organisation of social life – see **scientism**). Here Habermas works from the model provided by **hermeneutics**, which is to say the study of the interpretation of textual meanings. Communicative reason is thus initially understood as being akin to the dialogue that a reader sets up with her text. I come to a book, and in effect ask it questions (what are you about? what can you teach me?) to which it will provide more or less adequate answers. At this stage in his argument, Habermas is clear that communicative reason alone is not sufficient, and that it must be supplemented by **critical theory** in order to penetrate the systematic distortions that, due to political inequalities in society, have spoiled the possibility of pure communication.

In his mature work, communicative reason takes centre stage. Habermas drops the earlier model of critical theory, in order to argue that communicative reason represents the exercise of a basic competence or ability that all humans have, at least potentially. This is a capacity to engage each other in critical and rational argument. While it may be inhibited in any real society, not least due to political inequalities, it still provides a critical ideal, to which all communication should strive.

Habermas is therefore retaining from his earlier analysis the important idea that the exercise of reason should be a communal activity, and as such communicative rationality presupposes the possibility of dialogue. More precisely, he now argues that this is not primarily a hermeneutic process, but rather one through which participants in a conversation, or indeed any other social interaction, are required to justify what they are saying and doing. Ideally, if challenged, a speaker will be willing and able to provide evidence and reasons to support her beliefs about the world, and her right to be performing the actions in which she is currently involved. So, for example, if you command me to bring you a beer, I can challenge you either by pointing out that there is no beer immediately available (which seems to be an assumption that you are making about the world), or by asking what right you have to be bossing me about. If we are being reasonable, you must either provide a reasonable reply (for example, the off-licence around the corner is still open, and I'm your big sister), or accept my challenges and drop your command. It would be a breakdown of communicative reason if you insisted on enforcing the command, perhaps through threats, in the face of my reasonable challenges.

In Habermas's terminology, what happens as communication and interaction become problematic is that the participants shift to '**discourse**'. That is to say that they take a step back from the interaction, in order to reflect upon it, and debate its reasonableness. Such debates can be pursued at greater or lesser depth, depending on what it takes to convince everybody of the acceptable course of action. For example, 'I'm your big sister' might itself be challenged by the reply, 'But I'm not seven years old anymore!' We could then enter into a debate about until exactly what age big sisters have rights of command over younger brothers. We would have moved to discussing the normative principles that underpin the interaction.

This in turn highlights another aspect of communicative reason. It can be used to reflect upon, challenge and revise the taken-for-granted rules that we use to guide our everyday interactions. Social norms, from the rights of older sisters through to the legitimacy of forms of government, are accepted as part of the bundle of beliefs, values and skills that we are socialised into as we grow and live in a particular society (see **lifeworld**). Communicative reason is the resource through which we can reflect upon that bundle, when it becomes problematic. Taken further still, it is the resource through which we can reflect upon the goals that we are pursuing, personally or collectively. Instrumental reason presupposes given goals that are to be achieved, and focuses upon the calculation of the most effective means for realising them. (So, given that I want to buy a car, how do I quickly raise the money and get a good deal?) Instrumental reason can seem to be a monological thought process, which is to say that it looks as if one person can work out what are the most effective means in any given situation without discussing the matter with anyone else. This model of monological reasoning might also be taken to suggest that our goals are also decided upon monologically, or in other words subjectively. It is precisely this '**decisionism**' that Habermas seeks to challenge. Our goals are not, he insists, just a matter of personal whim. I can be asked to justify them: (Why do you want a car?). In pursuing a personal goal, almost inevitably I will come into interaction with other people – for example, because I need their help, or I am stopping them doing something they want to do. So these people have the right to challenge me, and I have the obligation to justify myself. To some degree, my justification will appeal to the norms and values that I, and hopefully my challengers, take for granted: (The car will allow me greater mobility). But again, deeper, underlying principles can be debated: (But cars cause pollution. There are already too many cars on the road. What's wrong with public transport?).

Further reading: White 1987; Honneth and Joas 1991

CONSCIOUSNESS, PHILOSOPHY OF

A set of presuppositions that are characteristic of much traditional philosophical and sociological inquiry, and that for Habermas account for the fundamental failure of either philosophy or sociology to offer adequate analyses of philosophical and social or political problems. In particular the philosophy of consciousness is criticised for failing to take account of the fundamentally intersubjective nature of human life, and the role that human skills in communication play in creating and sustaining social life. The philosophy of consciousness becomes a repeated target for criticism in Habermas's later works. It is seen to pervade the history of modern philosophy, and is exemplified by early modern philosophers such as Rene Descartes, through to **analytic philosophers** such as Gottlob Frege and Bertrand Russell, but also Continental philosophers including Husserl, Heidegger and Derrida (Habermas 1988a: 131–84). Only with the turn to the philosophy of **language**, initiated by philosophers such as Ludwig Wittgenstein and J. L. Austin, does it begin to be checked (see Habermas 1988b: 117–42).

The philosophy of consciousness may be summarised in terms of the primacy that it places upon the individual human being, rather than upon the processes of interaction within which that individual is involved. Thus, for example, the philosopher Kant is criticised for focusing, in both his theory of knowledge and his moral theory, on the isolated individual. It is that human who is imbued with certain cognitive processes, processes that allow her to make sense of her basic experiences and to shape them into the appearance of the taken-for-granted everyday world (see **transcendentalism**). To overcome the problem of solipsism, which is to say, here, the possibility of each individual constructing her own world and as it were retreating into it, Kant argues that these cognitive processes must be the same for all human beings. So, for Kant, each individual shapes her world in the same way, independently. This becomes problematic, not least when it begins to influence a philosophical account of scientific method. While not formulated in terms of the philosophy of consciousness, Habermas's early criticisms of **positivism** may be seen to make this point. Positivism presented scientific method as something that an isolated individual could follow. It is a set of rules that guide experimental work and theory formation, and that are underwritten by their rationality. Habermas's early enthusiasm for the work of the pragmatist philosopher Charles Peirce may be seen to lie, in no small part, in the fact that Peirce recognises that scientific discovery is a necessarily communal activity. Scientists do not work in isolation but in teams, debating and defending their results and hypotheses against the claims of rivals (Habermas 1971a: 91–112). An isolated scientist, however rational, cannot be her own effective critic. A theory of scientific method, for Habermas, must then explore the discursive processes through which hypotheses are defended. This, in effect, is part of Habermas's concern with the **validity claim** of **truth**, as it is explored in **universal pragmatics**.

The philosophy of consciousness is equally problematic when it seeps into moral or social theory. Again, Habermas is critical of Kant's moral philosophy because it presupposes that each individual in isolation can rationally calculate the morally correct way to behave. These separate calculations bring about a harmonious result (whereby every individual's moral decision is coherent with everyone else's), without the individuals having to talk to each other or to share experiences (1976a: 150–1). This, in effect, also lies at the root of Habermas's criticism of the contemporary liberal political theorist John Rawls (Habermas 1998a: 49–101).

Rawls suggests that, in order to work out a set of basic principles of justice that might be applicable to all societies, we should imagine a conference. The task of the conference is to set up a society. This is all very well, but, Rawls argues, if we as real people were setting up a society, we would try to make it as favourable to ourselves (or to people like us) as possible (so, of course, granting extra privileges to philosophers!). But that would be neither fair nor just, so Rawls modifies his thought experiment. The people at the conference have selective amnesia. They do not know who they are, or what talents they might have. Now if they design a society, they must approach the task rather more cautiously. They may be among the least talented, least healthy or just least attractive. Now, Rawls argues, the conference will design a fair society, which is to say one that respects everyone, regardless of their capacities and talents. The point for Habermas here is that, superficially, this looks as if it has taken account of interaction and discussion. Rawls is, after all, asking us to imagine a conference. The problem is that by imposing the selective amnesia (what Rawls calls a veil of ignorance) he has actually taken away all the individual differences that matter in real conversations. The conference has actually degenerated into a monologue. Real political and moral decision making, Habermas argues, requires real people to share and debate real differences of opinion and real experiences (hence **discourse ethics**).

Rawls also illustrates another point about the philosophy of consciousness, and this is that is it not always obvious. Much of Habermas's critical philosophical work lies in exposing the assumptions of the philosophy of consciousness despite an overt commitment on the part of the theorist under discussion to recognise and include social processes.

The problem of the philosophy of consciousness is two-fold. On the one hand, as the discussion of Rawls suggests, it is inadequate as an account of the justification or **legitimation** of moral claims. The justification of my command to you to get me a drink cannot be based on my self-justification. It must rather rest upon discussion between the two of us. You are an interested party, and you therefore have the right to challenge me: (Get your own drink!). The moral or normative implications of universal pragmatics, therefore, lie in the exploration of the intersubjective processes through which normative validity claims are rendered acceptable.

On the other hand, this is inadequate as a social theory. It fails to explain how social relationships can hold together. Habermas's mature work, revolving around universal pragmatics or the theory of communicative action, explores the use that ordinary people make of their skills in communication in order to create and sustain social relationships between each other. In particular, the ability to use **speech acts**, which is to say utterances that initiate or sustain some sort of social action, and so make something happen in the social world (like giving an order or making a promise), is fundamental to sustaining interaction. Any philosophical or social theory that neglects this dimension of social life is fundamentally flawed.

The flaw may manifest itself in either of two forms. The first, represented by Max Weber, is known as methodological individualism or atomism (Habermas 1987: 306). It is assumed here that all social actions and interactions can be analysed in terms of the actions of individual human beings. This is all very well, until it loses sight of the dependence of each individual upon those around her, and upon the culture within which she lives. While methodological individualism may recognise that individuals have to make sense of their social surroundings in order to be able to act within them, and as such it recognises that they require significant levels of skill and knowledge in order to be able to act competently, the analysis is cut short if it fails to recognise that the process of making sense is an intersubjective one rather than a subjective one. Without this recognition, we are back to Kant's moral agents, all making up their own minds and just happening to be able to coordinate their actions with each other.

The second form that the philosophy of consciousness takes is to treat society as what Habermas calls a 'macrosubject'. Here, the individual members of society drop out of sight altogether, and society as a whole is treated as an active subject. Habermas finds this approach to characterise a good deal of **Marxist** thinking, which has its roots in Hegel (Habermas 1979a: 140). Thus, from a Marxist perspective, history can be seen as the unfolding of the actions of society, where the key issue is the way in which society responds to the tensions and contradictions within its economic base. For Habermas, society can only change if ordinary members of society recognise that there is a problem (so that the contradictions of the economy, for example, must be experienced as disruptions of one's everyday life), and have the intellectual, cultural and technical resources to respond to the problem. For Habermas, **systems theory** in sociology similarly loses sight of meaningful human interaction (1988a: 368–85).

Further reading: Freundlieb 2003

CRISIS

A critical moment that requires decisive action in order to be resolved. Paradigmatic examples of crises can be found in medicine, where the disease reaches a critical point, and in religion with the notion of a spiritual crisis. If the medical crisis is not resolved, then the patient will die; if the spiritual crisis is not resolved, the soul is damned (Habermas 1976a: 213). While Habermas may take these examples as indicators of the meaning of the term, he is more interested in its application to society. Historically, he points to the crisis in the self-confidence of European Enlightenment culture that occurred when the Lisbon earthquake of 1755 challenged confidence in the ability to control nature and to sustain technological progress (and indeed in the notion that this is a divinely ordered and beneficent world). The development of nineteenth-century capitalism and industrialisation deepened the sense of crisis. Beyond the individual experience of urban and rural working conditions, **Marxism** and other social theories began to identify the unstable and unsustainable nature of the capitalist social structure as crisis tendencies.

In his earlier work, Habermas uses the concept of 'crisis' to support the **emancipatory** role of **critical theory** (Habermas 1976a: 1–8). That is to say that political emancipation will come about, in response to crisis, through a combination of decisive action and, crucially, self-knowledge. Crisis demands that the subject, be it an individual human being or a society, reflects upon itself in order to discover the illusions that it is harbouring about itself. Habermas has in mind here the approaches of psychoanalysis, where the patient is cured by being enabled consciously to recall traumatic events that she had previously blocked from her memory, and Marxist **ideology critique**, where the culture of the society works to conceal or legitimate political oppression and exploitation.

The concept of 'crisis' is developed by Habermas in the early 1970s, as he begins to change his theoretical position through an engagement with **systems theory** (Habermas 1976b). A crisis is now understood as a failure in a **system**. If a system is understood as a structure that is organised to fulfil certain purposes, by drawing resources from its environment and transforming them, then a crisis occurs when the system cannot fulfil those purposes, either because of a lack of resources or because it is badly organised and so cannot carry out the transformation required. Put more concretely, the economic institutions in a society (such as the means for producing goods and services, employing people, distributing finished goods, and so on) may be understood as a social system. It takes in resources (such as labour power and natural resources) from its environment, and transforms them into finished consumables. A crisis will occur if there are insufficient resources (such as a labour shortage or the exhaustion of fossil fuels), or internal disorganisation (for example, a lack of necessary technological skills, or poor social relations between employers and employees).

Habermas uses a systems theory approach to explore the way in which crises in one part of society have knock-on effects in other parts. Economic crises can lead to political crises (because the political institutions rely upon a steady source of consumer goods from the economy), and these in turn lead to crises of confidence in the government (**legitimation crises**) and in society as a whole (crisis in meaning), as the government seems to fail to fulfil its promises to the electorate, and as basic social goods, including a supply of consumer goods, but also social stability and a sense of justice, seem to be threatened.

The problem with an exclusive systems theory approach, for Habermas, is that it fails to explain the role that real people have in all this. Society may be modelled as a system, but at the end of the day it is made up of real people making real decisions. A systems crisis is nothing if people do not notice it, and crucially a system cannot solve its own crises. Real human beings must do that. This is where the notion that a crisis involves self-knowledge reappears. An economic crisis may be recognised through events that have an impact upon the everyday lives of people, hence the shortage of consumer goods, the rising price of fuel, increasing levels of unemployment, and so on. Similarly, as suggested above, political crises will be perceived in terms of the government's failure to fulfil certain manifesto promises. Crises can only be resolved if people have the ability to deal with them. This entails that, within the culture as a whole, there must exist sufficient capacity to learn and to adapt. There must exist the ability to analyse the sources of the crisis and to propose solutions. At the extreme, a crisis may be so acute that only radically new solutions and ways of thinking will resolve it. Such crises, if they can be successfully tackled, are for Habermas the stimuli to **social evolution**.

CRITICAL THEORY

An approach to the analysis of society that seeks to offer a political evaluation of that society, and to guide political practice. The term was coined by the **Frankfurt School** thinker Max Horkheimer in the 1930s (Horkheimer 1972: 188–243), and adopted by Habermas in *Knowledge and Human Interests* (1971a: 187–300) and, with a somewhat different emphasis, in *The Theory of Communicative Action* (1987: 374–403).

Horkheimer distinguished critical theory from what he called 'traditional theory'. Traditional theory typifies the basic assumptions that had been dominant in both scientific and philosophical inquiry since the seventeenth century. Traditional theory assumes that it is possible, and indeed necessary, to develop methods for acquiring knowledge that are valid for all times and in all places, and indeed that are valid regardless of the subject-matter studied. This entails, very importantly, that the methods of good science are the same regardless of who is carrying out the inquiry, and when and where they are doing it. It is therefore assumed that the subject-matter exists wholly independently of the scientist, and that what good methodology will do is to remove any idiosyncratic or subjective ideas, emotions or values that might clutter up and distort the scientist's perception and understanding. The end result of applying this method will be objective truth – 'objective' in the sense that it maps the way the object under investigation actually is.

While this sounds all very well and good (and indeed, to a degree Habermas is sympathetic to the aspirations of traditional theory), Horkheimer condemns such an approach for ignoring the thoroughgoing historical nature of perception and understanding. Human beings, even if they are scientists, do not exist in a cultural vacuum. They are informed by the values of their age, and come with preconceptions that are rooted in the historical development of their science. Further, they typically respond to the problems that the real world poses to them. While there may be certain values and perspectives that a good scientist ought to rid himself of (and Habermas offers the example of Stalinist genetics (1971a: 315)), the scientist cannot rid himself of all his values and preconceptions. As Habermas puts this, there can be no such thing as 'pure theory' (1971a: 302). Horkheimer thus argues that both the possibilities and the limitations of human thought and understanding are historically constituted. There can therefore be no objective knowledge in the sense intended by the traditional philosopher or scientist, for the very categories that the scientist uses to organise and express his knowledge are shaped by the political and cultural tensions of the society within which they are formulated. Knowledge is therefore always value-laden, and to some degree the object that is studied is a construction of the scientist. The task of a critical theory, therefore, becomes that of being aware of those conditions, and crucially of identifying the political values that infiltrate deep within the scientist's thought and perception. For Horkheimer, using 'critical theory' as a synonym for '**Marxism**', the task of the critical theorist is to identify the way in which values that serve the reproduction of the injustices of **capitalism** feed into their work and the work of others.

This is much the conception that Habermas puts forward in *Knowledge and Human Interests*, albeit Habermas's view is supported by a rather more subtle understanding of the nature of both natural and social science. While Horkheimer works with a simple dichotomy, Habermas suggests that there are in fact three types of science: natural science; cultural or social science; and critical theory. Each has a separate methodology. The methodology of the natural sciences is the closest to Horkheimer's traditional theory, in that there is the assumption of an independent world to be studied. While Habermas shares Horkheimer's concern that certain **positivist** self-understandings of natural scientists may blind them to the political and economic values that do infiltrate and shape their research, his appeal to the **pragmatism** of Charles Peirce provides him with a much more subtle account of the nature of good natural scientific method. Pragmatism allows the scientist to acknowledge that he is part of an on-going, historically and culturally shaped research project, without wholly abandoning the idea of objective knowledge (albeit that any claims to knowledge that the scientist puts forward are necessarily treated as mere hypotheses, to be accepted while they work and lead to effective technology, but to be abandoned as soon as they no longer help in making practical interventions into the physical world).

In contrast, the social or **hermeneutic** sciences recognise that they are engaging with an object that is not wholly separate from them. The social scientist is either a part of the society she is studying, or is relying upon the interpretative skills that she uses every day as a competent member of society in order to make sense of the material she is studying. The social scientist, in sum, is attempting to understanding the meaning of other people's actions and words. In order to do that she must bring her own presuppositions about the social world to her scientific inquiry. Those presuppositions will at once shape the interpretations she makes, but also those interpretations may challenge her presuppositions. For Habermas, the problem with this hermeneutic model is that it assumes that all communication between human beings is transparent. That is to say that, if one shares enough of the cultural assumptions and language skills of the person one is studying, one will be able to understand them. Critical theory challenges precisely this assumption.

Habermas offers psychoanalysis, as well as Marxism, as models for critical theory. The psychoanalyst is confronted by a patient with physical or behavioural symptoms that have no physical origin. The

origin must therefore lie in the patient's own actions, which is to say
that he is imposing the symptoms upon himself. He does not
acknowledge this, though. The process of psychoanalytic therapy
therefore attempts to trace the symptoms back to some traumatic
experience with which the patient cannot deal consciously. The
memory is repressed, but none the less manifests itself in the symptom. Crucially, the symptom is symbolic of that original event. It
talks about the event, as it were, in a private language, cut off from
the public communication that is the concern of the hermeneutician.
Critical theory, therefore, becomes an amalgam of natural and hermeneutic science. Its subject-matter is something that appears natural.
Its methodology is one of interpretation, albeit through the reconstruction of a private language.

In sociology, this is **ideology critique**. Again, society, which must
ultimately be the product of human actions, confronts its members as
if it were something natural. The workings of the economy provide a
prime example of this, as the laws of economic exchange appear to
have the same objectivity as the law of gravity (see **reification**).
Traditional theory within social science will fail to see through the
illusion of naturalness, and will attempt to explain social phenomena
as if they were natural, so that they provide explanations that link
diverse social phenomena together through causality – and hence, for
example, an economist might link changes in interest rates to changes
in employment levels, without needing to consider the meanings that
real actors give to these phenomena, and thus the actual free and
creative processes through which ordinary people bring about this
change. Traditional social science, remaining blind to the capitalist
values that shape it, serves only to reproduce or maintain the capitalist system, never to challenge it or to expose its exploitative nature.

In his later works, Habermas gradually abandons this model. In
part this is based in a fundamental shift from the problem that Horkheimer sets up. Horkheimer is concerned with the way in which the
cultural and political values of the scientist serve to constitute the object
of inquiry, which is to say that, thanks to his cultural presuppositions
the scientist preconceives the object in terms of certain sorts of concepts and ideas. Habermas's theory of cognitive interests echoes this
question of constitution. He argues, however, that the three different
types of sciences (natural, hermeneutic and critical) constitute their
objects differently because each is guided by a different interest (in
manipulating the natural world; in understanding and communication; and in political **emancipation**, respectively). Habermas comes
to regard this as a shortcoming of his theory. It focuses too much on

how the object is constituted, and too little upon how the **truth** of a scientific theory or hypothesis is tested and vindicated (1971a: 360–1). So Habermas begins to develop a theory that explains how claims to truth, but also to moral and political goodness, are justified – this is his account of **validity claims**, grounded in the theory of **universal pragmatics**.

This all begins to shift the understanding of what a critical theory might be. The idea that critical theory should guide political action is never lost, but the model of ideology critique is soon abandoned. What takes its place is, on the one hand, a moral, political and legal theory that explores the way in which claims to exercise **power** are **legitimated**. This becomes a question, not of unravelling ideological distortions, but rather of examining how relevant parties have been excluded from the processes of rational debate that should be used to justify political and legal decisions, and thus the exercise of power (see **discourse ethics** and **law**).

On the other hand, a new model of society is suggested that attempts to offer a new account of reification. Habermas develops the notions of **lifeworld** and **system** in order to explore the tension between the rich and meaningful everyday world (and thus, largely, the world as it is studied by hermeneuticians and experienced by ordinary people), and society confronting humans as something objective and natural. Now Habermas stresses the importance and inevitability of this objective (or systematic) aspect of society. Without it, complex social activities could not be organised. However, the expansion of systems (such as bureaucracies and economic institutions) is problematic. First, Habermas's commitment to questions of legitimation presupposes for him the effective use of communicative reason. That is to say that ordinary people must be capable of being involved in discussions to question and justify political beliefs and actions. Systems, however, work instrumentally, not communicatively. They are, to put it rather bluntly, tools designed to bring about given ends. They can be assessed in terms of their instrumental efficiency, but they remain insensitive to the question of the value of the ends that they serve. So, second, they also begin to take on a life of their own. As they increase in complexity, they cease to be simply means to desirable ends (and as such something that could be dissolved once its task was complete). They become ends in themselves, more and more intruding into and restricting everyday life. Life must increasingly be lived within the instrumental rules of the system. This is the phenomenon that Habermas explores in his account of the **colonisation of the lifeworld**.

35

Critical theory is thus now concerned with exploring what Habermas identifies as the 'pathologies' that come about through the inevitable expansion of systematic organisation in complex societies, and the concomitant erosion of scope for communication and critical discussion. Pathologies include a loss of **meaning** in everyday social life, the undermining of moral and other values, and psychological maladjustment (Habermas 1987: 143). The task of critical theory is to search for practical interventions that might resist and reverse such pathologies, and above all to defend the role of communicative reason in a social world that, thanks to its systematic organisation, is increasingly restricted to an **instrumental reasoning** that inhibits critical political thought. As a concluding aside, it may be noted that, in this aspiration, Habermas expresses a continuity with his earlier concerns about **decisionism**, and the abiding fear of the misplaced use of instrumental reason that has always been an underlying motivation of his work.

Further reading: Held 1980; Geuss 1981; Benhabib 1986; Wiggershaus 1994

DECISIONISM

The claim that value judgements, for example in ethics and political philosophy, and judgements about beauty or the value of art works, are not susceptible to rational resolution, and so can only be resolved through more or less arbitrary decisions, based on subjective caprice (1976a: 265). Much of Habermas's work during the 1960s may be seen to be concerned to counter decisionism, and thus to demonstrate that rational debate over the goals and values that underpin ethical and political decisions is both possible and necessary.

Decisionism is related, by Habermas, to **positivism** and to the prevalence of **instrumental reason** in late **capitalist** society. As an approach to the philosophy of science and language, positivism argues that meaningful statements are confined to those that can be verified through empirical observations. A scientific theory about the way the natural world works can be tested by observing that world and establishing facts about it. A bad scientific theory can be rejected rationally, for there will be no observations to support it, and all rational enquirers will be able to agree upon this. The positivist then argues that value judgements cannot be verified or falsified in this way. If I say, 'Democracy is the best form of government', there are no observable entities or characteristics in the world through which the statement can be verified. This is to say that there is no 'best-ness' out there in the real world to which I can point. Values do not exist in the world as facts do, for they are simply expressions of the way in which individuals respond to the world. Values cannot be derived from facts in a way that will be acceptable to everyone. At best, a value judgement is then reduced to an expression of personal opinion, so that 'Democracy is the best form of government' becomes 'I approve of democracy', and may simply be dismissed by anyone who has lived well under a dictatorship. Judgements of moral or political worth are thus treated in the same way as a person's preference for sugar in their tea, or for strawberry ice cream over vanilla.

If positivism undermines rational discussion of values (and it may be noted that it was a contributory factor in the decline of ethics, political philosophy and the philosophy of art in the English-language philosophy of the mid-twentieth century), then it undermines the possibility of rationally discussing the ultimate ends or goals of our actions. Such goals entail a value judgement, in so far as the goal is judged to be something worth pursuing. This worth is asserted as a mere matter of personal preference. The only issues that can be discussed rationally are the means by which that end can be achieved. The effectiveness of means is something that can be established and tested through empirical observation.

Habermas's objections to decisionism encompass both its inadequacy as an account of value judgement, and the implications that it has for politics. Habermas holds that at least some values can, and in a just society must, be discussed rationally. While we might accept that there is no point in attempting to have a rational discussion over the respective merits of strawberry and vanilla ice cream (because if I do not like vanilla, no argument is going to convince me of its merits), Habermas holds that there is a point in discussing the relative worth of political systems and even works of art. Such discussion can only occur if we recognise that instrumental rationality is not the only form that rationality can take, and that one may justify one's arguments by more than just an appeal to statements of empirical fact. Thus, to defend democracy over totalitarianism, I need not point out that it is merely empirically proven to be more efficient in realising certain subjectively desirable goals (such as the sustaining of economic productivity, or the avoidance of famines). Rather, I could begin to initiate a debate on what it means to live as a social being, of the aspirations that I have to freedom and creativity, and indeed on just why those supposedly subjectively desirable goals are so desirable. By bringing to light new and surprising aspects of our social and individual existence, and of how different forms of political organisation are integral to how we understand ourselves as human beings, our discussion makes us look upon the social world differently, exploring our values, and not merely dogmatically asserting them.

The political implications of an acceptance of decisionism may be seen in terms of the importance that Habermas gives to the vitality of public debate in just societies, and to the formation of public opinion. Any society that takes decisionism for granted will tend to abandon the cultivation of political discussion, and thus the rational formation of public opinion, in favour of merely eliciting aggregates of individual preferences (for example, through votes on party manifestos, or through public surveys and opinion polls). In effect, it will be assumed that what matters is the subjective opinions that individual citizens have separately, and not the possibility that such opinions could be modified or developed through rational debate. Individual opinions and expressions of political preference would be treated as mere givens, again as facts that cannot be questioned – so that my preference for liberals over fascists would be akin to my preference for strawberry over vanilla ice cream, and rendered as equally beyond moral questioning and rational debate, and – more worryingly – my political preferences might be subjected to the same form of manipulation and influence through advertising and propaganda as my preferences for ice cream. Crucially, without something akin to Habermas's defence of the rational debate and justification of political opinions, then a preference for fascism over democracy is no more wrong than is a preference for strawberry over vanilla ice cream.

Habermas's exploration of the notion of **emancipatory** science in *Knowledge and Human Interests*, and of **communicative rationality** in his later work (especially *The Theory of Communicative Action*) may be seen primarily as attempts to avoid decisionism.

DEMOCRACY

Literally, a society ruled by the people. In practice, what is known as direct democracy, where the citizens have a direct say in political decisions, is rare. Something akin to it existed in some ancient Greek states, in so far as all those judged to be citizens (so excluding all women and slaves) had the right to be involved in public discussions and votes over policy. In practice, most democracies are representational democracies, where the people are represented in government by elected senators or members of parliament who make decisions on their behalf. Habermas, throughout his career, has been concerned with the workings of democratic government and the accountability and responsiveness of government to its people. This concern is expressed in some of his earliest work, such as his study of the political attitudes of students in the late 1950s in West Germany (Habermas *et al.* 1961). *Structural Transformation of the Public Sphere* is in large part a social history of the development of democracy in Europe (Habermas 1989a). In his more recent work he has returned explicitly to the problems of the democratic organisation of government given the complexity and pluralism of late capitalist societies (Habermas 1996 and 1998a).

Habermas is most concerned to respond to the problem of life in complex, multi-cultural societies. He articulates the problem in terms of a distinction between *demos* and *ethnos* (1996: 495). As members of a *demos*, people are joined together in the same society, as citizens. *Demos* concerns one's existence as a political being. In contrast, *ethnos* refers to one's identity as a member of a particular cultural, religious or ethnic community. In a multi-cultural society the two must be separated.

Neo-conservative thinkers, such as mid-twentieth-century German political philosopher Carl Schmitt, are targeted by Habermas for assuming that modern political societies can only exist if they are grounded on a single homogeneous *ethnos* (1998a: 134ff). Schmitt, it may be noted, continues to have an influence on new right thinking in contemporary America. Habermas acknowledges the importance of the *ethnos*. In effect, it is the immediate **lifeworld** of ordinary people, and thus the source of the skills, values and beliefs that allow them to make sense of their lives, and of the events and people around them. Ordinary people must be socialised into an *ethnos* in order to acquire the competence to function in social life, and to develop mature personalities. But the *ethnos* cannot be allowed to be the basis of political life. Here Habermas alludes to the fact that we live in a modern, **post-metaphysical** society. That is to say that, in **modernity**, no single taken-for-granted worldview (or metaphysics) is any longer dominant, as it was for example in medieval Christendom. Substantial moral values can, therefore, no longer be allowed to shape the political sphere of the *demos*. Habermas's philosophy of **law** explores this requirement, by seeing law as the rules according to which human beings relate to each other as the citizens of a particular state (and not as humans *per se*).

Habermas summarises the requirements of *demos* under the concept of 'constitutional patriotism' (1996: 500). The constitution becomes the focus of citizens' common concern, as opposed to the substantial values of any particular *ethnos*. Indeed, Habermas suggests that a sense of common citizenship (as distinct from common ethnicity) may be formed through debates over the constitution. A constitution must none the less guarantee the procedures that secure the legitimacy of the law, precisely in that it determines the rights of participation in public debate that citizens must have. In effect, the constitution guarantees that all citizens have equal rights to challenge any legal reform, and to receive a reasoned reply to their objections, rather than the mere right to vote on the policies offered to them by political parties. Crucially, law and policy should not be supported through the eliciting of a mere aggregate of individual, and subjective, preferences (as a simple voting system allows). The acceptance or rejection of a law must go beyond mere preference, and must rather appeal to rational justification.

While basic constitutional requirements may be common to all just societies, Habermas recognises that different nations will realise the substantial details of their constitution and legal systems differently. This raises concerns of the continuing relevance of nationalism in the modern world (see 2001b: 58–129). Habermas thus remains a forceful proponent of international organisations, such as the United Nations and the European Community (1996: 500–7).

Further reading: Rosenfeld and Arato 1998; Schomberg and Baynes 2002

DIFFERENTIATION

A term from **systems theory** that refers to the process by which a **system** subdivides into specialist sub-systems, and thus a consequence of social change or **social evolution**. In biology, an organism may be considered as a system, in that it is an organised structure, designed to fulfil a series of functions. In the simplest organisms, such as the amoeba and other single-celled animals, all the functions (such as feeding, excretion, movement, reproduction) will be carried out by the one cell. It is an undifferentiated system. In more complex organisms, different cells will fulfil different functions. So, for example, the roots of a plant have the function of absorbing water and nutrients from the soil, the leaves have the functions of respiration and photosynthesis. The plant can therefore be differentiated into a number of sub-systems, each with different functions. As more differentiation takes place, new functions can be fulfilled (so that, for example, animals acquire nervous systems, increasing their autonomy and problem-solving functions). Once systems theory is applied to society, a society can similarly be understood in terms of the degree to which it can be subdivided into sub-systems with different functions. This is a measure of the complexity of the society. Thus, for example, in small-scale societies, the family unit is likely to be involved in economic production, the physical rearing of children and their education, and possibly religious and political functions. In industrial societies, while the family may still supply labour, it is no longer typically an economic producer. That function has been split off and assigned to specialist economic sub-systems. Similarly, while the family may still rear and socialise children, much of the task of education will have been taken over by a specialist educational sub-system (composed of schools, colleges and universities).

This systems theory account of differentiation can be complemented by an understanding of the impact that differentiation has within culture. As societies become more sophisticated, so social institutions, cultural beliefs and worldviews, and personality structures are increasingly separated. What this means can be clarified by imagining a small-scale society with very simple technology (or what the French sociologist Emile Durkheim suggested by his term 'mechanical solidarity' (see Habermas 1987: 87ff)). The binding-together of this society (which is to say its **social integration**), depends upon the fact that all the members of the society share the same cultural values, and will be occupied in a very similar range of activities, as no complex division of labour will have yet emerged. Because they will all have broadly the same experiences and the same values, they will understand themselves in more or less the same way. The contention is that a modern sense of individuality will not yet have emerged. As society becomes more complex, and people begin to take on specialist economic and other roles (as specialist sub-systems develop), so the homogeneity of their personal experiences, values and sense of self will begin to break down. Hence, there will come about a differentiation of what Habermas calls society (in the 'narrow sense'), culture and personality (1987: 147). People will become aware that there is a difference between a particular social role or office which they currently occupy, the cultural values and outlook that they accept, and their personality. So, for example, I am a university lecturer. But I have no problem with the notion that I might retire while my job continues, and is filled by someone who is very different to me – say, by an Indian woman who loves baseball and who, while having read Habermas carefully, is highly critical of him (as opposed to the present incumbent, me, an Anglo-Welsh male who loves cricket and is a Habermas fan). The tasks of the university lecturer might still be fulfilled just as well, despite the differences in culture and sense of personal identity of the person occupying the position.

Taking this a little further, differentiation here also suggests the differentiation of **validity claims**. That is to say as systemic and cultural differentiation takes place, so questions of **truth**, goodness and **truthfulness** come to be separated, as members of society come to recognise that their view of the world can be challenged on one of three levels: is what I believe true of the way that the world is; is it right to believe it; does that belief genuinely express the sort of person that I am? (So, for example, the issues of whether I am suitably qualified to teach a course on Habermas, and thus whether it is right for me to do that, can be separated from the truth of the claim that I am indeed the course teacher; all of which is quite separate from the question of what my belief that the cricket-player Ashley Giles is the greatest thing since sliced bread says about my personality.) Cultural differentiation and the differentiation of validity claims is explored by Habermas in his account of the **rationalisation of the lifeworld**.

DISCOURSE

The process through which the assumptions and claims made by participants in communication are subjected to discussion and criticism, in order to be accepted or rejected. The term becomes important in Habermas's technical vocabulary as he develops the theory of **communicative action** and **universal pragmatics** in the early 1970s (Habermas 1976e; 2001c: 99–100).

A basic contrast can be drawn between communication and discourse. Communication is the everyday activity through which people speak to each other, share information, and set up and sustain social relationships. Communication may break down. In particular, the information that is being shared, or indeed that is taken for granted by one of the speakers as being shared, might come into dispute (for example, 'You can't really believe that *Pravda* was a fair and objective newspaper!'). Or, one person's right to be saying or doing something might be challenged (for example, 'What right have you got to lecture me about Soviet politics?'). (See **validity claim**.) Ideally, these breakdowns will be resolved by resorting to discourse.

In discourse, what was taken for granted as true or normatively right in communication is treated as problematic, and everyone is free to contribute to the discussion. So, in communication I assert that *Pravda* gave objective reports of Russian life in the 1950s. You challenge me. My assertion is now treated as a hypothesis that needs to be tested. I am expected to bring forward evidence and arguments to support my view (just as a natural scientist might seek evidence to support a scientific theory). So, I give a dozen examples of *Pravda* carrying the same reports as the *New York Times*. You dismiss this as a highly selective batch of reports, and quote a dozen distorted reports of political trials, and so on. Ideally, one side will accept that its case is inadequate, and drop either the original assertion or the challenge. Everyone can then go back to communication. A similar process can go on concerning my right to say something. So here I might justify myself by pointing out that I studied Soviet journalism for my doctorate. You might challenge the academic rigour of my old university, and might add that you have spent a lot of time working with Soviet émigrés (and so on).

Discourse will ideally end in a renewed consensus between those taking part in the conversation. However, this ideal can be problematic. On the one hand, there may simply not be enough evidence to convince everyone, and perhaps some compromise will be necessary (see Habermas 1976b: 111–13). On a more sinister level, discourse may either be ended or avoided through the exercise of power. You may feel intimidated by me, and so not able to challenge me; or, rather than justifying myself through my academic credentials, I might just point out that I am in a senior position to you (teacher over student; professor over junior lecturer) and that disagreeing with me may adversely affect your grades or prospects for promotion. This **systematically distorted communication** is what Habermas's critical approach to reasoning seeks to identify and expose.

On the other hand, even if the process of discourse seems to be resolved rationally and freely, with everyone who wishes having had their say, and all now accept the conclusion, that conclusion remains provisional. Actual discourse cannot establish absolute truths, because actual discourse presupposes a bundle of taken-for-granted beliefs and values. While discourse makes one particular idea or value problematic, it cannot challenge everything at once. In order to reflect upon and resolve one problem, other information must be taken for granted as sound. In the above example, no one was doubting that *Pravda* was a Soviet-published newspaper, or that the Soviet Union existed. In the future new information may arise to challenge an old consensus; new ideas may arise to test the coherence of the conclusion. In which case, a new discursive process will have to arise. Discourse therefore establishes a working consensus, but (in line with Habermas's **pragmatism**) still demands of us a certain humility. Our most cherished beliefs about the way in which the world works, what happened in the past, and what will happen in the future, and what it is right and wrong to do, may come to be questioned. For Habermas, the importance of discourse lies in the fact that it provides a rationally justifiable way of challenging problematical beliefs.

DISCOURSE ETHICS

The normative theory that is implicit in the rules of communication that are presupposed by competent members of society. Habermas's contention is that, having outlined in **universal pragmatics** the kinds of knowledge and skills that are required by ordinary people to communicate with each other, and thus to create and maintain social relationships, one can recognise a strong moral dimension to these rules (see Habermas 1990: 43–115). At one level this is very straightforward. Universal pragmatics is a **reconstruction** of the rules that we follow in communication. Habermas points out that anything I say may, in principle, be challenged as to its **meaning**, the **truth** of what I am saying, my sincerity or **truthfulness** and, most importantly for ethics, my right to say what I am saying or to do what I am doing (see **validity claim**). Thus, for example, to be challenged over my right to assert that democracy is the best form of government is in part to ask me to justify that claim. At this point ordinary communication breaks down, and the participants resort to **discourse**, where for the moment the validity of my statement is treated merely hypothetically, and it can be subject to challenges and defences. So, discourse ethics emerges from the possibility of having to defend the rightfulness of what a competent speaker utters.

Habermas (along with his friend and sometime collaborator, Karl Otto Apel (Apel 1980)) develops this basic insight. Habermas first proposed the idea of a discourse (or, then, a 'communicative') ethics in the conclusion of *Legitimation Crisis* (1976b: 105–6), as a necessary element to a **critical theory**. In its fully developed form, it becomes a powerful tool for identifying what is wrong with actual moral debates. Habermas characterises it (in an allusion to the **Frankfurt School** thinker Theodor Adorno) as a minimal ethics (1990: 86, 121), which is to say it is not intended to allow the philosopher or moral theorist to propose substantial solutions to moral problems. The task of finding a solution remains that of the people who will be affected by that solution and who will have to live with it. Rather, discourse ethics ensures that the process through which that solution is reached, whatever it might be, is a fair and just one. It is about the *process* of moral decision making, not the *product*.

In his earlier work on discourse ethics, this critical potential was maintained through the concept of the **ideal speech situation**, which is to say a projection of a perfect interaction, in which participants could freely express themselves, and the final decision would be unanimous and based on the strength of better arguments alone. While Habermas argued that the ideal speech situation respected a set of counter-factual assumptions that ordinary speakers brought to a conversation (basically, in that we assume that everything is fair and above board until we have evidence to the contrary), the mature version of discourse ethics appeals rather to rules and principles that more precisely reconstruct our moral competence. Habermas offers two principles: the principle of universalisation (U); and the principle of discourse (D) (1990: 65–6).

The principle of universalisation holds that moral decisions are valid only if all those affected can consent to them. All must recognise the consequences of the decision, and must prefer those to the consequences of any other decision. This is an approach to ethics that owes much to the moral philosophy of Kant. Kant argued that a moral principle can only be acceptable if everyone would agree to be bound by it (so, for example, the principle that telling lies is okay cannot be a moral principle, because while a lie might be quite useful to me in the short run, if everyone could tell lies just as they chose then the social fabric would begin to fall apart into a large knotted heap of mistrust).

(U) alone is not enough. There are many ways to bring about a universal consensus, and not all need be moral, or, more to the point, not all need appeal to our ability to communicate. The problem with the Kantian method of resolving moral problems is that it does not actually require people to talk to each other. The universal applicability of a moral principle could be worked out, by an isolated individual, in an act of monological reasoning. The principle of discourse checks this. (D) specifies that normative validity is dependent upon agreement of all as participants in a practical (in other words, moral) discourse, which is to say that only agreement that is based on truly open and rational debate counts. To spell out the nature of discourse a little more precisely, this entails that all competent speakers and actors are allowed to take part; everyone can question anything that is said, and may introduce new assertions (including assertions of their attitudes, desires and needs) as they see fit, and no speaker may be coerced into withholding or withdrawing their participation (1990: 89). So, if consensus comes about through explicit or implicit threats to participants, or if the discourse is structured in such a way that certain issues cannot be raised, then there is no moral validity.

For Habermas the strength of discourse ethics lies in large part in the fact that it is a cognitive theory. That is to say that it presupposes that moral judgements can be justified through the argument. It is therefore explicitly opposed to all forms of emotivism, which argues that moral decisions are ultimately merely assertions of subjective opinion, and as such lie outside of the scope of rational debate (see **decisionism**). But Habermas also sees discourse ethics as a formal approach to ethics. This in effect takes up a point already made. Discourse ethics is about processes, not substantive outcomes. However, that in itself has another implication, for it means that people who engage in moral discourse bring with them a good deal of the cultural baggage that they acquire from their **lifeworld**. That is to say that the participants in moral discourse are not purely rational beings, but rather real humans, who are shaped as concrete personalities by their personal experiences and their upbringing. It is precisely the concreteness and diversity of these personal experiences, values and needs that makes practical discourse worthwhile. In practice, few if any moral decisions will live up to the ideal proposed, but that, in part, is Habermas's point. Real decisions can always be challenged in the light of new evidence, new experiences and new ideas.

For recent developments in Habermas's approach to ethics, and its application, see **genetics**.

Further reading: Benhabib and Dallmayr 1990; Rehg 1994; Kitchen 1997; Finlayson 1998; Hahn 2000: 173–256

DOUBLE STRUCTURE OF LANGUAGE

When using **language**, for example in speaking or writing, the language user can pay attention to either of two characteristics of language: that the sentence spoken or written is saying something about the external world; or that, in speaking or writing, one is establishing a social relationship with one's audience (Habermas 1979a: 41–4; Habermas 1976e). For example, if I tell you that 'Habermas wrote a book called *Postmetaphysical Thinking*', then on one level I am making a statement about a world that exists independently of me and of anything I say. But, in saying this to you, I am either establishing or maintaining a social relationship between us. I might speak in my role as a teacher (and you listen as student), or I might be making a peculiarly inept attempt to break the ice at a party. In Habermas's technical vocabulary, language has a propositional component (in that it refers to the world) and an **illocutionary** component (in that it invokes social relationships). The same propositional component can be coupled with numerous different illocutionary components (so that I can *tell* you that Habermas wrote *Postmetaphysical Thinking*, I can *ask* you if he wrote *Postmetaphysical Thinking*, and can even *promise* you that he wrote *Postmetaphysical Thinking*, as well as use it to show off my learning and introduce myself). Similarly the same illocutionary component can be coupled with an infinity of propositional components (so that I can also tell you that Habermas wrote *Legitimation Crisis*, and ask you if you would like to go to a concert on Friday night).

See also: **speech acts** and **universal pragmatics**

EMANCIPATION

One of three basic requirements that must be met if human beings are going to live in a flourishing and fair society. In his theory of **cognitive interests**, Habermas argues that human beings need to be able to understand and transform their physical environment through science and technology, to communicate with each other in order to organise small- and large-scale social interaction, but also to be free of oppression and exploitation, and hence emancipated (Habermas 1971a).

In this early stage of his work, Habermas contends that communication alone is insufficient to guarantee a fair and non-exploitative society. He argues that the sources of exploitation can be concealed by ideological distortions that seep into the language that we use, and the very ways in which we think and reflect upon the social world. Crucially, society confronts its members (and thus the people who create and sustain it through their everyday actions and interactions) as something natural, or at least as something governed by natural laws. An emancipatory science (or **critical theory**) is therefore required, alongside the natural and cultural sciences, that has the task of exposing our individual and collective self-misunderstanding, of seeing through this 'second nature'.

Habermas finds models for such a science in **psychoanalysis** and **Marxism**. Both strive to delve beneath surface appearances. The psychoanalyst is confronted by a patient who is seemingly afflicted by symptoms that have a physical cause. Her task is to expose, and bring back to the patient's conscious memory, the traumatic personal experience that is the actual source of the symptoms, to trace the symptoms as the patient's unconscious but none the less creative response to that trauma, and thereby to restore the patient's body to his own control. The task of Marxism, similarly, is to expose the illusion of naturalness and inevitability that conceals the social processes that serve to sustain economic exploitation and political domination. Again, such exposure will restore self-understanding and autonomy to society as a whole, allowing it to take charge of its own destiny.

The idea of critical theory is revised in Habermas's later work, and this concept of emancipation is dropped, not least in so far as the model of psychoanalysis encourages unrealistic aspirations for a wholly transparent and consensual society, which Habermas comes to regard as being unrealistic for any complex and large-scale social organisation.

FORMAL PRAGMATICS *see* **Universal pragmatics**

FRANKFURT SCHOOL

The philosophers, cultural critics and social scientists who belonged to, or were associated with, the Frankfurt Institute for Social Research. The figures most readily associated with the School are Max Horkheimer, Theodor Adorno, Herbert Marcuse, Erich Fromm and Walter Benjamin, with Habermas being considered as the major representative of a post-war 'second generation'.

The Institute was opened in 1924, but began to develop a characteristic and distinctive approach to **Marxism** when the philosopher Max Horkheimer became its director in 1930. The Frankfurt School approach can be characterised as an attempt to develop an Hegelian–Marxism that is appropriate to the conditions of twentieth-century **capitalism**. A major influence on the Frankfurt School is thus found in the work of the Hungarian Marxist Georg Lukács, not least in so far as his *History and Class Consciousness* (1971) offered a reading of Marx that was grounded in the German philosophical tradition of Kant and Hegel, but also in that it sought to modify Marx's account of capitalism by recognising the importance of the work of the sociologist Max Weber (not least in his analysis of the increasing role that bureaucracy and administration play in contemporary industry and government). To this, the Frankfurt School added an interest in **psychoanalysis**, and thus the project of fusing the work of Marx and Freud. Overall, the Frankfurt School, especially under Horkheimer's guidance, sought to pursue multidisciplinary research projects in which the empirical social science research would be directed and its results analysed by Marxist theory. An undoubted strength of the work carried out by members of the Frankfurt School lay in its development of a theory of culture – an area that had been comparatively neglected by earlier generations of Marxist theorists. This included not just sociological accounts of art and literature (from Leo Lowenthal) but also sophisticated Marxist philosophies of art (from Benjamin, Marcuse and Adorno).

Habermas became linked to the Frankfurt School early in his career. The work of Horkheimer and Adorno, and in particular their study *The Dialectic of Enlightenment* (1972), was an early influence on Habermas's intellectual development. However, it was not until 1956 that he became a member of the Institute, as Adorno's research assistant. It was under the auspices of the Institute that he conducted his first major research projects, on student attitudes to politics (Habermas *et al.* 1961), and on the public sphere (Habermas 1989a). They both represent the multidisciplinary aspirations of the School, combining empirical research, social history and philosophical argument. While Habermas formally left the Institute in 1962, leaving initially for Marburg and then Heidelberg after disagreements with Horkheimer, his work in the 1960s may still be seen to fall within the broad parameters of the School. In particular, the conception of **critical theory** that he outlines in the conclusion of *Knowledge and Human Interests* (1971a) draws together a number of Frankfurt themes. First, the very term 'critical theory' is borrowed from Horkheimer, in order to suggest a politically committed analysis of society. Second, Habermas's model of capitalist society owes much to the sort of Marxist models that the Frankfurt School had been developing, drawing as it does on Weber as well as Marx, and in recognising the way in which the exercise of economic and political power may distort the very ways in which we think and perceive social relationships (see **ideology critique** and **systematically distorted communication**). Finally, the models for a critical theory are drawn not just from Marx, but also from Freudian psychoanalysis.

From the late 1960s onwards (and, perhaps significantly, after Adorno's death in 1969), Habermas's work moves increasingly further away from its Frankfurt School origins. What makes Habermas's work distinctive is perhaps the greater range of sources upon which he draws. While the original Frankfurt School thinkers were innovative in trying to fuse Marxism and psychoanalysis, they tended to be resistant to other schools of philosophical, social or psychological thought. They were thus critical of the rival German philosophical schools of phenomenology and **hermeneutics**, and dismissive of much **analytic philosophy**, as well as of American **pragmatism**. Habermas's review of different approaches to social theory, *On the Logic of the Social Sciences* (1988b), may be seen as a deliberate attempt to break away from the narrow confines of Frankfurt thinking in order to embrace ideas from hermeneutics, pragmatism, the philosophy of language, and increasingly from **systems theory** approaches to sociology.

Habermas returned to reconsider the work of Horkheimer and Adorno in the 1980s. Appeals to their work play a major part in both *The Theory of Communicative Action* (1984a: 339–99; 1987: 374–403), and in *The Philosophical Discourse of Modernity* (1988a: 106–30). The argument of *The Dialectic of Enlightenment* is acknowledged as a key source of inspiration. In particular the explorations of the tensions within late capitalism, whereby the development of rationality is entwined within the increasingly repressive nature of human society, finds strong echoes in Habermas's own conception of the **colonisation of the lifeworld**, albeit that Habermas remains critical of Horkheimer and Adorno's restricted understanding of reason. Highlighting the role that **instrumental reason** plays in contemporary society, for Habermas they neglect the all important place of **communicative rationality**.

Indeed, throughout his career, Habermas has used appeals to communicative reasoning in order to combat the resignation or quietism that pervades, in particular, Adorno's work. Adorno hones his critical powers against capitalism to such a point that he becomes sceptical of the possibility of any action, however critically motivated, to do anything but ultimately reinforce the capitalist status quo. He thus retreats into a purely critical stance, at best awaiting the crisis that will bring about the fall of capitalism, albeit he can do nothing to hasten its arrival. In contrast Habermas wants a more nuanced theory, one that can advocate political interventions into society, and that can acknowledge the political gains that have been achieved through, for example, the expansion of democracy and the development of the welfare state. While never complacent about these achievements, or indeed the compromises and hidden exercises of power that they may entail, Habermas sees in the human capacity to communicate, and thus in the ineradicably social nature of human existence, sources of both theoretical criticism and the justification of political action through which capitalism can and must be challenged.

Further reading: Jay 1973; Connerton 1976; Arato and Gebhardt 1978; Bronner and Kellner 1989; Wiggershaus 1994

GENETIC STRUCTURALISM

The theoretical framework of the child psychologist Jean Piaget (so called because it is concerned with the development – and thus genesis – of structured stages). Piaget seeks to explain the development of an ordinary child's cognitive ability. He does this by suggesting that a child's understanding of the physical world, the social world and her own psychological states must proceed through a number of stages. The infant is initially in a symbiotic stage, where she has not yet differentiated between herself and the world around her. This differentiation occurs at the ego-centric stage, albeit that no differentiation will have yet been achieved between the physical and the social world, and everything is understood from the child's own perspective. The socio-centric stage establishes this differentiation of the physical and the social. The egoistic perspective breaks down as the child begins to be able to imagine the world from other people's perspectives. In addition, the child here gains a greater control of language, so that she can at once separate between the word and that to which it refers, and use language to bring about effects in the world (for example by giving orders or making requests – see **speech act**). In the final universal stage, achieved with adolescence, the child becomes capable of hypothetical thought, and seeks a rational justification both for her factual beliefs and for the moral values that guide her actions. A similar form of analysis is found in the work of Maurice Kohlberg on children's moral development (Kohlberg 1981).

This approach is important for Habermas, not merely as an account of the growing competence of a person (or 'ego-development') (Habermas 1979a: 69–129), but also in that it provides a model for other forms of explanation. In particular, it becomes a model for **social**

evolution (Habermas 1979a: 130–77; 1979b). Societies are similarly seen to proceed through a series of stages of growing complexity and **differentiation**. Further, just as Piaget is charting a process of learning, so Habermas argues that societies evolve through a process of learning such that they are able to understand and handle ever more complex and demanding challenges. As with Piaget's model, Habermas stresses the point that later stages cannot be achieved without the prior mastery of earlier stages.

GENETICS

The scientific study of the inheritance of, and variations in, the traits and characteristics of individuals and populations. Advances in this science have had major implications for medical and other technical interventions on the human body and on human populations.

Habermas's principal writings on genetic technology are included in *The Postnational Constellation* (2001b) and in *The Future of Human Nature* (2003b). While the former draws together three short essays on human cloning, the latter ('The Debate on the Ethical Self-understanding of the Species') is a substantial essay, primarily concerned with preimplantation genetic diagnosis (PGD) and eugenics. In PGD, genetics is used to establish the presence of certain traits, such as potential or actual disease or disability, in the foetus before implantation in the womb. Eugenics is the attempt to manipulate genetic inheritance in order to improve a population. Habermas's disquiet over the potential for genetic control of human reproduction centres upon the impact that it would have upon the communicative and ethical relationships that serve to integrate human society. Habermas's worries are articulated on four more or less distinct levels: the self-understanding of the individual; the intersubjective relationship between individuals; the status of the individual in law; the ethical self-understanding of the species as a whole.

Before turning to the substance of Habermas's arguments, their theoretical background, in terms of both ethical and social theory, may be usefully outlined. Habermas's arguments rest ultimately upon the model of **discourse ethics**. Discourse ethics is primarily concerned with the procedures through which normative claims are justified. Ideally, justification occurs through the free and open discussion of all parties who are affected by the decision. This is a broadly Kantian approach to ethics, and open discussion may be seen to approximate Kant's notion of the kingdom of ends, in which all moral agents treat each other as ends, and never merely as means. In part, Habermas's concern over genetic technology lies in the fact that it reduces certain individuals to means, and thus inhibits their participation in the discussion and justification of norms. In his more recent writings, Habermas has more explicitly acknowledged the limitations of discourse ethics, in so far as it failed to acknowledge fully the place and importance of the concrete values that are part of the normative framework through which we evaluate and make ethical sense of our world. The concern with genetics is that it may undermine the very possibility of such substantive ethical values.

In terms of social theory, Habermas evokes his model of late **capitalism** and the **colonisation of the lifeworld**. In brief, Habermas's argument is that the meaningful lifeworld, and with it the opportunity for rational debate, has been eroded by the intrusion of the instrumental and impersonal forms of organisation that are characteristic of social **systems**. With respect to genetics, Habermas argues that the development of genetic science and technology is increasingly driven by purely economic goals (principally of profit maximisation) or the development of the intrinsic logic of the science, and as such it is increasingly unable to recognise or allow meaningful debate of the ethical and political challenges that it poses.

Turning to the details of Habermas's discussion of genetics, the first problem that Habermas poses concerns that of the individual's self-understanding in a society in which genetic technology has free rein. Cloning or PGD presupposes that the physical and possibly intellectual or emotional attributes of a future person can be chosen prior to their conception and birth. In what Habermas terms 'liberal eugenics' – as distinct from the 'authoritarian eugenics' of the Nazis – the people making the choice are most likely be the future person's parents. Liberal eugenics is thus understood as a political framework that allows individual freedom, on the part of the parents, to intervene in the life of their offspring, typically by buying genetic services from a free market (2003b: 48–9). The future child is thus part of the parents' life project, which they are given the freedom to pursue as best they can (2003b: 60). The defenders of such liberal eugenics would argue that such genetic interventions are continuous with the educational interventions that parents make in their child's development, and as such pose no new ethical problems.

Habermas's initial concern can be identified through reference to the colonisation of the lifeworld. If the genetic services that are made available are those that are profitable (or that facilitate the working-through of scientific research projects (2001b: 166–9)), then they are governed by the system, and not by the lifeworld. There is no guarantee that such services will meet real needs (for example, in terms of health care), nor indeed that they will be chosen on rationally defensible grounds. Habermas points to the danger that a 'media circus' might bring in distorting our ability to understand genetics and thus to make choices concerning genetic technology (2003b: 22). Further, the intrinsic momentum of these systems suggests that genetic technology, including cloning, will develop, regardless of ethical objections to it voiced at the level of the lifeworld. The subsequent arguments that Habermas offers may be seen to be substantiating this claim that genetics is breaking away from (or indeed breaking asunder) the lifeworld, by detailing precise points of tension.

The problem of self-understanding is one such point of tension. Habermas identifies three elements that characterise the growth and social development of a child prior to the possibility of genetic intervention. First, one's genetic inherence will have been a matter of 'fate' (2001b: 163). Second, this fate is manifest in a body that is one's being – which is to say that in developing physical autonomy, one comes to take one's body for granted. It is you, and expresses your will and personality. To be self-conscious of one's body, and thus to treat it as an object that is somehow separate from you and possessed by you, is an attitude that is secondary to and made possible by the more fundamental state of being one's body (2003b: 50–1 and 53–4). Finally, one's social and psychological development occurs through the medium of language, and the core capacity that one develops is that of being able to enter into communication with others, to present one's own viewpoint, and to reject or challenge the viewpoint of others (2003b: 62–3). Genetic modification undermines these three elements.

If one has been genetically modified, then one's genetic inherence will be to a greater or lesser extent causally determined. This is significant not least because it begins to blur the conceptual distinctions that, until this point, have been a fundamental resource within our lifeworlds (2003b: 42). The distinction between the 'grown' and the 'made' breaks down. An ethical language that makes sense when related to the human being (or indeed any other natural object) as grown ceases to make sense when applied to that which has been manufactured. More precisely, it may be suggested that if a human being is understood as made, then it is increasingly subject to instrumental thinking (as is any other manufactured object). It can be assessed only in terms of its effectiveness and efficiency in realising its pre-given and unquestionable end, and not in terms of its moral existence as an end in itself.

This leads to the second and third elements. Again, the conceptual distinctions contained within lifeworlds as they now exist are seen to be inadequate for the self-understanding of the genetically modified person. Habermas suggests that any such individual must look upon their own physical and mental capacities instrumentally. They must understand themselves as being made, not grown, as being causally determinate and not fateful. Their primary relationship to their body will thus be one of 'having' – their bodies will be their possessions, to be judged in terms of their instrumental efficiency – and not one of being – where they realise who and what they are through the process or quest of bodily existence (see Habermas 2003b: 34). The purpose for which they exist has been given by another, and in Habermas's phrase, they 'may interpret, but never revise or undo [their designer's] intention' (2003b: 64). Habermas is here making a crucial difference between genetic modification and education. Education will give the child the capacity to say 'no' to the very goals that the parent is attempting to encourage in it. Because genetic modification is a causal and instrumental process, it offers no resources for challenging the designer's goals morally. The very ground for one's existence is an instrumentally manufactured body, not a fatefully given one. What might then have been a fateful burden (for example a naturally inherited ability that one might be encouraged to use, or a disability that one must manage (see Habermas 2003b: 62)) becomes a given. It can be reinterpreted, as Habermas suggests, but only at the cost of further separating oneself from one's body, and thus of instrumentalising oneself.

The second level of Habermas's argument, the question of the impact that genetic technology would have upon the interaction between individuals, is already anticipated in noting the impact that genetics has upon socialisation. The interaction between the child and its parents, if those parents are its designers, necessarily falls short of the ideals of meaningful interaction that are presupposed in socialisation. The child cannot say 'no' to the parents' intentions. The child has thus been objectified – its right to enter into communicative action and moral discourse undermined – rather than engaged with as an equal. Further, the relationship between the geneticist as physician and the child as patient is similarly compromised. Here Habermas makes an important distinction between therapeutic genetic interventions and genetic enhancement. The former implies that the role of the physician is to remove or remedy a potential disability. In terms of the communicative relationship between the physician and the (as yet unborn) patient, an assumption is being made, by the physician, that the future person would, unequivocally, agree to the genetic therapy. Genetic therapy is thus acceptable where the goal is one 'of avoiding evils which are unquestionably extreme and likely to be rejected by all' (2003b: 43). Thus, the physician relates to the patient as a subject – as a second person with whom they are in dialogue. In the case of genetic enhancement, however, the physician cannot make that same assumption. There is no guarantee that the future person would agree to the enhancement. The communicative relationship is thus broken, and the patient is treated as an objectified third person that can be manipulated, and not as a second person to be engaged.

This analysis may be taken further. Habermas suggests that genetic modification inhibits not merely the patients' interaction with their designers, but also with all other human beings. The point here is that genetic enhancement, by partially objectifying the human agent, may compromise their ability to enter freely into discussion, precisely because the enhancement may have curtailed their capacity to reflect critically and openly upon specific purposes and norms, or more generally, through the inappropriateness of the existing categorical structures of the lifeworld for articulating their position. Genetic modification thereby becomes a new form of **systematically distorted communication** that has, under various guises, concerned Habermas throughout his career. When systematic distortion is the result of the exercise of macro-political forces, it typically works by silencing sections of the population (specifically in such a way that they are themselves unaware of that silencing) or tacitly excluding certain topics from public and open discussion. Systematic distortion of communication is thus a result of the colonisation of the lifeworld, precisely in so far as it renders the goals of the system no longer amenable to rational discussion. Genetic modification is thus presented by Habermas as a micro-political complement to the overarching processes of colonisation. The power of the designer systematically distorts the communicative capacity of the patient (2003b: 63). For Habermas, there is a danger that the genetically modified person is then (explicitly or implicitly) denied the dignity that is entailed in mutual recognition and respect for autonomy (2003b: 34).

The phenomenon of systematic distortion of communication leads to the third level of Habermas's argument: the legal status of those who have been genetically modified. Habermas poses the basic pro-

blem of whether or not a constitutional **democracy** within a plur-
alist society can formulate laws that recognise the rights of genetic
modification (2003b: 22). Habermas's approach to constitutional
democracy, that is developed at length in *Between Facts and Norms*
(1996), follows on from his notion of discourse ethics. Ideally a **law** is
drawn up and agreed to only by the people who will be subject to it.
All who could be affected by a law have the right to articulate their
opposition to it. The constitution of a democratic society must
guarantee this. Further, the cultural pluralism of contemporary
societies requires a **post-metaphysical** approach to law and politics,
which is to say that legal and political decisions cannot be informed
by the particular (metaphysical) values of one cultural group – which
is to suggest that law-making works at a level equivalent to morality,
rather than ethics. Put another way, constitutional democracies must
safeguard the traditional liberal freedom of individuals and groups to
pursue their freely chosen substantive goals in life. The liberal euge-
nicist may then argue that the geneticist (and the prospective parent)
must have the right to pursue their goals (of a desirable child).
Habermas replies that this entails an inherent contradiction. The very
process of genetic enhancement imposes a goal upon the future child.
The freedom of the designer is not merely in conflict with that of the
child, but violates the child's liberal freedoms. More subtly, the child
is unable to participate freely in the discussion that validates any law
making genetic enhancement permissible. Either the child does not
yet exist, in which case validation of the law presupposes a highly
dubious consent; or the capacity of the existing child to participate is
compromised by its very genetic modification. Genetic enhancement
cannot then be legally validated within the framework of a democratic constitution, precisely because those most directly affected by
the process cannot give their free consent to the law.

Habermas's final level of argument is that of the ethical self-
understanding of the species – and thus the theme signalled in the
title of the essay. The key term is 'ethical'. Habermas has distinguished the formal procedures of morality from the substantial
(lifeworld) values of ethics. The key move that Habermas makes at
this stage of the argument is to suggest that morality is not the most
fundamental level to be considered in ethical theory. Morality itself is
underpinned by a very broad cultural agreement on the substantial
nature of ethics. Habermas suggests that the ethics of all global civilisations is underpinned by broad conceptions of human autonomy,
responsibility and dignity that were established in the axial period
(the eighth to the third centuries BCE) in the cultures of China, India,

Israel and Greece. It is precisely this ethics that is being disrupted by genetic modification, not least in what Habermas sees as the instrumentalisation of the 'preperson' (Habermas 2003b: 39 and 71). The understanding of what it is to be human, and thus of what it is to be part of humanity and crucially to participate in the historical and cultural development of humanity, is challenged by genetic technology. The disruption to the ethical notion of a common humanity has already been seen clearly in the distortion that genetic enhancement brings to communication. The disruption of the historical self-understanding of humanity may be seen in the relationship between generations, and in the impact that genetic technology would have upon social learning. For Habermas, societies since the axial age have begun to institute rational mechanisms that allow them to adapt to the problems of social change through discursive means (manifest as much in the development of new science and technology as in growing sophistication in political and moral debate). Already Habermas's concerns over the forestalling of this process through the colonisation of the lifeworld have been noted. Genetic technology poses a further threat, precisely in so far as it has the potential to reduce human development and adaptation to one of instrumental manipulation, rather than increased learning capacity. Habermas is thus suggesting a nightmare scenario in which genetic technologists attempt to anticipate the capacities that humans will need in the future, and to engineer them into the next generation, rather than providing that generation with the cultural competences to respond to problems on their own terms. In effect, this is the relationship between the individual designer and the individual child, writ large. The designer imposes the child's purpose and meaning upon it, rather than allowing it to discover that purpose for itself.

HERMENEUTICS

The theory of textual interpretation. Hermeneutics emerged as a response to the problem of interpreting Biblical texts, and in particular to the problem of the identification of corrupted texts. It developed during the nineteenth century as a general theory of the processes that would lead to the correct interpretation of written and spoken texts, and indeed of human actions and non-verbal artefacts, like buildings or works of art. For Habermas, hermeneutics is important as the basic account of the methodology that is appropriate to the social and cultural sciences, in distinction to the natural sciences (see **scientism**). He looks in particular detail at the application of hermeneutics to the study of history by Wilhelm Dilthey in the late nineteenth century, and to the work of the dominant hermeneutician of the twentieth century, Hans-Georg Gadamer (Habermas 1988b: 143–70).

Within the context of his theory of **cognitive interests**, Habermas links hermeneutics to humanity's deep-seated interest in communication (1971a: 140–86). That is to say that, in order to flourish, human beings must be able to organise themselves into social groups, and to do that they must be able to make sense of each other's actions and utterances. Thus hermeneutics, as the science of interpretation, is the systematic refinement of a basic human ability. Dilthey recognises something of this as he strives to distinguish between the methods used by social scientists (and in particular by historians) and those used by natural scientists. Here Dilthey offers an affecting image. The natural scientist stands outside nature. He is not its creator. He can only explain how it works. In contrast, the historian is part of the very history she studies. She is a human being and humans created history (Habermas 1971a: 149). She can then understand history in the way that God, who created nature, must be able to understand the natural world.

The basic task of the historian is thus to find common ground between herself and her subjects. For Habermas, Dilthey's approach is marred by the continuing influence of **positivism**, and what Habermas would later come to call the philosophy of **consciousness**. That is to say that Dilthey assumed that the work of the historian was a largely monological process. The historian works as an individual, observing historical events, and being linked to them through what Dilthey called 'experience' (*Erlebnis*). Only vaguely does Dilthey recognise that what is going on here is not a process of observation, but rather one of communication.

The historian is in a form of dialogue with her subjects. This may seem an odd reflection. The historical subject, being typically dead and buried, is seemingly in no position to discuss anything with anyone. This, none the less, is a crucial point of hermeneutics, and one that is developed at length by Gadamer. Let us assume that the historian is studying a manuscript. It is of course literally mute – it cannot answer back. But the process of interpretation is understood as one of addressing questions to this manuscript. What sort of manuscript are you? Are you a legal document, or a sacred text? The hermeneutician will come to the manuscript with certain presuppositions. The most obvious of these is that it is a certain sort of manuscript and of a certain age. So, imagine that the hermeneutician presupposes it is a sacred text. But, upon reading it, she finds that there are oddities. Let us say, perhaps, that quotations from the scriptures are distorted, the names of secular leaders are introduced. Her dialogue has begun. The manuscript unsettles those first presuppositions of the hermeneutician. The idea that the text is a straightforward sacred manuscript is clearly inadequate. The hermeneutician must formulate a new question. Perhaps she will ask if it is a text from an heretical sect. Again, a reading will test this assumption.

This is an example of what is known as the hermeneutic circle. The process of interpretation runs from a set of general assumptions that the reader brings to the text, and then the particular details of the text challenge and demand the refinement of those assumptions. The refinement is the basis of another reading, and perhaps further challenges from the particulars of the text. More subtly, what this means is that the particulars of the text will only make sense in terms of an overarching general assumption. Any given sentence can mean many different things, depending upon the context within which it is used. Mistake the context, and one misunderstands the sentence. So, when the hermeneutician goes back to the text, to reread it in the light of a revised general presupposition, elements that had been read previously may begin to mean something different. A seemingly sincere sentence begins to stand out as ironic; an error of transcription becomes a deliberate pun; and so on.

While Dilthey presupposed that one could come to a definitive reading of a text, later hermeneuticians generally question this. The hermeneutic circle is endless, and our understanding of a text is continually open to revision. In part this is because of the actual complexity of the presuppositions (or what Gadamer calls the prejudices or pre-judgements) that we bring to a text, and in part because we cannot avoid working from some set of presuppositions. There is no acultural point of pure theory from which we can look down objectively upon a text. We engage with it because we have prejudices. If we did not, we would be either wholly indifferent to the text or, more problematically still, we would lack the hermeneutic skills that were forged in learning our own culture, with its particular **language** and set of pre-judgements about the world.

So we do not come to a text with a simple assumption that, say, it is a sacred text. Rather, we carry with us our whole culture and language. We will have a certain preconception of what a sacred text is, though that preconception may not be shared by the original author of our manuscript. We will have notions, perhaps vague and unarticulated, of how humans should live their lives, and what counts as a meaningful action. Again, our author may not share these views. Our language may not easily express what the author says in his. So what we take for granted may be challenged by the text. It will remain problematic until those presuppositions are brought to the light and re-examined. The past, as the novelist L. P. Hartley remarked at the beginning of *The Go-Between*, 'is another country. They do things differently there.' For Gadamer, the creative engagement with the past, or indeed with the culture of another country, brings about a 'fusion of horizons' – that is to say, a contact between two different worldviews, two different complexes of prejudices, two different ways of doing things.

Habermas is critical of hermeneutics on two levels. While he is content that hermeneutics grasps the basic ability that humans have to make sense of each other's actions and utterances (albeit that this endorsement is heavily qualified by his development of **universal pragmatics**), he is concerned that politically and morally it leads to relativism. This is to say that if there is no escaping culture, then it is not clear how one can make a moral judgement that has any claim to universality. In effect, a moral judgement becomes little more than the expression of the values that are already inherent in your culture – or, put otherwise, an expression of your prejudices. To say that 'Fascism is an evil' would be no more than saying that my culture disapproves of fascism, or that it can make no sense of the fascist worldview. In his later work, Habermas clearly distinguishes between the hermeneutic problem of interpretation and the moral problem of justifying a normative assertion (see **discourse ethics**).

Habermas's second point follows, in part, from this. He sees the hermeneutician's understanding of the social, and thus of social science, to be limited. If hermeneutics claims to be exhaustive of social science methodology, then it can only do this because it has failed to recognise the social role of **ideology** and **reification** (Habermas 1980; 1988b: 171–5). That is to say that hermeneutics presupposes that the meanings of social actions are in principle interpretable for any competent social agent. This neglects the fact that some social processes present themselves as if they were natural processes. Dilthey was aware of this, recognising that economic relations did not obviously lend themselves to hermeneutic analysis (Habermas 1971a: 183). Certain social actions are subject to quasi-causal forces. In his early work, Habermas explores this in terms of the need for an **emancipatory** science that will free humanity from its enthralment to these alien forces. In his later work, he explores this in terms of the need for such causal or instrumental forms of social organisation and the threat that they pose to our everyday ability to make sense of our lives (see **colonisation of the lifeworld**). In both versions, strong moral and political claims are being made as to how human life should be lived, that would sit uneasily with hermeneutics' relativism.

Further reading: Thompson 1981; Holub 1991: 49–77; How 1995; Roberts 1995; Teigas 1995; Hahn 2000: 463–500; Harrington 2001

HISTORICAL MATERIALISM

The theory of historical change and development proposed by Karl Marx, and fundamental to most versions of **Marxism**. Marx argues that social change is led by changes in the economy, and most specifically at the level of technology innovation. In Marx's terminology, social change is driven by developments in the 'forces of production'. The point is that, as technology improves, so too will the ability of society to produce goods and services. However, that productive potential will only be properly exploited if it is organised in the right way. The organisation of production, in what Marx calls 'relations of production', is thus vital to the understanding of social change. The relations of production entail that one particular class will be dominant in that society, albeit that its dominance will allow it to control the economy and make full use of the forces of production. Developments in forces of production therefore bring about revolutions, as the proponents of the new technology must forcibly displace the old dominant class and transform the relations of production. Once the relations of production have changed, so too will the rest of society (the superstructure), including the society's culture, belief systems, educational system and even family organisation.

Marx postulated six basic stages (or 'modes of production') in the development of society. He begins with a period of 'primitive communism', which is to say a technologically undeveloped and therefore poor society. However, the poverty leads to equality, as there are insufficient resources available for any section within the society to secure more than its basic share. All this changes as technology develops, and the society divides into classes. Extra production entails a surplus that one group can appropriate for its own use. A class society is thus one where one group controls the economy (and thus

the society as a whole), while the other groups carry out the productive work. Yet this inequality grants the dominant class leisure
time that may be used to further improve the forces of production.
So Marx takes us here through two modes of production. The first is
based upon slavery (and hence the subordinate groups in society are
slaves, owned by their masters, the dominant group); and the next is
feudalism, where the serfs are tied to the land, legally obligated to
work for their master or to provide part of their produce to their
master, while not strictly being the master's property.

The crucial development comes with the rise of **capitalism**.
While slave societies and feudal societies relied on natural forms of
power, such as human or animal muscle, water or wind power, industrialisation radically transforms the forces of production. However, if the
potential of steam, for example, is to be fully exploited, it cannot work
with the small-scale production units typical of feudalism. So the feudal
system breaks down, the serfs are freed from their ties to the land,
allowing them to form the basis of a labour force that can move to large-
scale production plants (the manufactories of newly expanding urban
centres). The dominant class are the owners of capital (machines and
raw materials), while the subordinate classes own only their ability to
labour, and exchange this ability for wages on the labour market.
Marx suggests that, as the forces of production continue to develop,
then the material inequality between classes will cease to be justifiable
(and indeed, perhaps, that human labour will cease to be justifiable, as
all production becomes automated). Thus revolution will bring about
socialism, leading to the perfect justice of Communism.

To this list of six modes of production Marx adds a problematic
seventh, namely oriental despotism. He suggests that, outside Europe,
economic development is not happening, and that oriental societies
are stagnating. Their only hope for development is invasion by the
industrialised West.

Habermas, in his reconstruction of historical materialism, identifies
several problems with this account, problems that his own theory of
social evolution is designed to correct (1979a: 130–77). First,
Habermas questions the primacy that Marx gives to the economy.
For Marx, the economy is always the 'base' of society, the most fundamental group of institutions that serves to determine the nature of
the rest of society. Habermas suggests that the role of the base may
shift between different institutions, including the family and the state
(see **principle of organisation**).

Second, according to Habermas, this appeal to the economy highlights a basic flaw in Marx's thinking. Marx suggests that human beings

are primarily **labourers**, which is to say that humanity may be defined by its ability to transform its environment, and to do so through conscious and reflective activity. While Habermas does not deny the importance of labour, he argues that it must be complemented by the human ability to **interact** with other humans. Humans are social, communicative creatures. Once this is recognised, not only will the economy cease to be the only base available to society (for communicative structures such as the family may be as important), but we also become aware of a gap in Marx's argument. Marx fails to explain how real people bring about social change. Social change cannot just be a result of labour. People must organise themselves together (into revolutionary groups, political parties, armies or whatever), and that requires their communicative or interactive abilities.

If interaction is ignored, and with it the full richness of human beings as creatures who make sense of their world and who are motivated by the sense they make of it, then Marx's account at best becomes the story of a 'macro-subject'. Society becomes the real hero of Marx's historical materialism, and not the people who make up society. Any adequate account of social change must, in contrast, explain the involvement of ordinary people, and crucially how a crisis in the economy (or elsewhere in society) is interpreted by those people, and how those people find the resources to respond creatively to the crisis. This also means that a theory of social evolution cannot unfold with the inevitability that Marx gives to his account. In practice, the people within society may not be able to deal with problems. Societies may regress or dissolve as readily as they progress and evolve.

Finally, bringing these points together, Habermas highlights the inadequacy of Marx's justification of his six modes of production. For Habermas, key points in human history (such as crucial developments in early Greek, Hebrew and Chinese culture) are ignored. The distinction between slavery and feudalism is, in terms of the technology used, largely arbitrary. Oriental despotism is an ambiguous embarrassment to the theory, and tends to leave historical materialism as a whole as little more than a simplified narrative of European history.

Further reading: Schmid 1982; Rockmore 1989; McCarthy 2001; Owen 2002

IDEAL SPEECH SITUATION

The conditions for free and transparent communication. The concept played an important role in the early formulations of Habermas's theories of **communicative action** and **universal pragmatics** (Habermas 1979a: 1–68; 1984a; 1987), although it was subsequently replaced by Karl-Otto Apel's notion of an 'unrestricted communication community' (Apel 1980; Habermas 1990: 88).

The ideal speech situation can be understood as the projection of the conditions for a perfect discussion. In Habermas's early accounts, what is most important about these conditions is that they entail that there is no imbalance of power between the participants to the conversation. This means that nobody can force his opinions upon anyone else, and cannot exclude somebody from the discussion, or prevent them raising problems or challenges. If such conditions held, then Habermas states that any agreement that the participants came to would be based upon the force of rational argument alone.

The notion has its origins in the work of the nineteenth-century American **pragmatist** philosopher Charles Sanders Peirce. In reflecting upon the methods of natural scientific inquiry, Peirce first argued that scientists work communally, so that discoveries are not made by individuals but rather by teams of scientists who discuss and criticise each others' ideas and evidence. Only then will formulations of scientific laws and hypotheses be accepted as true. In practice, the actual discussion of scientists will be marred by the lack of relevant information, and possibly by hierarchies of status and power within the community. Junior researchers may feel inhibited about challenging their superiors, and even if they do challenge them their arguments may easily be suppressed or ignored. So any actual agreement that scientists come to must be provisional. New evidence and new ideas may challenge it in the future. Peirce therefore contrasts any actual agreement with an ideal agreement, achieved in 'the very long run' as Peirce puts it, which is to say at the end of the history of science. This ideal community of scientists will have all the information it needs and will debate freely and rationally, and thus be able to discover true natural laws.

The images of an 'ideal community of scientists' and an 'ideal speech situation' have a utopian ring about them, suggesting the goal of perfect societies at the end of human history. Habermas is keen to reject such an interpretation of the ideal speech situation (Habermas 1982: 261f). Initially the concept can be seen as a critical tool. It does not describe a realisable set of conditions, but is rather used to highlight the imperfections of actual communication. To some degree all real communication will be distorted, not least by the imbalances of power that silence some of the parties who should be involved in the discussion, and should have the right to protest against any decisions made (see **systematically distorted communication**).

Habermas further justifies the importance of the ideal speech situation by arguing that it is a counter-factual assumption typically made by all participants to a discussion, as they enter that discussion. What this means is that, in order to take part in discussions with others, we must assume that the discussion will be transparent until we have evidence to the contrary. It is difficult to see how we could genuinely enter into a conversation with somebody who, from the first, we assumed was lying to us, or was trying to trick us. At best we might humour him, and pretend to go along with his fantasies or inventions, but that is not communication. It certainly would not have the goal of reaching mutual agreement, which, for Habermas, is what communicative action is all about. So, genuine communication entails that the participants presuppose each other's sincerity or **truthfulness**, and the moment at which this presupposition becomes dubious is the moment when communication begins to break down. This approach allows Habermas to spell out the sort of assumptions that we must make as participants in communication. Beyond assumptions about the truthfulness of the participants, we assume that everyone who is sufficiently competent, and who has an interest in the outcome of the discussion, is allowed to take part. All these participants can question anything that anyone else says, and everyone can introduce new ideas and topics as they see fit. To enter a genuine conversation entails that one accepts that the views and opinions you are prepared to put forward will not only be challenged, but could be found wanting on grounds of rationality and evidence. As I enter a conversation, I must accept that my opinions could be changed by it (Habermas 1990: 89).

In practice, actual communication rarely if ever realises these conditions. People do feel hesitant or intimidated about introducing topics or challenging others. They stubbornly refuse to acknowledge relevant evidence or to accept that their position is inconsistent. A rhetorical flow of words or a finely tuned metaphor may carry more weight than a carefully made argument. This does not, for Habermas and Apel, serve to undermine the fact that communication does presuppose openness and transparency, and further, that any person who enters a conversation cynically, with the aim of manipulating the other participants and so forcing agreement rather than allowing agreement to arise through the power of reason alone, is effectively contradicting themselves (see **performative contradiction**). The notion of an ideal speech situation or an unrestricted communicative community may thereby be seen to underpin the normative side of Habermas's work. It is through this notion that Habermas can criticise not just imperfections in scientific debate and inquiry, but also imperfections in moral, political and legal debate, again precisely because actual debates will systematically exclude certain people, or inhibit the raising of certain complaints or topics. The notion of an ideal speech situation explains why this state of affairs is morally and politically wrong.

IDEOLOGY

Within **Marxist** social theory, the dominant culture of a society that serves to maintain and legitimate the rule of the dominant class. The concept remains important in Habermas's early work, albeit less so in his later work. This is in part due to the influence of the first generation of **Frankfurt School** thinkers, alongside neo-Hegelian Marxists such as Georg Lukács and Ernst Bloch, on the young Habermas. Their work was characterised by a much greater interest in culture than was shown by Marx or the earlier Marxists. For the Frankfurt School and their contemporaries, culture was a key site of political struggle and expression, and this led to a subtle account of the nature of ideology.

The original Marxist notion of ideology may be summed up by Marx's remark that the ideas of the ruling class are in every epoch the ruling ideas (Marx and Engels 1977: 64). This is to say that, through its power to control significant parts of culture, such as religion, education and latterly the mass media, the ruling class can propagate a view of the world and a set of values that serves to justify its position of power. Thus, for example, the mediaeval European church may be seen to have offered an account of the social (and indeed natural) world as a God-given hierarchy. God had given each person his or her place, and to challenge it would be defiance, not just of earthly authority, but of divine authority too.

There is, however, a more subtle notion that may be found in Marx's well-known (and perhaps little understood) comment that religion is the opium of the masses (Marx 1975b: 244). The point here is not just that religion provides a narcotic as a cushion against the harsh realities of everyday life that might serve to stifle political unrest (for example, by promising the meek and oppressed their reward in heaven). More importantly, opiates encourage dreams, and dreams of a better and more just life frequently constitute the substantial contents of ideologies. Thus, for example, Christianity offers promises to peacekeepers and those who minister to the poor, and powerful images of a Last Judgement in which the wicked will be condemned. As an ideology, the political sting is taken out of such ideas by linking them to an afterlife. A politicised reinterpretation of the ideology turns it into a demand for immediate social change and justice. Such a reading is important to the work of Ernst Bloch (Habermas 1983a: 61–77). Bloch and other twentieth-century Marxists take this interpretation of ideology further, by arguing that the content of ideologies is also symptomatic of the concerns of the oppressed. This is to suggest that ideologies have a utopian content, again a dreaming of a better life. But, just as the **psychoanalyst** may find in the dreams of her patients clues to their neuroses, those dreams are not to be taken literally. Most utopian visions would be singularly unpleasant places within which to live. However, treated as symptoms, they provide an important clue to the forms that oppression is taking, and thus what must be done to change it. This approach allows the Marxist analyst to find within culture complex strands of visions, longings and aspirations, as ordinary people are seen to use cultural resources to cope with and make sense of their lives (rather than merely accept an imposed vision from the ruling classes) (see **ideology critique**).

In Marx's later writings the concept of 'ideology' is abandoned in favour of an analysis of what he calls 'commodity fetishism'. That is to say that he suggests that the need for an overt culture to legitimate or conceal the dominance of the dominant class ceases to be necessary in **capitalism**. While, in earlier forms of society, the politically dominant group directly controlled the economy (for example by owning slaves, or by directly benefiting from the labour of serfs), in capitalism the relationship between the owners of capital (for example, the factory owners) and the people they employ appears to be an equal and fair one. It is a relationship that is regulated through the market for labour (and a worker will be paid a fair day's wage for a fair day's work). There is no direct exploitation, as there was with slave-ownership or feudalism. As Habermas puts this, the ruling class can now convince itself that it does not rule (Habermas 1976b: 22). Marx's point is that the cultural achievement of market exchange comes to confront those involved in it as if it was a natural process. Market exchange is therefore inevitable, and the inequalities that come out of it are fair. It is this approach which is taken up and generalised as a theory of ideology, again by the likes of Lukács and the Frankfurt School, under the concept of **reification**.

Further reading: Larrian 1979

IDEOLOGY CRITIQUE

An approach to the analysis and interpretation of culture that has been dominant in much **Marxist** social theory. The approach is typified by treating the contents of culture as an **ideology**, which is to say a set of ideas that serves to legitimate the political position of the ruling class, but, by seeing culture as a determinant response to political oppression and economic exploitation, seeks to find in it the resources to understand and expose the injustice of that society. A 'critique' is therefore properly understood not merely as a criticism of the content of ideology, but also as an analysis of its origin and motivation.

Ideology critique can be seen to be an important element of Habermas's early work, both in practice in the account of the ideological aspects that surround the development and decline of the bourgeois **public sphere**, and in more theoretical work, in his engagement with **positivism** and his defence of a model of **critical theory** in *Knowledge and Human Interests* (1971a). With his shift towards **systems theory**, and the associated development of a theory of **communicative action**, from the 1970s onwards, the theory of ideology is abandoned in favour of analyses that turn upon the problems of legitimacy and a legitimation crisis (1976b), **systematically distorted communication** (1970a), and ultimately the **colonisation of the lifeworld** (1987: 318–31). Here a theory of ideology is replaced by a focus on the way in which political inequalities and structural aspects of social systems distort and inhibit the possibility of communication and subject the exercise of power to rational justification.

While the early chapters of *The Structural Transformation of the Public Sphere* (1989a) are primarily concerned with the rise of public political debate in eighteenth-century Europe, Habermas also looks to the associated ideological aspects of an emerging bourgeois culture, and in particular to the literary culture that allows for the shaping of bourgeois notions of subjectivity and personal autonomy. Habermas's contention is not just that the eighteenth century sees the emergence of the economic conditions that allow for a bourgeois class of property owners and professionals to emerge, but also that this new class strives to articulate its sense of who and what it is. At the level of the individual, this is 'an ideology of intimacy' that entails the gradual development of techniques to express a sense of self-identity, not least through the ability to articulate and justify one's personal thoughts, emotions and values (Habermas 1989a: 43–51). The popularity of the letter and the novel became crucial in this development. In effect, a letter became a means of presenting oneself to a public (as the readership of a letter would not necessarily be confined to its immediate addressee), articulating thoughts and feelings, rather than merely conveying information. The novel builds upon this (not least in so far as early novels were often written in the epistolary form, as a series of letters). The novel provides models for the self-understanding and expression of the bourgeois self.

At a more general class level, this development entails the self-understanding of the bourgeoisie as representative of humanity as such. The ideology of intimacy serves to conceal from the bourgeoisie its own dependency upon the economy and property ownership. As such it is able to champion its own freedom and autonomy as being those of all human beings. It presupposes that anyone can enter the privileged realm of property ownership if they are sufficiently motivated and hard-working. The second part of *The Structural Transformation of the Public Sphere* (1989a: 89–140) explores the way in which a number of the major philosophers and political thinkers of the eighteenth and nineteenth centuries reflect and struggle with the contradictions of the social and economic position of the bourgeoisie. The specific tension to be managed is that between the bourgeois as members of a specific class, and as such dependent upon certain economic privileges from which others are more or less actively excluded, and their self-presentation as representatives of humanity as such. The all important point of Habermas's analysis is that, while bourgeois ideology might conceal and distort the true political and economic position of the class, it also fostered the ideals of rational debate and the equality of all human beings. As such, there is an important truth content that may be redeemed from its distortions and misrepresentations. As ever with ideology critique, the problem posed is that of how these ideals are to be transformed into realities. This, in effect, becomes the question that Habermas pursues throughout his career.

In his more theoretical works of the 1970s, Habermas explores two forms of ideology critique. The first he finds in positivism. The positivist is concerned to defend a rigorous model of scientific research. At its core this model entails that the scientist should be guided by facts, and never by her personal values. Science should never be polluted by 'the sewage of emotionality' (Habermas 1976a: 265). The idea, for example, of a Nazi physics is a distortion of real science. However, while Habermas is sympathetic to this as a requirement of the natural sciences, he is aware that, paradoxically, it can itself become a form of ideology. The moment at which a commitment to this principle makes the natural sciences dogmatic, blinding it to the subtle values systems that might influence and structure its work, is when science itself becomes ideological. Habermas suggests, for example, that much scientific research is actually driven by the values of a capitalist culture, and as such much scientific research, and indeed the very commitment to the importance of technological development, becomes an ideology that serves to justify and sustain the capitalist system (Habermas 1971a). In illustration of this we might consider contemporary arguments that justify further genetic modification of crops on the grounds that they will increase agricultural productivity, and thus help to alleviate global food shortages. The counter-argument, that sufficient food is already grown globally to feed everyone but is poorly distributed, highlights the point that the problems of poverty and starvation are social problems. Addressing such problems through more technology conceals, rather than addresses, the real issue.

In *Knowledge and Human Interests* Habermas argues that a model for a critical theory, which is to say a theory of society that would allow political intervention to challenge injustice and oppression, can be based upon the examples of **psychoanalysis** and Marxism. In both cases, their appeal can be seen to lie in their development of a sophisticated ideological critique. In psychoanalysis Freud presented dreams as being what he called 'the royal road to the unconscious', which is to say that, through dreams, one has a glimpse of the problems that the patient has repressed into their unconscious mind. A dream is thus symptomatic of some deeper traumatic experience, which the patient cannot yet handle consciously. However, this symptom is quite determinate. It is not a random image, but one that responds to the problem the patient faces. The task of the psychoanalyst is to retrace the steps to that real problem, in order to allow the patient to confront it consciously. Habermas can be seen to treat ideology critique in a similar manner. The elements of a culture are similar to dreams. That which cannot be spoken about publicly, or that which is repressed by the dominant culture (for example, the early bourgeoisie could not confront their own economic position without unravelling their new-found sense of self), will seep through and manifest itself, albeit often in a distorted form akin to the dream. It will, for example, be found in the tensions and contradictions that mar the texts of great philosophers (and as *The Structural Transformation of the Public Sphere* demonstrates of the political philosophies of Kant, Hegel and John Stuart Mill, for example). Ideology critique, as part of critical theory, is therefore intended to turn its critical gaze upon contemporary culture, in order to expose the contradictions and tensions there that betray the deeper problems that we are, as yet, unable as a society to bring to consciousness and debate publicly.

ILLOCUTIONARY FORCE

The power of an utterance to create a social relationship between the speaker and listener (Habermas 1976e). The idea of illocutionary force was first proposed by the **analytic philosopher** J. L. Austin when he distinguished what he called **speech acts** from cognitive utterances. Put another way, Austin argued that there were two forms of speech. In one, cognitive utterances, the speaker simply asserts some fact or opinion about the world (for example, 'The capital of France is Paris'; 'I have a headache'). In the other, the speaker does something by speaking (for example, 'I declare you man and wife'; 'I sentence you to three years' hard labour'; 'I promise to meet you at nine'). It is this second group of speech acts that have illocutionary force.

Habermas, following the philosopher John Searle, develops Austin's original insight to argue that all utterances have both a cognitive (or 'propositional') content and an illocutionary force (see **double structure of language**). When I say that 'The capital of France is Paris', then the cognitive content is certainly to the fore, but I am still involved in a social relationship with the people listening to me. For example, I might be teaching them geography, or answering a quiz question. If I say, 'Why don't we spend a weekend in Paris?', then the illocutionary component of the utterance comes to the fore. I am asking you a question, and I am perhaps involved in organising a holiday for us. But, in asking this question, I assume that there is indeed such a place as Paris. As Habermas puts this, while in statements I assert my knowledge of the world, in the question I merely mention it. It is still, however, important, and a suggestion, promise or order might fail because the presuppositions it makes about the world are false (for example, 'Let's fly to Paris next weekend.' 'We can't; all the available flights are already booked.').

If an utterance can be challenged on the grounds of what it assumes about the world, then it can also be challenged on the grounds of its illocutionary force. I assert that Paris is the capital of France, and the rather irritating student at the back of the geography class demands to know what right I have to be teaching him about

France – have I ever been there? I promise to lend you this copy of *Knowledge and Human Interests*, but you protest that it is not my copy, so I have no right to lend it to anyone else. (On the challenging of utterances, see **validity claim**.) These examples indicate that, in making an utterance, the people I am talking to must come to respect my right to make that utterance (to perform the action that it entails). Only then will the utterance succeed in its goal of bringing about a specific social relationship between the speaker and his or her audience, and crucially to do so on the grounds of the free consent of all involved (and not because they are threatened, coerced or tricked by the speaker).

INSTRUMENTAL ACTION

Action that is governed by **instrumental** or purposive rationality, and that is intended to manipulate the natural world. As such, instrumental action is contrasted to both social **action**, which is performed between persons in the social world, and **strategic action**, which is a specific form of social action in which one person takes an instrumental attitude to other people (but not to natural objects). Habermas uses the concept widely, and in subtly different contexts, throughout his career (see, for example, Habermas 1971a; Habermas 1979a: 40).

In his earlier writings instrumental action is linked by Habermas to the human ability to **labour**. Human beings transform their physical environment by treating it as a mean to the ends that they desire. Instrumental actions can then be assessed in terms of their efficiency in achieving any given end. While the older generation of the **Frankfurt School** thinkers, such as Marcuse, tended to see the instrumental attitude to nature as repressive, and thus as a part with the repression of human beings, Habermas challenges this assumption by pointing to the fundamental importance of instrumental reason in the development of the natural sciences. Habermas argues that scientists conceive of the natural world as an entity that is governed by universal laws. The regularity and universality of these laws is such that any action performed on the natural world will have a consequence that, in principle at least, is predictable. The task of the scientist is to establish what these rules (and thus what the predictable consequences of actions) are through practical experiments. The consequences of experiments and other interventions in the natural world (for example, through new technologies) can be assessed instrumentally in order to refine our understanding of the natural world. For Habermas, instrumental action only becomes problematic when it is applied inappropriately in the social world (as strategic action).

INSTRUMENTAL REASON

The rational choice of the most appropriate means for the achievement of any given end. Instrumental reason appeals to knowable facts about the world, and in particular to the causal relationships that can be established between means and ends. The most appropriate means are therefore those actions and resources that are judged to realise the desired goals most efficiently (be this in terms of the least use of resources, the lowest cost, or the speed of the achievement). Instrumental reason is fundamental to the development and application of technology, and thus to the control of the natural world. In so far as the social world can be understood to be shaped by causal relationships between social facts, instrumental reason can be used in social administration and the formation of social and economic policies.

Max Weber is a major source for Habermas's reflections on instrumental rationality (see Habermas 1984a: 143–272). While Weber recognises that instrumental rationality is not the only form that reasoning can take (see Weber 1946a: 293), he suggests that instrumental reason is becoming increasingly dominant in the culture and organisation of **capitalist** societies, not just through science and technology, but also in governmental and commercial bureaucracies. Increased instrumental rationality can be a good thing, if it leads to the removal of wasteful and ineffective ways of doing things. However, Weber sees its dominance as leading, on the one hand, to a 'disenchantment of the world', by which he means that substantive traditional meanings are lost – literally, the world loses its magic – so that human agents increasingly live in a disorienting world that seems to make no sense and that has no grounding or compelling values. On the other hand, it leads to the erosion of freedom, as bureaucracies become an 'iron cage' that constrains human action, forcing it into narrowly instrumental channels and stifling spontaneity. These two problems are rooted in the fact that instrumental reason does not simply become dominant, but becomes the only form of rationality acknowledged within capitalism. If this is accepted, then it becomes impossible to reflect rationally upon ends. Ends are mere givens, at best chosen through subjective whim (and thus what Habermas calls '**decisionism**'). In so far as ends embody values or meanings, these values are reduced to something that is purely subjective. The individual agent must choose arbitrarily between the multitude of competing values and goals that society presents to them, with no set of values or meanings being demonstrably better than another. Throughout Habermas's career, he may be seen to be seeking to establish an account of rationality that at once encompasses instrumental rationality (and so recognises its importance in the development of science and technology), while also finding alternative accounts of reason that will restore the possibility of rational reflection on, and thus rational choice of, ends. This he achieves in his account of **communicative reason**.

INTERACTION

The relationship that exists between two or more people, when they share an understanding of the social norms and rules that should guide their **actions**, so that they have reciprocal expectations about their respective behaviour. So, if I am in interaction with you, I can anticipate how you will respond to what I say or do because I know that you share broadly the same understanding of the world, and of the rules of morality and even etiquette that should govern our actions. We can thus make sense of each other's actions and utterances.

'Interaction' is a synonym for **communicative action** in Habermas's earlier works (Habermas 1971b: 92). However, the context from which Habermas explores and develops this 'interaction' in his earlier works differs from that in which he explores 'communicative action' in his later works. This is because 'interaction' is tied up with the theory of **cognitive interests** (Habermas 1971a), and in particular a reading of the early works of the German philosopher Hegel (Habermas 1976a: 142–69). Interaction is explored in terms of a model of the most fundamental characteristics of human beings. These characteristics are the human ability to transform the physical environment (and thus use **labour**); the use of **language**; and finally social existence, so that humans interact with each other. Labour, language and interaction are the three media through which a person can deal with the world around them. Interaction is the medium through which people deal with the social world. In interaction one recognises that one is dealing with other people, and not with mere objects (as one would when labouring).

In the context of the theory of cognitive interests, Habermas is arguing that it is in human beings' interest, if they are to develop and flourish both individually and collectively, to become more sophisticated in labour (through better technology), language use (through better understanding of the meaning of each other's actions and utterances), and through better social organisation (crucially in that interaction should be free of political repression and exploitation). 'Interaction' is thus used by Habermas to explore the abuse of power, and the human interest in **emancipation**. Habermas's point is that oppression and the abuse of power spoil the purity and transparency of interaction. For example, anti-Semitism, like most forms of prejudice, works by undermining the humanity of the Jew. The relationship of the anti-Semite to the Jew thus comes to be, at least in the anti-Semite's eyes, a relationship between a human and a non- (or sub-) human. The preconditions of interaction, where the two people would respect the same set of moral rules and would respect each other's autonomy, are destroyed. The anti-Semite treats the Jew like an object to be manipulated and exploited, not as another human being who is to be recognised as such. Habermas's argument is that the exercise of power typically works by making the social realm of interaction appear to be natural. The exercise of power can conceal and legitimate itself because of this, for once social relationships or human beings are made to appear as part of nature then they can no longer be changed – or, at best, they can be changed only by technological manipulation and thus labour, and not through negotiation or the exercise of any collective human will (see **ideology** and **reification**).

LABOUR

The manipulation of the natural environment through the use of technology, guided by **instrumental reason**. This term plays an important role in Habermas's early work, and in particular in the theory of **cognitive interests** (Habermas 1971a). There it is seen as one of three fundamental characteristics of what it is to be human. While the concept of labour is perhaps most familiar in the work of Karl **Marx** (Habermas 1971a pp. 25–42), Habermas finds the concept being developed previously in the early works of the German philosopher Hegel (Habermas 1976a: 142–69). It is through labour that human beings engage with the physical world around them, transforming it. Humans are not the only creatures to transform their environment, however, as both Hegel and Marx make clear, humans exercise choice and autonomy in making these transformations (in contrast, say, to a bee, that acts merely according to instinct). Such transformations allow humans to develop, learning more about their environment, but also about themselves and they build ever more complex technologies. While Marx stresses this aspect of labour (see Marx 1976: 284), for Habermas the young Hegel gives a more adequate account by recognising that labour is necessarily entwined with the human ability to use **language**. Only through language is the human being freed from his animal nature. While the animal responds immediately to its desires, using whatever capacities nature has given it to satisfy them, once a human has mastered language, he can manipulate the object of desire in his mind before he acts upon the world. It can imagine new tools, and explore different ways of manipulating natural objects. The human being learns by testing these purely imaginary possibilities against the real world – inefficient and ineffective ideas will be exposed by the failure of one's plans. However, such failures lead to new and more refined knowledge, and so, for Habermas, labour provides the foundation of the natural sciences.

LANGUAGE

In his early writings, and specifically within the context of the theory of **cognitive interests**, Habermas treats language use as one of the fundamental characteristics of what it is to be human, alongside the ability to **labour** and human social **interaction** (Habermas 1971a). In his later writings, after what he considers to be a 'linguistic-turn' in his work, language plays an even more fundamental role in so far as it is seen to be fundamental to the organisation of social life and to the development of an individual's sense of personal identity (Habermas 1984a and 1987).

Language has a somewhat ambiguous role in Habermas's theory of cognitive interests. The human capacity to use language is linked to the **hermeneutic** sciences, which is to say to those disciplines that deal with the problem of interpreting spoken and written statements, and of interpreting human actions. This is because language is the medium through which human beings express themselves and make sense of the actions and utterances of others. Language is therefore entwined with the human ability to communicate, and thus to act meaningfully. It is the meaningfulness of human action, along with the need to interpret it, that serves to distinguish the social sciences from the natural sciences. The natural sciences explain phenomena, including the behaviour of animals, in terms of their causes. Social sciences, such as **history**, must understand the **actions** of human beings, because such actions are meaningful. Humans act not through blind causal determinism, but rather because their actions have a meaning for them, and are a response to the meaning that they find in the actions of others. Actions will be understood, both by the actors themselves and by those who witness the action, through language.

The ambiguity of Habermas's early theory arises once it is recognised that language is also important for the two other distinctive human characteristics, labour and interaction. While labour is the ability to transform the environment, for example by using tools, the difference between a human being transforming his environment and the behaviour of a non-human animal, such as a beaver building its dam, lies in the fact that the human is acting consciously and wilfully, while the beaver is presumably driven by instinct. It has no choice but to build its dam in the way that its nature prescribes. However, because humans have language, they can conceptualise and think about their environment, and manipulate it in their imaginations before they manipulate it in practice. Hence, labour presupposes language, if labour is to be free and imaginative.

Similarly, interaction between human beings again presupposes language, precisely because interaction is free and meaningful, and not causally determined. Human beings can interact with each other because they can communicate through a common language. However, such interaction can be spoiled or distorted by imbalances and abuses of power. At this stage in his career, Habermas argues that such abuses can be analysed through reference to language. Abuses will either go unnoticed, or will be tolerated as inevitable or natural, precisely because there is no language available to articulate the suffering and abuse that are being perpetrated. Members of the oppressed group may be unable to communicate their oppression to others, for those others may not hear or be able to understand what is said if the oppressors already presuppose that the oppressed are sub-human (as were African slaves, or Jews to an anti-Semite) or irrational (as were women throughout much of European history) and thus incapable of communication and rational or coherent use of language. The lack of a suitable language may even inhibit the ability of the oppressed to articulate their situation to themselves. The slave who internalises his master's image of him as intellectually or racially inferior, or the woman who accepts that she is emotional and incapable of sustained rational thought, will be unable to make any sense of the injustices of their own condition.

If language has a complex position in the early work of Habermas, as his theories of **universal pragmatics** and **communicative action** develop from the 1970s onwards, Habermas's approach to language becomes clearer. The fundamental role that language use plays in all human activity now becomes a core theme of Habermas's arguments, and in particular he explores the role that language use plays in the construction and maintenance of social relationships. Crucially, while the younger Habermas focused on language from the perspective of hermeneutics, and thus on the problems that meaningful human action posed in terms of its interpretation, the mature Habermas approaches the problem of language through ideas borrowed from **analytic philosophy**, and in particular the idea that language is used not merely to convey information but also to perform social actions (see **speech acts**). For example, when I say 'I promise to be at the cinema by five', I am not simply imparting information, but rather creating a social bond with you, one that you can expect me to fulfil or you will want to know the reason why. Habermas's concern with language is thus placed within a broader concern with what he calls 'communicative competence', which is to say the ability of humans, not merely to share meaningful information, but also to create social relationships and to realise social interaction between each other.

LAW

Habermas has been interested in law throughout his career, and his more recent work, *Between Facts and Norms* (1996), is very much the culmination of years of research. This work has embraced the nature and development of legal systems, the processes of justification, interpretation and application of laws, as well as the role that law plays in the integration and organisation of societies. The philosophy of natural law is discussed in early essays (1976a: 88–141), and the historical development of the legal systems in Western **democracies** is discussed in *The Structural Transformation of the Public Sphere* (1989a). *Legitimation Crisis* (1976b) and *The Theory of Communicative Action* (1984a and 1987) address the question of the legitimation of law and its role as a sub-**system** within society.

That is to say that Habermas is concerned with law as a mechanism for organising complex social structures. As a system, law has a status akin to economic and administrative structures. It allows people within society to relate to each other as agents who will act according to the law, and thus will act predictably (1987: 365). Such predictability takes a great organisational burden away from the communicative skills that we use in more intimate and personal relationships. If both you and I respect the same law, and we know this fact of each other, then, as we come to coordinate our actions together, we need not worry overly about making sure that we both understand the situation and the projects in which we are involved in the same way. It is rather like two chess players. One may be playing to practise experimental strategies in preparation for a major championship, while her opponent is just passing the time during a lunchbreak. Providing each obeys the rules of chess, neither need know or discuss the other's motivations. The game, and the interaction it entails, will proceed effectively.

So law is important for organising complex societies. As Habermas notes, it is often all that is 'left of the crumbling cement of society' (1999b: 329). But this leaves open the question of the legitimacy of law. What makes for good and acceptable law? One account might suggest that a good law is one that is instrumentally effective in maintaining social order. The precise content of the law would then be largely irrelevant. What would matter would be its consistency (so that like cases are treated alike, and there is a largely predictable consequence arising from breaking the law), and its workability (so that it must, in practice, be enforceable). This leads to what is known as a **positivist** philosophy of law. The legitimacy of the legal system is understood primarily in terms of its internal consistency. New law and interpretations of old laws must strive to be consistent with existing law. The history of the legal system may then be understood as an on-going attempt to increase its consistency. As a simple example, consider traffic laws. Once a country has decided that one drives on the right, then all other traffic regulations must be consistent with that rule (for example, cyclists must display a rear light on the left side of their bicycles). Crucially, such a view of the law is wholly indifferent to its moral content. Just as no one would claim that driving on the left is morally superior to driving on the right, so the positivist is suggesting that law has little or nothing to do with morality. Law is concerned with the systematic organisation of society. This is the position that Habermas attributes to the **systems theorist** Niklaus Luhmann (Habermas 1976b: 98–9).

Against the positivist, Habermas pits the natural law tradition. This argues that law is grounded in a series of basic moral values (1976b:

99). The seventeenth-century political philosopher John Locke, for example, identified a series of natural rights (to life, liberty and the enjoyment of property). These were basic freedoms that all humans should expect to enjoy in a just and fair society, so they had to be incorporated into any just legal system. So, for the positivist, a legal system could be acceptable if it denied the right to private property, providing that it did so consistently. Not so for Locke. However consistent it might be, such a legal system would be perpetrating a moral wrong against its subjects. This approach to law, then, shifts the question of legitimation away from the positivist position of 'legality', as Habermas calls it, to legitimacy proper. A natural rights approach suggests that, in examining the question of legitimacy, it is not even enough to ask whether the law is acceptable to those who are subject to it. Real people may misunderstand what is in their real interests; they may simply accept legal traditions without reflecting upon them; or they may be gulled by the **ideologies** of their society. Legitimacy therefore comes to imply not actual acceptance of the law, but rather the possibility of rationally justifying it.

It is this tension between different legal philosophies that interests Habermas. But before we turn to the way in which this tension is worked out in *Between Facts and Norms* (1996), one sociological implication of the tension should be highlighted. In *The Theory of Communicative Action*, precisely by treating law as a system, Habermas begins to express his concern that, while law may serve to organise and stabilise social life, it may also infringe upon personal freedom and render our lives largely meaningless. This, in effect, is to highlight the place that law has in the **colonisation of the lifeworld** (1987: 362). Briefly, Habermas's argument is this. However well intentioned a law might be, precisely because it encourages individuals to relate to each other instrumentally (which is to say in terms of their predictable behaviour as law followers), rather than communicatively, it begins to constrain the ways in which we act. This is not simply a matter of the obvious constraints that law puts upon our actions, by making some of them illegal. Rather it is a more subtle process.

Consider, for example, the relationship between a doctor and her patient. The process of consultation and diagnosis should be a largely communicative one. The resultant treatment will follow from that diagnosis. But, if the relationship comes to be colonised by the legal system, then the doctor may begin to relate to her patient increasingly cautiously and instrumentally. The patient is someone who will sue if anything goes wrong. Notice that the patient is then also treating the doctor instrumentally. Doctors become devices that diagnose diseases, and the patient's communicative participation and the doctor's fallible hermeneutics skills in understanding her patient's complaints are all ignored. In response the doctor, rather than treating the patient as an individual, subjects him to a standard series of tests and treatments, knowing that she is then covered should anything go wrong. The end result is that a legal system that, very sensibly, is designed to safeguard vulnerable patients, comes to waste scarce medical resources and reduce the quality of the patient's care.

In summary, a positivistic theory of law, one that looks only to law as an organisational system, is in danger of losing sight of the real and meaningful values that laws should promote and protect. The colonisation of the **lifeworld** can, in large part, be characterised in terms of the way that it inhibits reflection on and critical discussion of those values, marginalising the natural law tradition. In *The Theory of Communicative Action*, a core problem for Habermas is to find ways of checking this process of colonisation. He talks grimly of creating 'bulwarks' between our everyday meaningful lifeworld and the system (1992c: 444). *Between Facts and Norms* is more optimistic. Habermas begins now to suggest that a properly understood and properly legitimated law will serve as a 'sluice' between the democratically formed values or opinions of the lifeworld and the administrative and economic systems that organise our lives (1996: 345–8). This is to suggest that law can have a creative, rather than a merely restrictive role in the formation of the community. Such a role will be grounded in Habermas's alternative to both positivist and natural law traditions.

The key to Habermas's philosophy of law rests perhaps in the title of *Between Facts and Norms*. It is all to do with the tension between law as a fact and law as a norm (or, as the original German title perhaps makes more clear, between the facticity and the validity of law). This again echoes the tension between positivism and natural rights approaches. On one level, Habermas argues, the positivists are right. For ordinary citizens, law confronts them as a fact, something that they must obey – or else; just in the same way that a failure to respect the law of gravity can lead to a painful fall. This encourages an instrumental or strategic approach to the law: I will exploit it to my own benefit, and will try to get away with breaking it. But, Habermas is quick to point out, most citizens do not think about the law in this way. They respect the law, not because of the painful consequences of not respecting it, but because they think that it is right. I do not steal. This is not because I am afraid of getting caught.

It is because I think that it is wrong to steal. This particular law, therefore, has a moral legitimacy for me. This suggests that law does have a strong moral content, as the natural law theorists suggest.

Habermas continues to defend something of the positivist position. He recognises that law cannot be equated with morality. He notes three differences. Morality encourages moral agents to act appropriately, to do their duty. Typically, then, one is granted moral rights (and thus the respect of others) if one is acting morally oneself. In contrast, law grants citizens certain unconditional rights, and typically does so in order to secure the possibility of their acting freely, without external constraint, as citizens. There is a key shift in vocabulary here, between 'human' and 'citizen'. Morality is concerned with human beings *per se* (or at least it is for Habermas). Hence, human rights are the moral rights that all humans should enjoy, regardless of their particular historical or cultural situation. In contrast, legal rights apply to the citizens of particular nations. Citizenship is about one's public relationships with others in a particular society. My rights as a British citizen may then differ from Habermas's as a German citizen, precisely because British and German societies are organised slightly differently. Notice that this gives significant ground to the positivists. Law seemingly does not require the same rigour of justification as morality.

The next difference concerns the scope of law and morality. On the one hand, the law is narrower in scope, because it only concerns what one does as a citizen. So, there are many immoral acts that are not legislated against. (For example, most forms of lying are not illegal. Slander and libel may be seen as special cases, precisely because the lie may adversely affect the victim's status as a citizen.) On the other hand, law is wider in scope, touching on many issues that are morally neutral (such as the side of the road we drive upon).

The final difference is perhaps the most important, and concerns the way in which laws and morality are justified. Anyone familiar with Habermas's work will expect him to turn to the arguments developed within **discourse ethics** at this point. Within discourse ethics, he argues that a moral principle is acceptable if everyone who is likely to be subject to its being obeyed has a say in debating it. This he formulates in two principles. The first of these, the principle of universality (U), claims that a moral principle is valid only if all those affected can accept the consequences of its general observance. The principle of discourse (D) claims that the agreement of all (and thus the satisfaction of (U)) must be achieved through practical discourse, which is to say through open and free debate, where agreement depends on the strength of better argument alone. Initially Habermas supposed that law would be subject to (U) and (D), just as are moral principles. However, if law applies only to the citizens of particular states, and not to humans *per se*, then it cannot claim universality. A valid law must satisfy (D), but not (U) (1996: 104–18). There is even a slight difference in (D). The purity of moral discourse is compromised by a more pragmatic turn in legal discourse. Law must work, and so good laws may not be morally perfect, but may be the best that can be achieved given citizens' current values and concerns, and given current limitations on policy, the judicial system and so on (1996: 452).

Further consideration of the idea of the discursive justification of law takes us to the heart of Habermas's legal philosophy. In order to clarify what is entailed in legal discourse, he turns to the concept of sovereignty. The sovereign is the person or body who imposed law upon a society. The sovereign is thus typically conceived of as being separate from the subjects of that law. It is precisely this point that Habermas challenges. A law can only be considered to be legitimate if the sovereign who debates and offers justification for the law is at one and the same time the citizen who will be subject to that law. This entails that any just society must secure certain rights for its citizens that guarantee their participation in the discursive process that leads to good law. Before we outline exactly what those rights are, we may note here how Habermas is continuing to handle the tension between positivist and natural law theories. He is stressing, much as he did in his account of discourse ethics, that the philosopher's concern is not with the content of the law, but with the process by which the law is instituted and accepted. This allows him to accept the positivist position that legitimate law may vary in content between one society and another, while at the same time accepting the natural law criticism that legitimacy must still depend on something more than just consistency. What legitimacy depends upon is a process that includes every citizen.

Habermas suggests five groups of rights that all citizens should possess (1996: 122–3). The first is a block of traditional liberties (so that the citizen is free to do what he likes, until that freedom of action begins to infringe upon the freedom and wellbeing of others); the second group guarantees the individual citizen's membership of the legal community; the third group concerns due process of the law, so that all citizens have legal recourse should their rights be violated. These three groups secure the freedom of citizens to act as they like, within the constraints of this particular society. The fourth group is the most distinctive. All citizens should have the right of participation in political debate. Only then is the legal system guaranteed legitimacy. The final group includes traditional welfare rights, such as rights to pensions, education, a minimum wage and so on, without which individuals cannot act freely.

In summary, what Habermas's position amounts to is the claim that, through full participation of all citizens in the formulation and justification of the law (the public use of reason), a society can articulate its self-understanding. Law in effect becomes expressive of the sort of people we are (1996: 461). In reflecting rationally on law, citizens are not solely considering their own interests, but also the interests of others within their community, and how they should relate to them. Only if the interests of others are considered can any objections to a law be sympathetically received and rationally answered. The law thereby becomes the language through which citizens deal with each other (1996: 455). An unjust law will be resented by at least a portion of the population, and if that resentment is not engaged with and defused, the injustice remains.

It may be noted, in conclusion, how this position throws into question the pessimism of the thesis of the colonisation of the lifeworld. While that thesis is not dropped, Habermas's initial grim picture of law colonising the lifeworld is now modified. Law is now, on the one hand, an expression of the lifeworld. The processes of debate and political participation allow for the formation of what he calls **communicative power**, focusing the self-understanding that is present in the lifeworld. This self-understanding is then more or less adequately institutionalised in law, thus the state's exercise of **administrative power**. But this is not the end of the process, and nor are its consequences inevitably negative as the thesis of colonisation suggests. Now Habermas opens the possibility that the self-understanding of the community is actually developed through the formation of law. If the law is perceived as unjust, if it is challenged by sections of the community, then this is an indictment not just of the law but of the communal self-understanding that produced it. Bad laws (and one may hazard a guess that many bad laws are currently being proposed throughout the world as part of the supposed 'war against terror') raise uncomfortable questions about the sort of people we think we are.

Further reading: Matustik 1993; Bernstein 1995; Chambers 1996; Deflem 1996; Cooke 1997; Rosenfeld and Arato 1998; Hahn 2000: 257–422; Marsh 2001; Schomberg and Baynes 2002; Eriksen 2003

LEGITIMATION

The general acceptance of a government, political system or legal system by the majority of the people subject to it. The concept can be linked to the distinction, made by the German sociologist Max Weber, between 'power' and 'authority'. The mere exercise of power may be seen as the exertion of brute force by, for example, a state, against people who do not acknowledge the right of the state to use that force. Consider the many repressive regimes of the twentieth century (such as that of Pol Pot in Cambodia, or the more recent time of Robert Mugabe's rule in Zimbabwe), or the expansion of British imperial influence in the eighteenth and nineteenth centuries. Authority may entail an exercise of force, but this time with the consent of the people coerced. A magistrate imposes a fine for a traffic offence, but we pay up, accepting the authority of the court; the government makes a policy decision with which we disagree, but we accept it, because that government has come to power through a free and fair election. Legitimacy is thus a characteristic of authority. At its most basic, authority may be understood as the use of power that has legitimacy. Habermas's use of 'legitimacy' raises further issues, though. Max Weber and, crucially for Habermas, the social theorist Niklaus Luhmann (see **systems theory**), assume that the exercise of power is legitimate if the people in fact accept it. The sociologist need only look to the people's overt expressions of content or dis-content with their rulers. Habermas looks rather to the reasons that ground that acceptance, in order to argue that authority is only gen-uinely legitimate if it can be backed by a rational justification. Habermas's conception of legitimation may be seen to be linked to his overriding concern with **communicative reason**.

The exploration of legitimation may be traced back to Habermas's earliest work. His study of the attitudes of students to politics in post-war Germany is an initial step in this project (Habermas *et al.* 1961). For his English-speaking audience his study of the development of European politics and political discussion, *The Structural Transformation of the Public Sphere* (1989a) is more relevant. Here Habermas charts the gradual development of public debate of political issues, and the need of governments to make themselves rationally accountable to their people (see **public sphere**). He expresses his concern that the possibility of public debate is being eroded in contemporary society, as the public is increasingly expected merely to choose between the election manifestos of two or more competing political parties, with no opportunity to debate more fundamental issues, or indeed for public debate and scrutiny to feed into the election process. The mere fact that a party has won the election according to the existing rules seems sufficient to guarantee it (and the political system as a whole) legitimacy.

In his mature work, from the 1970s onwards, legitimation begins to be tackled in terms of Habermas's growing interest in systems theory. So, in his reconstruction of **historical materialism**, he explores the different forms that the legitimation of the exercise of power takes as societies increase in complexity (Habermas 1974a; 1979a: 130–77). In early societies, the justification of social hierarchies and the enforcement of law will typically depend upon appeals to more or less consistent mythical narratives (for example, by explaining the authority of dominant groups in terms of their inheritance from mythical progenitors). With the development of polytheistic and then monotheistic religions, the particularistic mythical narratives are brought into a more systematic and abstract theology. This, in effect, represents a step forward in rationalisation. People are not looking for justification just in terms of a good story, but rather in terms of something like general underlying principles from which consistent consequences can be deduced. So, on the one hand, these grounding principles and values can become increasingly open to scrutiny and challenge (and the development of new religious movements, such as Christianity or Islam, may be understood as exactly such challenges). On the other hand, political rule and the rule of law must be seen to be applied consistently, so that everyone faces the same law and is treated alike. Inconsistencies in legal principles and their application will become increasingly problematic, and tend to undermine the authority of the ruling class. The people can now see that a ruler is being unfair. The emergence of modern law and politics comes as all classes in society perceive themselves to be subject to the same secular legal system. Politics and law are no longer grounded in substantial religious principles, but rather in increasingly general moral principles (such as appeals to human rights, or to the utilitarian demand to maximise the overall happiness of the population), that again are subject to increasingly rigorous rational scrutiny.

Legitimation Crisis (Habermas 1976b) is, as its title suggests, centrally concerned with the problem of legitimacy, and in particular within contemporary **capitalism**. While the **crisis** in legitimation is but one alongside three other crises that may afflict modern societies, it is the legitimation crisis that serves not only to highlight the continuing instability of capitalism, but also for Habermas the hope of the transformation of capitalism into a more just form of social organisation. In brief, Habermas holds that capitalism, even in its contemporary form of welfare-state democracies, is still structured in the interests of the owners of capital, and is thus fundamentally unjust and exploitative. If a capitalist state is to survive, it must conceal this injustice and secure (a spurious) legitimacy for itself. At one level this legitimacy is secured through the production of plentiful supplies of consumer goods, and the relative security that the welfare state provides. However, this leads to increasingly bureaucratic or administrative interventions in the everyday life of citizens. The welfare state intervenes, for example, in education, health care and the social services, and is supported by legal and financial sanctions. Crucially, Habermas suggests, the welfare state therefore entails a highly instrumental way of thinking about itself and its activities, which is to say that it is concerned with the efficient realisation of its plans, rather than with the value of these plans and their goals. This makes the welfare state highly vulnerable to failures and inefficiencies if, for example, the consumer goods that the public demands are not made available, or, perhaps more significantly, as apparently top-heavy and over-bureaucratic state institutions seem to hinder their freedom and wellbeing. Such problems lead to a legitimation crisis not directly, but rather indirectly, because the **instrumental reasoning** of the welfare state inhibits the possibility of the use of **communicative reason**, and thus of proper discussion about the role of government and the purposes of the welfare state. This is compounded by the fact that the population itself is increasingly well educated and critical, and thus resistant to the state's attempts to indoctrinate it. As Habermas puts this, meaning cannot be administratively generated, which is to say that the government administration cannot dictate to the people what they should think of it, or indeed what they should make of their lives. In practice, we continue to see a growing discontent with modern government in the industrialised world through, for example, falling attendance at elections (as the electorate fails to perceive a difference between the rival parties, or considers them to be avoiding the pressing issues of the day such as environmental crisis and global injustice), and the rise of popular protests (for example against the invasion of Iraq, or now routinely at G8 summit meetings). All may be seen to be symptomatic of a crisis in the legitimacy of modern forms of government.

In Habermas's later work, he returns to this theme, first in his theory of the **colonisation of the lifeworld** (Habermas 1987: 318–31), where he explores in more depth the part that administrative ways of thinking play in eroding the communicative rationality that is fundamental to everyday life, and in his study of **law** (Habermas 1996), where he is increasingly concerned with the possibilities for the rational justification of the constitutional frameworks of modern societies.

LIFEWORLD

The stock of skills, competences and knowledge that ordinary members of society use, in order to negotiate their way through everyday life, to interact with other people, and ultimately to create and maintain social relationships. The term was originally coined by the German phenomenologist Edmund Husserl, and was developed as a concept in sociology by his pupil Alfred Schutz. Habermas adopts the concept from them in his some of his earliest essays (1971b), but considerably develops the concept after he becomes interested in **systems theory** in the early 1970s (1976b; 1984a; 1987).

Habermas may be seen to use the term lifeworld initially in order to emphasise the competence of ordinary people as social agents. In doing this he is correcting a bias, or at best a gap, in the social theory of the first generation of the **Frankfurt School**, as well as in the work of many American sociologists of the period, who tended to emphasise the coercive power that society had over the individual. This is perhaps best encapsulated in Theodor Adorno's description of modern capitalism as a 'totally administered society', which is to say a society in which our every act, and even thought, is subject to administrative control. While, as we will see, Habermas has his own worries about the impact of bureaucracies and the capitalist economy on people's freedom, he resisted the bleakest parts of Adorno's account. At some level, society must be created and sustained by human actions. A social theory that fails to take account of that is flawed.

The lifeworld becomes a core term in Habermas's vocabulary in the 1970s. In *Legitimation Crisis* he begins to explore the relationship between the lifeworld and what he calls the **system**. The system is basically society as a coercive power. Habermas's concept of 'lifeworld', however, has already begun to gain a certain independence from that of Husserl and Schutz. The crucial move for Habermas lies in his development of **universal pragmatics**, and thus in a recognition of the role of ordinary people's ability to communicate with each other, and thus to use language, in the creation and sustaining of social interaction. The lifeworld is not a mere stock of cultural resources, but part of a complex process of interaction, through which we use language to establish, maintain and repair social relationships to others. For example, I give you an order to get me a beer. You challenge my right to do this (see **validity claims**). I may now be expected to justify myself, and part of my justification will lie in appealing to local, taken-for-granted customs (and they are part of the lifeworld). So I point out that around here it's the job of the newcomer to fetch the beer. You reply that, as the newcomer, you have no idea where the nearest off-licence is, and after a certain amount of negotiation perhaps I come to realise that the newcomer fetching the beer was a stupid custom in the first place (see Habermas 1987: 121f). The lifeworld is thus not merely a resource upon which I draw, for it is also something that itself may be disputed. It is fluid, and as much the focus of negotiation between people as it is the focus of taken-for-granted agreement. Habermas argues that one form that the development of societies can take is through what he calls the **rationalisation of the lifeworld**, whereby the content of the life-world is subject to increasingly rational challenges and justifications.

The tension between lifeworld and system is central to Habermas's understanding of contemporary society. Habermas's contention is that, as societies become larger and more complex, so the resources of the lifeworld are stretched to breaking point ('overburdened') by the demands of organising social interaction. We use our lifeworld competences, typically, to maintain our relationships with people we know. The interactions involved require that we share a view of the way the world works, of what is of value in it, and bring our respective actions into some sort of coordination (so that somebody does go and fetch the beer). But large-scale societies require the coordination of not just a couple or even a couple of dozen people, but of many thousands or millions. For Habermas, such coordination cannot be achieved through establishing common meanings and common interpretations and uses of the resources of the lifeworld. Rather, we obey more or less meaningless signals. We respond to the power exercised by a bureaucracy or a police officer, or the exchange of money in a shop. While certain lifeworld competences will still be evident, such as our ability to recognise a police officer or a €10 note, the social context has been massively simplified. I need no longer inquire into the bureaucrat's motivations or understanding of the situation, nor she into mine. The shop assistant need not inquire into what I intend to do with my purchase. All I need is the knowl-edge of how the person will react to my action. The interaction between us is then a largely predictable sequence of actions and reactions. While this use of systematic rules relieves the burden placed upon the lifeworld, and allows large-scale social organisation, it also

poses a danger. Precisely because social systems rely upon impover-
ished forms of interaction, as they intrude further into everyday life
(for example, as the state bureaucracy comes, through the work of the
health, education and social services, to interfere more in the role and
structure of the family), so they erode at once the complex cultural
meanings of the lifeworld, and undermine the freedoms that it gives
ordinary people. Adorno's totally administered society remains, thus,
a threat that may never be realised completely, but one that still
represents an erosion of important human qualities. It is this threat
that Habermas analyses as the **colonisation of the lifeworld**.

MARXISM

Those schools of social, economic, political and philosophical inquiry
that are inspired by the work of Karl Marx and Friedrich Engels. The
interpretations of Marx's work are in practice extremely diverse, and
the direct line of influence for Habermas comes from neo-Hegelian
or Western Marxism (as opposed in particular to the interpretations
that were dominant in the old Soviet Union and in Mao's China).

The key figure in the development of Western Marxism, at least
from Habermas's perspective, is the Hungarian Georg Lukács.
Lukács's *History and Class Consciousness* (published in 1923) interpreted Marx as the inheritor of the German philosophical tradition,
and thus sees in Marx's social theory a reworking of Hegel's idealist
metaphysics. In Lukács's hands, Marxism is thereby presented as a
humanist philosophy, concerned with the ability of ordinary people
to take control of their lives. He opposes supposedly scientific readings of Marx that argue that Marxism outlines the laws of historical
progress, and that human intervention to change or hasten the outcome of those laws is in vain. Habermas's own discussions of Marx
highlight the tension in Marx between his humanism and a vestigial
positivism that leads to a self-understanding grounded in the model
of the natural sciences (see Habermas 1971a: 25–42).

History and Class Consciousness was highly influential on the key
figures within the **Frankfurt School**, such as Theodor Adorno and
Max Horkheimer, not least in the recognition of the place that
Hegelianism can play in the interpretation of Marx, but also in terms
of certain key ideas, such as '**reification**'. However, the Frankfurt
School began to break from Lukács's approach due to a growing
scepticism over the revolutionary potential of the proletariat. In
effect, this was to work out an implication already present in Lukács's

arguments. Lukács recognised that **capitalism** had transformed itself since the period in which Marx wrote. Marx's social theory alone was therefore inadequate. It lacked the resources necessary to make sense of the development of corporate capitalism (within which the market becomes dominated by increasingly fewer, but larger, firms), and of the rise of the bureaucratic organisation of society. Marx had therefore to be complemented by the work of the German sociologist Max Weber. It is precisely this transformed, late capitalism that, for Adorno and Horkheimer, indicated the loss of a revolutionary proletariat. Indeed, the whole political structure of capitalism appeared to change, as an increased material affluence that was not predicted by Marx was seen to be entwined in a loss of freedom, as administrative structures increasingly regulated everyday life.

It is broadly this form of Marxism that Habermas inherits, in part through his reading of Lukács, Horkheimer and Adorno immediately after the war, and during his period as a research assistant to Adorno in the 1950s. Initially, Habermas may therefore be seen to be unproblematically a Marxist theorist, albeit one who recognises the limitations of Marx's work, and thus the need to complement it through the work of Weber and other sociologists. The account that he gives of his work as **critical theory** at the conclusion of *Knowledge and Human Interests* (1971a: 246–300) is thus basically a Marxist one. The task of critical theory is to unmark the ideological distortions within society, and thereby restore autonomy to individuals within society and to society as a whole.

As Habermas's work develops in the late 1960s and 1970s, Marx becomes just one source of influence amongst a very wide range of influences and sources. Thus the 1970s see a major engagement with Marxism, and the continual use of a number of key Marxist terms (such as base and superstructure, and historical materialism), but those terms are increasingly being challenged and reinterpreted (see Habermas 1976b and 1979a: 130–77). In *The Theory of Communicative Action*, which is in part a grand overview of the development of social theory, Marx is still, inevitably, there, but now alongside not just Weber but also a wide and diverse range of other social theorists, such as Emile Durkheim, Talcott Parsons, G. H. Mead and Erving Garfinkel. However, finally summing up what critical theory is about reflects Marxism's concerns, not least in terms of the need for social theory to inform political practice and to act to expose the injustices of contemporary capitalism.

The most recent phase of Habermas's work may suggest a drifting away from a Marxist agenda towards a more liberal one. Habermas freely engages in debates with liberal philosophers such as John Rawls (Habermas 1998a: 49–101) and Richard Rorty (Habermas 1999a: 343–82). He is concerned in his legal theory with the notion of constitutional **democracy**. A term like 'justice' seems to replace a term like '**emancipation**' that had appeared in his early writings. However, while Habermas's writings may be more sober, and increasingly attuned to what can be done within the scope of modern welfare states, there remains a radical and critical intent that at least has its roots in his Marxist inheritance. He remains a staunch critic of the failings of capitalism.

MEANING

In his early writings, Habermas approaches meaning through **hermeneutics**, which is to say that meaning is understood as a property of human actions (including speech and writing), and human artefacts (such as books, works of art and buildings). The task of the hermeneutician, as a student of the process of interpretation, is to understand how we can extract meaning from what is, *prima facie*, just matter (be this the physical movements of our bodies, the noises made when we speak, the marks we make on paper when we write, or objects that the artist, builder or toolmaker produces) (Habermas 1971a: 140–86; 1980; 1988b: 143–70). The hermeneutic approach to meaning, while explaining much about the processes of interpretation and understanding that go on as human beings make sense of each other's actions, leaves the concept of meaning somewhat vague. As the examples above show, it embraces a wide range of phenomena, from the abusive gesture that I make with my hand, through the subtle nuances of rhyme and expression that I put into a poem, to the movements of whole armies or even populations in the conquest and occupation of territory. In his later work on **universal pragmatics** and a theory of **communicative action**, Habermas turns to **analytic philosophy** for inspiration, in order to give a more focused account of the concept of meaning. More precisely, Habermas is concerned with identifying the conditions under which competent human beings find the speech and actions of others to be meaningful (Habermas 1979a; 1999a).

Two broad approaches to the problem of meaning can be identified in analytic philosophy. What is known as the formal semantic approach focuses on sentences, and asks how a sentence can be meaningful, regardless of who utters or writes it, and regardless of the context within which it is used. For example, what would make the sentence, 'Habermas is a German philosopher' meaningful? Notice first that this is not an issue about the **truth** of the sentence. 'Habermas is a French philosopher' is as meaningful as 'Habermas is a German philosopher', although only one of the sentences is true. Second, given that the philosopher's concern is with the sentences regardless of who says them, what they know, or where they happen to be; the point is to find out what general conditions have to be met in order for any sentence, in any context, to be meaningful for anyone who hears or reads it. This approach to meaning tends to focus on sentences that assert something about the world, and understand the conditions that make those sentences meaningful in terms of the scope that the audience has either to imagine the world described by that sentence, or to check the facts asserted. So, 'Habermas is a German philosopher' is meaningful because I understand how Habermas could be a German philosopher (whereas, say, I could not understand how a triangle could have four sides or Tuesday could be squishy), and so I understand what sort of evidence to look for in order to establish the truth of the sentence. Put simply, the meaningfulness of the sentence is related to the fact that it refers to things, people and events out in the world. Many debates in analytical philosophy have been built upon this simple foundation.

An alternative approach focuses on what is known as the pragmatic aspect of language. Here the primary concern is with how specific people make sense of a particular sentence uttered in a particular context. At its extreme, this approach can suggest that the generalisations of the formal semantic approach are mistaken. There are no general rules of meaning. Meaning depends upon the particular context within which a sentence is uttered, and upon the knowledge and presuppositions that the audience brings to that context. In effect, this is closer to the hermeneutic approach to language and meaning, at least in so far as hermeneuticians also stress the importance of the pre-understanding that humans bring with them when trying to interpret writings and other meaningful actions or objects. So, in order to understand an utterance, I may need to know something about the person's motivations in saying what they did – or, as the English philosopher R. G. Collingwood once remarked, the problem with the formal semantic approach is that it does not inquire into the speaker's tone of voice. The same words can have very different meanings if spoken ironically or sarcastically (so that 'Habermas is a German philosopher' could in fact be questioning the worth of

German philosophy as a whole, or sarcastically dismissing the claim of a glorified sociologist to be a philosopher).

The pragmatic approach puts even greater stress on the particular details of the context of the utterance. So, in order to understand 'Habermas is a German philosopher', I must know something about that context. If it is said in reply to my question, 'What is the capital of Peru?', it is meaningless (and I am likely to assume that my respondent has misheard my question, and has not understood me). Philosophers such as Wittgenstein talked about the form of life or the language game within which an utterance is made, indicating that the rules that govern meaning vary subtly with context. The question, 'What is the capital of Peru?', makes sense only in certain contexts, such as a geography test or a quiz show (and even here there can be problems, for the question might appear to be so simple in a university examination that it could seem baffling to the candidates).

If the formal semantic approach focused on assertions, then an advantage of the pragmatic approach is that it can deal with different uses of language, such as questions, the giving of orders, and exclamations of surprise (see **speech acts**). Again, there will be distinct rules governing what makes an order meaningful (so that a military captain ordering a sergeant to 'take an enemy gun emplacement out' makes sense on the battlefield, while a request to 'take the dog out' would be bizarre in the same situation).

Habermas recognises the advantages that the pragmatic approach has over the formal semantic. None the less, he is critical of the pragmatic approach for its excessive focus on the details of particular encounters and exchanges. Meaning seems to fragment into many different bundles of rules, with little or nothing in common. Habermas's programme of **universal pragmatics** (or what he later called 'formal pragmatics') attempts to embrace the insights of pragmatics, while also seeking to identify various rules that must govern meaningful language use regardless of context. He focuses upon the ability of ordinary language users to make utterances – which is to say that he is less concerned with the meaning of sentences (as is formal semantics) than with the conditions and rules that govern utterances, which in turn is to say the use of sentences in particular circumstances. He can then seek to identify the knowledge that all competent speakers must have if they are going to use language appropriately, regardless of their cultural background or the particular context within which they are speaking and acting, in addition to the particular knowledge required of that context. What this entails is a recognition of the conditions that make an utterance acceptable to its audience. So, for example, 'Habermas is a German philosopher' is unacceptable and therefore meaningless as a reply to 'What is the capital of Peru?', just as 'Take the dog out' is unacceptable and meaningless in the midst of a battle.

Further reading: Cooke 1994

MODERNISM AND POST-MODERNISM

'Modernity' typically refers to the period of European and American history that began with the end of the Renaissance (and thus around the beginning of the seventeenth century), and therefore 'modernism' is the culture that is characteristic of this period. A modernist culture can be broadly characterised in terms of its commitment to values that were fully articulated in the European Enlightenment (of the seventeenth and eighteenth centuries). Reason and scientific inquiry are to be used to bring about technological and political progress. The perfection of human social life may thus be envisaged and sought after. The received political, moral and religious values of the previous period, the middle ages, are subject to criticism, and increasingly demands for rational justification of the exercise of power led to the overthrow of the authority of the feudal state and church.

The more problematic term 'post-modernism' may refer, rather obviously, to a culture that comes after 'modernism' (although the actual dating of this cultural period is a matter of some dispute), and more profoundly to a culture that challenges the most fundamental presuppositions of modernism, not least in terms of the assumed perfectibility of humanity, and thus of the idea of political progress, and the assumption of the universal validity and applicability of reason and science. The terms are important for Habermas in that he presents himself as defending the 'unfinished project' of modernity in the face of its post-modernist opponents. This is made explicit initially in an address given in 1980 (Habermas 1983b), and subsequently developed at length in *The Philosophical Discourse of Modernity* (1988a).

Habermas points out that the term 'modernity' was originally used in the fifth century CE to distinguish between the Christian present and the pagan past (1983b: 3). It is not until the eighteenth century that it takes on its current sense, specifically with the refinement of a new understanding of human history. For the medieval Christian, the present was a break from the pagan past, and one that would be as nothing compared to the break between the present and the new post-apocalyptic age to come, after the Last Judgement. Even for the Renaissance thinker, history was still cyclical rather than progressive (with every possibility that their golden age might once more regress into silver and bronze ages). In contrast, the Enlightenment thinker saw himself as already living in the new age. Progress is guaranteed. It is after all an age of revolutions (be they political, agricultural or industrial), and of the stabilisation and growth of the 'New World' of America. The tools to perfect humanity already exist and are being put to use.

But modernity's very difference from the past leaves it with a problem. How is it to justify its own superiority and distinctiveness? This, for Habermas (1988a: 7), is the crucial issue that underpins the project of modernity. Christianity had a clearly defined worldview that gave it self-justification. Similarly, the ancient Greeks and Romans could distinguish themselves from their barbarian contemporaries and primitive pasts. The critical questioning of all value systems entails that the modernist cannot fall back, complacently, on a given set of values. Religious truths, for example, could no longer be accepted just through the dogma of divine revelation. Increasingly the Christian Bible itself came to be something that could be subject to rational, scientific investigation, its moral and theological claims only acceptable if independently justified by reason and evidence. But that leaves open the question of the grounding of reason and scientific evidence themselves. Some rationally defensible ground must be found in order to justify the Enlightenment project.

Habermas presents the history of modern philosophy very much as a struggle with this question, from Descartes's search for certainty in his belief in his own existence ('I think therefore I am'), through the British empiricist philosophers' search for certainty in empirical experience (all of which falls apart with the sceptical genius of David Hume), to Immanuel Kant and his **transcendental** argument that the human mind constitutes the world that it perceives. In his *Critique of Pure Reason*, Kant explores the foundations and also the limits of human knowledge. In the *Critique of Practical Reason* he offers a rational foundation to morality. In the *Critique of Judgement* he attempts to bring his philosophical system together, bridging the gulf that he perceives to exist between scientific knowledge of the material world and the human freedom and rationality that grounds our capacity for moral action. In part he does this by seeking a foundation to the human sensitivity to beauty in the fusion of our material bodies and rational minds.

Kant is the culmination of the Enlightenment. He offers the most profound justification of the modern age and of its aspirations to scientific, moral and political progress, and yet ultimately he cannot bind his whole system together coherently. In the end, he leaves humanity as all powerful and rational, with a moral capacity that makes it the very justification of the existence of the natural world, and yet also finite, limited in its scope and vision, unable even to understand properly its own freedom. For all its moral superiority, humanity is no more invulnerable to the hazards of the natural world than any other animal. After Kant, Hegel and his successors, the Young Hegelians, attempt to overcome these weaknesses. In large part, Hegel attempts to do this by reinvigorating the historical dimension of modernist thought. Kant may then be seen to have articulated problems that will be resolved through historical progress. The limitations and tensions that he identifies are not givens, but stimuli to historical, intellectual and political progress. The Young Hegelians respond to this prospect in one of two ways. The Left Hegelians, and pre-eminently Karl Marx, stress the need for revolutionary progress into the future, transforming the organisation of society. The conservative Right Hegelians stress the need to perfect existing social structures. The Left Hegelians seek the justification of modernity in the **emancipation** of the repressed; the Right Hegelians seek that same justification in the perfection of the market mechanisms and civil society of nineteenth-century **capitalism**.

It is at this point that Habermas's responses to the post-modernist critics of modernism begin to emerge. First, he makes the point that modernism has always been a self-critical movement. Self-doubt is part of its very nature. So, to a degree, post-modernism is little more than that self-doubt being carried on in a new guise. Second, and perhaps more important, this self-doubt has, at least since the nineteenth century, entailed a criticism of the social organisation of modern (which, in effect, is to say capitalist) society. That criticism can take either of two forms, represented by the Left Hegelians and the Right Hegelians respectively. Habermas is effectively situating himself as the inheritor of the Left Hegelians. In continuing the unfinished project of the Enlightenment, he is seeking to diagnose the roots of political repression (not least in his account of the **colonisation of the lifeworld**), as a means to the realisation of a political emancipation. In contrast, the post-modernists are situated as the inheritors of Right Hegelianism, and as unwitting **neo-conservatives**.

The point at issue is the status of reason. The Left Hegelian embraces the prospect of rational progress. But Habermas is critical of Marx for ultimately considering only the role of **instrumental reason** (which is to say Marx's model for social change cannot escape that of natural science and technological intervention in the material world). With only a limited grasp of the nature and importance of communication (and thus what Habermas calls **communicative reason**) in creating and sustaining social relationships, Marxism is in danger of degenerating into authoritarian social engineering. But the Right Hegelians fare no better. They stress the importance of individual freedom, and see the free market as a way to realise that freedom, and thereby again fail to recognise the importance of communication in social life. The Right Hegelians offer a society that is bound together by people treating each other instrumentally (as means to satisfy their subjective desires through market exchanges). In order to check the imperfections of the market their society too must resort to the rule of an authoritarian state (Habermas 1988a: 51–74). To escape this impasse, the post-modernists follow Friedrich Nietzsche, and attack reason *per se*. The Enlightenment commitment to reason and to the rational founding of its project must be abandoned, not least because the appeal to reason is seen as little more than the guise taken by the exercise of power (or, in Nietzsche's terminology, the 'will to power') (Habermas 1988a: 83–105).

Habermas's reply is to accept that instrumental reason is at fault, albeit that his analysis of the place of instrumental reason within the organisation of complex societies is more subtle than that offered by the post-modernists. Instrumental reason has a role, not just in technology (which is a point that Habermas has explored and defended throughout his career (see Habermas 1971a)), but also in the **systematic integration** of society. That is to say that large social structures cannot be maintained by people just using their ability to communicate and negotiate with each other. Instead, 'relief mechanisms' such as the market or bureaucracies come into existence, serving to massively simplify social relationships, and thus to focus people's interaction upon precisely defined tasks (such as, say, in the case of a market, buying vegetables). Here people do quite legitimately treat each other instrumentally. Problems only occur as these relief mechanisms begin to intrude into all aspects of our social life, eroding our capacity to communicate with each other. This is what Habermas means by the colonisation of the lifeworld. Habermas's point is that the Hegelians and their post-modernist successors have failed to distinguish between the necessary role of instrumental reason in social life and its corrosive abuse. Put otherwise, they have failed to distinguish instrumental reason from communicative reason. In recognising the abuse of instrumental reason, they abandon communicative reason with it. The end result of this, for Habermas, is that the postmodernists ultimately leave themselves without the resources to mount an effective critical challenge to contemporary society. As soon as an Enlightenment commitment to the true and the good is abandoned (alongside commitments to reason and historical progress), then one has lost the capacity to judge one political system as being better than any other.

See also: **post-structuralism**

Further reading: Lyotard 1984 and 1985; Bernstein 1985; White 1987; Honneth 1995; Passerin d'Entréves and Benhabib 1996; Fleming 1997; Trey 1998; Babich 2004

MONEY

An example of a **non-symbolic steering medium**, which is to say that money is used in modern economies to guide the actions of individual people, in order to maintain the integrity and stability of the economy as a sub-**system** within society, and indeed society as a whole. Habermas argues that money serves to organise societies and social interaction 'horizontally', in so far as it serves to bring about the integration of a society (in contrast to **power**, that 'vertically' organises society into separate strata).

Money binds society together by facilitating exchange between people. Exchange may be seen to have been important in integrating small-scale tribal societies, prior to the use of money. In such societies, either ritual gifts or women were typically the objects of exchange. The gift bound two groups through the obligation to return the gift, and the exchange of women bound lineages together through marriage ties (Habermas 1987: 161). In contemporary society, money works as a more efficient mechanism, not least in that it can sustain far more complex forms of social organisation. It has the advantages of being precisely quantifiable, and as such allows for the minute calculation and control of exchanges and the resultant social interactions; it can be accumulated and stored, and as such can be utilised when most appropriate, maximising its organisational efficiency; and it circulates readily about the social system, bringing all of society rapidly under its sway. Thus, in contemporary society, nearly all our actions are guided in one way or another by monetary considerations, from our choice of education, training and work, through to our choice of partner, the number of children we bring up, and the schooling those children receive.

Habermas's concern, expressed in his account of the **colonisation of the lifeworld**, is that this dominance of money (and power) over our lives begins to erode our freedom. This is not merely due to the fact that our actions are to a large degree restricted or at least shaped by the availability of money, but also because money is non-symbolic, and thus it places the organisation and control of most key institutions outside the scope of debate through communicative rationality. A company, for example, can be challenged if it is making insufficient profits (for profits are precisely measurable in monetary terms and are taken as a guide to the efficacy of the company). But that reduces the challenge to a purely quantitative one. It is making an insufficient quantity of money. To ask whether the company should be making money at all (because, for example, its products are so important to the wellbeing and needs of so many people that they should be subsidised and distributed by the state) becomes almost meaningless. It requires that the ends, and indeed the very nature, of a company (and even the wider market mechanisms of which it is a part) are subjected to rational debate, and for Habermas that would entail a debate in which everyone affected by the actions of the company had a say, and their voices would be heard and respected. The difficulties of revising the regulations for world trade that presently confront the World Bank and the G8 countries may be seen, at least in part, to rest upon this very problem.

NEO-CONSERVATISM

For Habermas, an intellectual position that is opposed to what he calls the 'project of modernity', which is to say is opposed to scientific and historical progress, and to the rational justification of moral, cognitive and aesthetic beliefs (Habermas 1989b: 22–47). The neoconservative position is typically characterised by a recognition of the problems and pathologies of **modern** society (and, as such, is reacting to what Habermas analyses as the **colonisation of the lifeworld**). However, lacking what Habermas sees as the appropriate intellectual resources to understand these problems adequately, it turns instead to a wholesale rejection of reason. This, often despite the neo-conservative's best intentions, leaves it unable to challenge the very problems that it identifies. Habermas distinguishes between 'young conservatives', 'old conservatives' and 'neo-conservatives' (1983b: 14–15).

The young conservatives stress the importance of aesthetic experience, and use this as a substitute for reason. This may be seen to have its roots in early Nietzschean thinking, in his appeal to the aesthetics of ancient Greek tragedy, as a way of making suffering acceptable, and in his rejection of the 'Apolline' reasoning of Socrates. Nietzsche's argument is that Socratic reason treats everything as a problem that can be rationally resolved. That which is irrational (including great art) is repressed. This line of argument is taken up in the twentieth century by the French thinkers Georges Bataille, Michel Foucault and Jacques Derrida (see **post-structuralism**). Habermas's point here is that, in abandoning reason for rhetoric, which is to say in abandoning the possibility of changing people's minds or challenging their acts by the force of better argument, one is abandoning oneself to forms of coercion and manipulation where only the most aesthetically pleasing position matters, not the rationally justifiable one (Habermas 1988a: 161–293).

The old conservatives, again reacting to the pathologies of the modern world, retreat to a pre-modern position. Habermas presumably has in mind here contemporary communitarian philosophers, such as Alisdair MacIntyre, who attempt to reinstate the values of communal belonging in the face of the fragmentation of life in late capitalism.

Finally, the neo-conservatives retain a commitment to science, but deny that science has any influence on political, moral and social questions. In effect, this entails curtailing the scope of reason. While both the young conservatives and the old conservatives reject **instrumental reason**, precisely because they see it as having at best no relevance to, or at worst a corrosive effect on, moral reasoning, the neo-conservatives accept instrumental reason in its place, which is to say within the natural sciences. Echoing **positivism**, questions of moral or aesthetic value are thereby placed outside the scope of rational debate, and are left to subjectivity or tradition.

Habermas's general argument against all these versions of conservatism is that they lack an adequate conception of reason. By confining their arguments to instrumental reason, they remain trapped within what Habermas calls the 'philosophy of **consciousness**', which is to say that they remain blind to the importance of inter-subjectivity and thus to **communicative reason**.

NON-SYMBOLIC STEERING MEDIA

The mechanisms used to organise activity within social **systems**. Within **systems theory**, the analysis of a society is approached by treating the society as a system, which is to say that as a whole it is composed of a set of elements organised together according to a relatively simple set of rules. For a society to work as a system, the people who are members of that society must be able to recognise and respond appropriately to the demands that the system places upon them. This is where non-symbolic steering media come in. In effect, they provide the cues to certain types of action, that in turn allow the goals of the system to be realised. Habermas identifies two important examples: **money** and **power** (1987: 202). Money is the simpler example. When I buy goods from a shop, I am responding to the cues given to me by the price of the goods (and the money I have available to spend). My purchase will in turn provide a cue to the shopkeeper to order more of those goods, and to the supplier to produce more, and so on through possibly many thousands of social events (as people are employed, resources made available and distributed, more money is invested, and so on). In all this, no one need ask why I want the goods, or how they fit into my overall plans. That is to say that the way in which I make sense of my purchase, and give it meaning (for example, is it a present for my partner; a treat to myself after a hard day's work; a replacement for the old one that the cat broke?) is largely irrelevant to the working of the economic system. Hence Habermas's claim that the steering media of systems are non-symbolic. They are separated from the meaningful resources that we draw upon in everyday interaction (see **lifeworld**).

While symbolic media may be vital to the organisation of large and complex societies (for ordinary people's basic skills in creating and sustaining interaction cannot be expected to embrace the large-scale institutions of an ancient empire, let alone a modern corporation or government administration), they pose a double threat. On the one hand, as social interaction is guided increasingly by non-symbolic media, that interaction loses its vestigial meaning (so that one merely follows the demands that the system places upon one), and free human choice becomes eroded (as it becomes increasingly difficult to escape the systems) (see **colonisation of the lifeworld**). On the other hand, rational critical debate is undermined. Because money and power are non-symbolic steering media, and money and power regulate the actions of the economic and political sub-systems respectively, Habermas argues that it becomes increasingly difficult to subject those sub-systems to rational scrutiny and debate. Symbolic steering media encourage **instrumental** responses that focus upon assessing the efficiency of an action in achieving a given goal (and thus I approach the economy in terms of finding the most effective way to spend my money so as to realise my personal happiness). As such they discourage the use of **communicative rationality** to challenge the systems, and to assess both the means and ends available (so that, obedient to the workings of the market, I no longer ask myself if my happiness is really served by buying yet more CDs, and even if I continued to ask the question, could I live with the consequences of the loss of income that my withdrawal would bring about for so many record companies?).

PERFORMATIVE CONTRADICTION

Where my action is at odds with the basic assumptions that I must make in order to act so. Habermas offers in illustration a canonical example of the role that the notion of performative contradiction has played as a critical tool in the history of philosophy. Descartes argued, in the seventeenth century, that I cannot doubt my own existence. To do so is a performative contradiction, for I must exist in order to doubt. Therefore to doubt my existence contradicts the existence which is the precondition of my doubt (Habermas 1990: 80).

Habermas uses the notion of performative contradiction to strengthen his defence of **discourse ethics**. Habermas wishes to establish that the rules that govern our everyday ability to communicate with each other have ethical implications, not least in so far as they determine the conditions of critical discussion through which moral claims and actions can be justified. Thus, if I tell a lie, I am involved in a performative contradiction. The argument runs like this. When I enter into communication, I must initially assume that everyone else is telling the truth and is being sincere. If I do not, it is not clear how I could make sense of what is being said to me. Everything I heard would be ambiguous. Although in practice I may realise that people are lying to me or are being insincere, and I might drop my assumption, at that point genuine communication has broken down.

So, what happens if I lie? I seem merely to be taking advantage of the necessary assumption that others are making to the effect that I am telling the truth. As it stands, this is simply to treat them **strategically** (as things that I can manipulate, rather than as people with whom I should engage communicatively, seeking mutual agreement). While this may be wrong, it is not obviously a contradiction. Habermas's point, however, is that one cannot take a rigorously strategic approach to social interaction. I cannot systematically assume that I can treat all human beings as mere means to my self-advancement, and wholly dismiss their moral status. While this might seem to work for a particular lie, as soon as I am challenged, or as soon as I am asked to justify my amoral stance, I am drawn back into communicative action. Even if I insincerely defend myself, I still presuppose the sincerity of those who challenge me. If I refuse to justify myself, retreating into an egoistic and solipsistic silence, then I have still not side-stepped the contradiction. In practice I have deepened it. In order to avoid answering, I have still used my social competence (my ability to choose not to speak and thus to shun company). The retreat contradicts my very existence as a socialised and socially competent human being.

POSITIVISM

An approach to the philosophy of science and the theory of knowledge, characterised by the primacy that it places upon the natural sciences as the principal or only source of sound knowledge claims.

Positivism has its origins in the work of the French philosopher and social theorist Auguste Comte (1798–1857), who sought to establish a methodology for the social sciences through which they would be able to discover the laws that govern the development and change of societies. The knowledge of such social laws could be exploited in order to engineer societies, just as natural scientific knowledge of the laws of nature is the basis for technological interventions in the natural world.

In the early twentieth century, a more sophisticated version of positivism emerged, typically known as logical positivism. This is characterised by a concern with the methodology of the natural sciences and the nature of language and meaning. It is argued that the natural sciences proceed by generating theories and descriptions of the world that are verifiable, which is to say that the only statements that have any meaning are those which can be confirmed (or verified) through empirical observation. Thus, for example, the claims that 'The earth orbits the sun once every 365.25 days' and 'Eating unripe bananas causes stomach cramps' are verifiable. This 'verification principle' entails, on the one hand, that all scientific enquiry (including that of the social and historical sciences) should model itself on the methods of the natural sciences (and thus conduct empirically verifiable experiments, resulting in causal explanations of observable phenomena); and on the other that any statement that is not verifiable is metaphysical nonsense. The consequences of this second point include the rejection of all religious and theological language as nonsense (because, if an omnipresent and omnipotent God is unobservable, no statement of the sort that 'God exists' can be verified and thus can never make any sense), and the rejection of all value statements, including those in ethics and aesthetics. If there is no observable property of 'goodness' or 'beauty', then claims such as 'Murder is wrong' and 'Cezanne was a great painter' are either meaningless or reducible to the claims 'I disapprove of murder' and 'I like Cezanne's work'.

While Habermas may be seen to engage with Comte's account of the development of society in his theory of **social evolution**, it is in his early writings that Habermas engages more fundamentally with the later positivist philosophy of science. This he does through his two contributions to what is known as the *Positivism Dispute* (Habermas 1976c; 1976d) – a series of exchanges, initiated by the philosopher of science Karl Popper and the **Frankfurt School** theorist Theodor Adorno, on the nature of scientific method and particularly on the nature of the social sciences. Here Habermas both questions the accuracy of the positivists' understanding of natural scientific methodology, and defends the idea that the methodology of the social sciences must be radically different to that of the natural sciences, and thus that the positivist attempt to unify the sciences on a natural scientific model (what Habermas calls **scientism**) is in error.

The first argument concerns the positivists' view that all that matters for good science is a set of rules that the scientist should follow in pursuing her enquiry. Such rules would include not merely the demand that her scientific theories can be verified through (experimental) observations, but also a guarantee of her impartiality (so that results are not distorted by personal value judgements or idiosyncratic perspectives on the world). Results are ideally expressed in quantitative, mathematical formulations. The scientist is seen as a neutral observer of a world that exists independently of herself. Habermas is not wholly unsympathetic to this argument. However, in stressing this impersonal methodology, positivism neglects the fact that the process of scientific research must be a communal process. Scientists do not work in isolation, following set rules (as if they were playing a game of solitaire). Rather, they work in teams whose results may be challenged and debated by other, rival teams. Crucially, Habermas borrows an argument from Karl Popper, who notes that even in verifying a theory the observation of facts is insufficient. The scientist does not simply point at the world (for example, at the slide under her microscope) and assume that it is self-evident that what she sees there verifies her theory. She must explain why what she observes is a verification of the theory. Popper suggests that this is like the process found in courts of law, where the evidence presented before the court must be demonstrated to be relevant to determining the guilt or innocence of the accused. The evidence can never speak for itself. For Habermas, this is to argue that science itself relies on processes to which positivism is blind – processes of social interaction, of negotiation and communication. This is an early glimpse of the importance that communication, and what Habermas will call **communicative reason**, will have in his later philosophy and social theory.

Habermas's second argument may be seen to take up this concern with the nature of social interaction and communication, in order to argue that causal explanation is typically inappropriate in the social sciences, precisely because social processes are processes of communication. Such processes rest upon the capacity of social agents to make sense of their social world, to interpret the words and actions of others, and to explain their own actions and statements to each other. In sum, the social world is one of meanings, not of causal relationships. (For example, I go to work each morning, not because anything causes me to, but because I recognise my obligations to my students and colleagues, and my need for an income to pay my mortgage and keep me in the style to which I have become accustomed. I no doubt could, and perhaps should, become accustomed to a simpler lifestyle, but right now I freely choose not to.) The social world is not therefore generated and sustained through causal forces, but rather through the creative and meaningful actions of its members. Social science, then, must have a methodology grounded in **hermeneutics**, which is to say in the sciences of interpretation.

However, Habermas does acknowledge that society can often appear to those who belong in it (and whose thoughtful, meaningful intentions and actions must sustain it) as if it were a natural force. For example, the economy must be the product of the free actions of human agents, choosing to trade goods and services, to invest and to save and so on, and yet the laws that govern the economy, and that are formulated by orthodox (which is to say positivist) economics, confront those very economic agents as natural laws, seemingly as independent of human influence as are the laws of mechanics or optics. For Habermas, this transformation of meaningful actions and interactions into meaningless and seemingly objective forces – this process of **reification** – is indicative of the political inequalities and repression inherent in society. The law-likeness of certain social processes cannot then be taken for granted, and handed over to a social science that, like economics, borrows the mathematical methodologies of the natural sciences; it must be exposed through critical examination in order to **emancipate** society from repression.

Habermas explores this approach to the hermeneutic and critical social sciences in *Knowledge and Human Interests* (1971a) and *The Logic of the Social Sciences* (1988b). In *Knowledge and Human Interests* Habermas offers an historical account of the emergence of positivistic approaches to the sciences. He notes repeatedly how those theorists who have the potential to break from the sway of positivism – including C. S. Peirce in his account of the natural sciences (see **pragmatism**), Wilhelm Dilthey on history, and Karl Marx and Sigmund Freud on emancipatory science – all compromise their insights and revert at crucial moments to positivistic models of scientific inquiry. For example, Marx's emphasis on the potential that humans have freely to transform their own societies is undermined by an emphasis on iron laws of social development that echo Comte's sociology, and that place social change beyond the will and control of social agents; Freud presents **psychoanalysis** and its 'talking cure' (through which seemingly physical symptoms are given meaning, and brought back under the conscious control of the patient) as a stopgap before more effective chemical treatments become available for mental illness.

In his later writings, Habermas is less concerned with the threat that positivism poses to the social sciences (in part because he sees the arguments as having been taken up effectively by others). However, the problem of balancing natural scientific and hermeneutic models of social science remains, and is pursued not least in his debates with Niklaus Luhmann concerning the state and scope of **systems theory** (as an approach to social science that is grounded in natural science and in particular in cybernetics). This culminates in the complex model of society as **system** and **lifeworld** that is articulated in *The Theory of Communicative Action*.

In his most recent writings on **law** (1996a), Habermas turns to the problem of legal positivism. Positivism in the theory of law (or jurisprudence) refers to an understanding of law that stresses law as it is exercised in a particular society, in contrast to an approach that stresses how the law ought to be. A positivist approach is thus primarily concerned with the consistency of the system of law, and the procedures by which changes in the law are instituted. It therefore seems to require no deeper moral justification of a law than that it is consistent with existing laws and has been introduced according to accepted principles. Like positivism in the natural sciences, on Habermas's account, legal positivism underestimates the role of communicative reason in deliberating upon the validity of the law, and in interpreting law and determining its application. It is Habermas's contention that consideration of the scope and nature of communicative reason will bring to light resources for questioning the legitimacy of law that will go beyond the mere acceptance of an arbitrarily given system and its inherent procedures.

POST-CONVENTIONAL MORALITY

A concept borrowed by Habermas from the moral psychologist Lawrence Kohlberg, that refers to the most advanced stage of moral reasoning. Kohlberg offers three basic stages in the development of a person's moral decision-making capacity (albeit that these are subsequently subdivided into six stages): pre-conventional; conventional; post-conventional. At the pre-conventional stage the young child responds merely to the direct consequences of its actions. Thus a good action is one for which it is rewarded, and a bad action is one for which it is punished. At the conventional stage, the child begins to recognise that there are principles or rules underpinning moral judgements. Thus, a good action is now one that conforms to accepted rules, and a bad one breaks those rules. At this stage, the rules themselves are taken for granted, as conventions. It is only at the post-conventional stage that the adolescent begins to require justification of the rules. The adolescent therefore begins to distinguish between the mere fact that there is a moral convention, and the normative question as to whether that convention should exist (see Habermas 1979a: 156).

Habermas uses this term to characterise moral decision making, not merely at the level of the individual, but also at the level of societies as a whole. In his theory of **social evolution**, he suggests that the development of societies may be understood in terms of the increasing rationality of their technological, moral and political, and artistic cultures. This growth in rationality is itself characterised in terms of an increasing ability to reflect upon activities, and to demand increasingly general justifications for them (see **rationalisation of the lifeworld**). Hence, a post–conventional society may be characterised in terms of the widespread capacity of its members to challenge existing norms and conventions, and to demand rational justifications for continuing to obey them (see Habermas 1976a: 142–3, 1979a: 95–129).

POST-MODERNISM *see* **Modernism and post-modernism**

POST-METAPHYSICAL THINKING

A characterisation of philosophical thought in **modernity**, once the metaphysical assumptions that dominated philosophy prior to the twentieth century have been challenged. Post-metaphysical thinking rejects idealism and the philosophy of **consciousness**, ultimately abandoning a pursuit of grand, all inclusive absolute truths in favour of an examination of the concrete, intersubjective and discursive processes through which claims to truth and moral goodness are questioned and justified. In practical terms, it may be seen as an approach to philosophy that is sensitive to the cultural pluralism of contemporary society. Habermas discusses post-metaphysical thinking very much as an adjunct to his engagements with modernism (1992b: 3–9 and 28–53).

The metaphysics of nineteenth-century German idealism may be briefly illustrated through reference to Hegel. In his *Encyclopaedia*, Hegel sought to expose the basic logical structure of all existence. The *Encyclopaedia*, through three parts, devoted respectively to logic, the natural world, and to the psychological and cultural realm, charted the development of spirit (*Geist*) from mere subjectivity, gradually unfolding itself through a series of ever more subtle logical distinctions, through its manifestation in the natural world and its gradual coming to self-consciousness in human culture. This self-consciousness, a recognition on the part of the spirit of itself in the seemingly alien material and cultural world, is absolute knowledge. The world therefore exists supported by a purely ideal and subjective process. This process encompasses and accounts f or everything.

Post-metaphysical thinking rejects this, almost point by point. The very idea that truth and the inquiry into truth should be a purely logical process – a subject thinking itself into existence and to a closure in self-consciousness – is rejected. Hegel is condemned for having constructed nothing more than a vast intellectual edifice into which are shoe-horned the results of the empirical sciences; and if the facts contradict the theory, hard luck for the facts: pure thought dominates. The rise of the empirical sciences in the nineteenth century, and the achievements of industry and technology, throw that whole approach into question. Within the natural sciences, it is empirical research that drives inquiry, not abstract reflection. This is picked up by **positivism**, but to the point that philosophical argument is wholly subordinated to the natural scientific model. All metaphysics, which is to say anything that cannot be verified by appeal to empirical evidence, is dismissed as nonsense. At best philosophy is left to clarify the methodology of scientific research.

Analytic philosophy takes a more promising turn, around the beginning of the twentieth century, in the hands of such thinkers as Gottlob Frege, Bertrand Russell and G. E. Moore. It begins to recognise the importance of **language** in any philosophical inquiry, albeit in an initially rather restricted way. The early analytic philosophers were concerned with language as a way of communicating information about the world. They were therefore primarily interested in the way in which language refers to, or hooks onto, the world. The post-war generation of analytic philosophers, and in particular Ludwig Wittgenstein (in his later works), J. L. Austin and Gilbert Ryle, began to recognise the role that language and language use play in sustaining social relationships. We do not simply, or even primarily, use language to communicate; rather, as Austin puts it, we do things with words – we promise and command, baptise and launch ships ('I name this ship ... '), challenge and question.

This linguistic turn recognises the fundamental role of inter-subjectivity in human life, and as such challenges what Habermas calls the philosophy of consciousness. The philosophy of consciousness assumes that explanations should be proposed in terms of the activities of individual subjects. At one level, this is Hegel's macro-subject, the spirit, unfolding itself over the natural world and through human history. On another level, it is the assumption of early analytic philosophers (and indeed positivists before them) that problems of language and knowledge are ultimately to be explained in terms of the thought processes and perceptions of the isolated individual. The linguistic turn of Wittgenstein and Austin shows that humans are irreducibly social beings, and as such their thoughts, perceptions and sense of self-identity, as well as their values and skills, rest upon their interaction with each other.

Politically, post-metaphysical thinking entails that one can no longer take for granted a particular worldview. The all-embracing aspirations of Hegelian idealism, whereby one puts forward a theory that accounts for everything, are to be rejected. Any such aspiration to a theory of everything is in danger of neglecting or undermining any counter-view. Post-metaphysical thinking, precisely in that it rejects the philosophy of consciousness and embraces intersubjectivity, stresses the need for dialogue between worldviews. For Habermas, this poses a problem, and is a continual tension in his work. For some post-modern philosophers, the rejection of metaphysics entails the rejection of the Enlightenment aspiration to truth. In its place comes a cultural relativism or perspectivism, embracing both beliefs about what is truth, and values that express what is politically and morally right. What one believes is relative to one's social or cultural circumstances, and there is no place outside of culture from which anyone can judge what the truth or the good may be. While wishing to reject such relativism, Habermas equally does not want to allow just one set of values, or one worldview, to inform and shape his thought. His solution, and thus his preferred interpretation of a post-metaphysical political philosophy, is to look to the processes by which political and moral disputes are conducted, and not thereby to stipulate the contents or end results of any such dispute. While there may be correct and incorrect ways in which to conduct a moral debate (see **discourse ethics**), the topics, substantial resources and outcomes of that debate depend upon the particular groups and individuals represented in it.

POST-STRUCTURALISM

A term covering the diverse thinkers who emerged, especially in France, in critical response to structuralism. Structuralism has its roots in the work of the linguist Ferdinand de Saussure. In particular, Saussure argues for an analysis of language that focuses upon the structured relationships between elements (such as sounds and words) within it, rather than upon the relationship of those elements to the non-linguistic world. So, for example, what allows the word 'cat' to have meaning is its differentiation from words like 'rat', 'bat' and 'sat', rather than the way in which it refers to furry animals that meow. This allows an analysis of the highly general and abstract structures that make everyday spoken and written language possible, and thus a turn away from historical accounts of particular languages. This approach to the analysis of meaning was taken up in such disciplines as social anthropology (pioneered by the work of Claude Lévi-Strauss), Marxism (Louis Althusser), literary theory (Roland Barthes) and psychoanalysis (Jacques Lacan). Structuralism played a significant role in Habermas's own thought, largely through the influence of the linguist Noam Chomsky on his idea of a **reconstructive science**, and of Jean Piaget's **genetic structuralism** on his accounts of the development of the individual personality and on his theory of **social evolution**.

Post-structuralism may be characterised in terms of its scepticism towards the scientific aspirations of the structuralists. Structuralism appeared to develop rigorous methods of analysis that seemed to generate results that had a universal applicability. The structuralists situated themselves, as scientists, outside all human culture. Structuralism presented itself as a pure theory, in the sense that it seemed to be unaffected by any particular cultural or personal values. Lévi-Strauss's analysis of mythologies is a case in point. Lévi-Strauss grounds his analyses, justifying their validity, by claiming that the structures found in mythologies throughout the world reflect the universal workings of the human mind. It is precisely this aspiration to objectivity and universality that the post-structuralists challenge. Once structuralism is itself seen as a product of a certain culture, then the fixed point that would guarantee the objectivity of its analyses disappears. Post-structuralism thereby abandons a key element of **modernism**, which is to say the commitment to finding an ultimate rational grounding of its science, and political and moral practice. It is precisely this abandonment of what he calls the 'incomplete project' of modernity (1983b) that motivates Habermas's antipathy towards much post-structuralist thought. This may be illustrated by reviewing his reactions to the work of Michel Foucault (Habermas 1988a: 238–93) and Jacques Derrida (Habermas 1988a: 161–84).

Habermas clearly admires Foucault's work as an historian, and their accounts of the pathologies of contemporary society cover similar ground, not least in Foucault's concern with the repressive nature of much psychiatric and other medical science, and the influence of **positivism** on social and penal policy. But Habermas challenges Foucault over the philosophical underpinnings of his work. The influence of the work of Friedrich Nietzsche on Foucault is significant. Nietzsche poses a fundamental challenge to the project of modernity by questioning the role and nature of reason. A suspicion that the post-structuralists tend to share against the project of modernity is that the commitment to universal rationality actually serves to exclude or repress the interests of marginal groups. Foucault himself explores this in his early study of madness (1971). Madness becomes the 'other' of reason, to be excluded from civilised society within asylums. Anything that challenges civilisation can thus be condemned under the label of insanity. Nietzsche allows this general suspicion to be pushed further. In an earlier work, *The Birth of Tragedy* (1993), Nietzsche outlines his own suspicions of the influence that the ancient Greek philosopher Socrates has upon Western thought. The commitment of Socrates to rationality, so that the whole world is approached only in terms of problems that can have definitive and rationally calculable solutions, excludes what Nietzsche theorises as the 'Dionysian', which is to say the emotionally excessive, ambiguous and tragic. In his later work, this process of exclusion becomes more clearly seen as an exercise of what he calls the 'will to power'. 'Truth' is reduced to whatever set of beliefs allows a group to survive, and to exercise its power over others. Socratic 'truth' thus ceases to be something that can be grounded in universal reason, and instead becomes a tool to repress and exclude others.

Again, Habermas may be sympathetic to this line of analysis. His work has always been sensitive to problems of political oppression and exclusion. Yet, for Habermas, Nietzsche's approach leaves unanswered a crucial question. If all 'truth' is merely an expression of the will to power, how is one to justify one's preference for any one truth over another? The consequences of this within Foucault's work may be understood as follows. Consider Foucault's championing of the voice of certain repressed groups, such as prisoners and homosexuals. Foucault can offer a highly plausible analysis of how and why such groups are excluded from power, and in particular of how dominant conceptions of truth (and thus of the scientific acquisition and justification of knowledge in general) serve to marginalise them. The problem is that if their voices are brought to the fore, on Foucault's Nietzschean grounding, all that this can entail is the substitution of one voice (one truth) for another. There is no way of justifying this as political progress, or the achievement of a more just society.

Habermas's overall argument against Foucault is thus that, while he recognises the pathologies of contemporary society, he ultimately remains confined within what Habermas calls the 'philosophy of **consciousness**', which is to say that he has an insufficient grasp of the nature and importance of **communicative reasoning**. It is in the possibility of rational discussion between free and equal persons that Habermas finds the resources to justify the political emancipation of the oppressed.

Habermas makes a somewhat similar point against Derrida. Derrida is equally condemned as remaining within the philosophy of consciousness, albeit that he might recognise the problems that arise from it. Habermas is primarily concerned with Derrida's work on **meaning**. From within the philosophy of consciousness, and thus from within the framework that shapes much modernist philosophy of **language**, there must exist some ground that secures the meaning of a word. Derrida thus criticises Edmund Husserl's appeal to 'ideal meanings', supposedly already known by the language user and thus by which they understand the words they hear or use. This is an example of what Derrida calls the 'metaphysics of presence', and in effect the belief that there exists something that can fix meanings. Here Derrida can turn back to Saussure's structuralism, and radicalise the importance of the relationship between elements within a structure. If there is no grounding 'presence', then meaning cannot be secured by referring to something outside language. (The furry, meowing animal is no longer present, at least not in the sense that it might, once and for all, pin down how I make sense of the word 'cat'.) Rather, there is only a now shifting set of relationships. Words will change their meaning in different cultural contexts. Novels, poems and letters will be read and re-read, their interpretation continually shifting, and, if there exists nothing against which readings and interpretations can be compared, then all are equally valid or true.

Ultimately, Derrida abandons any distinction between reason and rhetoric, so that the justification of one interpretation over another depends, not on either its consistency or its link to something present and grounding, but merely on the rhetorical excitement it creates. It is here again that Habermas turns to communicative rationality, not least in so far as Derrida, through a criticism of the **analytic philosopher** John Searle, attacks the **speech act** theory that lies at the basis of Habermas's own theory of communicative action. Habermas's point is that the conflation of reason and rhetoric is in turn the conflation of different uses of language. What Habermas calls the **rationalisation of the lifeworld** entails, in no small part, the development of the ability to distinguish between three different ways of using language. Language can be used to convey information about the physical world. Within such language one makes claims to the **truth** of what one is saying, and empirical and other evidence can be used to justify one's claims against those who seek to challenge them. Conversely, language can be used to establish social relationships, for example by promising or ordering. Again, the right to use language in that way can be challenged, and justifications can be given. Finally, language can be used artistically or expressively, disclosing a perspective on the world. Derrida is conflating the first and third forms of language use, and as such attempting to turn philosophy into literature.

Habermas's position against the post-structuralist might be summarised so. He acknowledges that they have recognised problems in the philosophy of consciousness. Derrida's attack on the metaphysics of presence is justified. No statement is secured in its truth or meaning simply by gesturing towards the physical world. It is not enough to point at the furry meowing animal. One will have to be prepared to argue that this is relevant evidence (and, for example, that this is a cat and not a kitten). Similarly, Foucault is right in his suspicion of the use of science in social policy (and this echoes much of Habermas's earlier work on **scientism**, as well as his later work on the **colonisation of the lifeworld**). But the abandoning of certainty does not entail abandoning the project of modernity as a whole. It rather involves recognising the need for a continuing process of rational debate in order to prevent a slide into the rhetorical or aesthetic justification of another political barbarism.

Further reading: Kelly 1994; Best 1995; Healy 1997; Ashenden and Owen 1999

POWER

Habermas has been concerned with the use and abuse of political power throughout his career. In his earlier works, and in particular within his theory of **cognitive interests**, power is treated as one of the constitutive elements of human social existence, with human beings having a fundamental interest in the abolition of the unjustifiable exercise of power (Habermas 1971a). In his later work, Habermas shifts to the problem of how the exercise of power is justified (1976b), and within the **systems theory** approach that characterises studies such as *The Theory of Communicative Action*, power is theorised as one of the **non-symbolic steering media** through which complex societies are organised (1987).

In the early work, Habermas approaches power as something that compromises the autonomy of individuals and social groups. At its simplest, this may be understood as the way in which a master may coerce and limit the actions of his servant. Clearly, if the servant must do what the master commands, then he or she cannot act upon his or her own initiative. More subtly, following the work of Karl **Marx**, Habermas suggests that the coercive nature of power in **capitalist** societies lies in the fact that it is concealed. While the dominant classes in pre-capitalist societies overtly use their power to constrain and exploit the subordinate classes, within capitalism the processes of exploitation and domination are concealed by the seeming fairness and inevitability of market exchange. The ruling class within capitalism can convince itself that it does not rule, for the mechanisms through which it exploits the subordinate classes are hidden within the processes of commodity exchange. Neo-Marxists such as Georg Lukács and the **Frankfurt School** further argue that this process of concealment seeps into the very ways of thinking that are current in capitalism. Our language and thought are distorted, as power systematically inhibits the possibility of critical reflection on the real sources of political power (see **reification**). Precisely because the existence of power is inhibiting the possibility of rational thought, it is also inhibiting the possibility of human beings making rationally informed, and thus autonomous, decisions about their own actions. Humans therefore have an interest in being emancipated from political oppression.

As Habermas comes to abandon this model of **critical theory**, he comes increasingly to see power more as a resource or mechanism that circulates about society. While the abuse of power is still harmful, he becomes more interested in the social mechanisms that give rise to that abuse, and the scope that still exists for challenging it. So, on one level, the exercise of power becomes something that requires **legitimation**, and that in terms entailing not merely that the people subject to power accept that the power-holder has a right to its use, but also that the reasons given for that right are good and appropriate reasons. If legitimation was merely a question of popular acceptance, then the justification of a particular exercise of power would be entirely relative to that particular situation. (So, if slaves believe that, because of the rules of military conquest, in losing a battle and becoming prisoners they lose their right to be free men, then slavery in that situation is justified.) Habermas is looking for processes of justification that can be made universal. So, if the enslavement of a human being is a violation of his human rights, then even if he personally accepts his condition, it is still wrong. It is this line of thought that leads Habermas both to his theory of **discourse ethics** and to his later discussions of **law**.

On a second level, power is a mechanism that allows for the working of complex societies. As a non-symbolic steering medium, it provides the rules according to which social hierarchies are organised and according to which people in those hierarchies act. Habermas's contention is that power, along with other non-symbolic steering media such as **money**, can facilitate the organisation of more complex social activities than could be achieved by individuals using only their capacity to communicate with one another. For example, a large bureaucracy is composed, in basics at least, of a series of quite precisely defined offices, with rules governing the relationships between each office. Thus, if a senior manager wishes to realise some particular goal, she is likely to delegate tasks (and the power to accomplish those tasks) to her subordinates. They in turn might delegate to their subordinates, and so on. The act of delegation is regulated by the rules that define the offices of the managers involved. Most importantly it may require very little proper communication between the offices. Neither need be in any doubt about what the other can and must do. The right to delegate does not have to be justified (as it is enshrined in the nature of the office), and so on. Power thus simplifies social interaction, ultimately to the point that the actions of the other person are wholly predictable. I issue an order, and you comply with it. It is irrelevant whether you want to, or whether you agree with it. You just do your job.

Habermas's concern – and this is explored in his account of the **colonisation of the lifeworld** – is that such exercises of power, even if initially legitimate (in the sense that good reasons can be given for the existence of the office, and of the appointment of this particular person to that office), can erode communication and thus, again, autonomy. Precisely because they are systematically organised, administrations depend upon instrumental reason. This is once again the point that anyone within an administration typically relates to their superiors and subordinates in terms of the predictability of their actions. Decisions can be debated in terms of their efficient contribution to the realisation of a given project. But, if administration does not require communicative action and **communicative reason**, then the possibilities for debating the value of that overall project are seriously inhibited. The administration's commitment to instrumental reason renders it insensitive to the sort of challenges and justifications that are typical of communicative reasoning. Thus, for example, arts bodies in the United Kingdom have long complained of the difficulty of justifying their activities to governments, and thus of receiving suitable funding and other state support. Within their own sphere, they can justify the arts in terms of its intrinsic value and its expressive capacities (and thus, perhaps, in terms of the **validity**

claim to **truthfulness**). Government administrations on the other hand seek quantitative justifications that can be used to demonstrate the efficient use of the funds given. Hence, arts projects are justified not in artistic terms but because of their contribution to tourism and the balance of payments, or their contribution to educational and social services projects. Activities that cannot justify themselves in such a way, which is to say instrumentally, are excluded and their continued existence threatened.

PRAGMATISM

An approach to philosophy, and in particular to the philosophy of science, that developed in America towards the end of the nineteenth century. It instigator was Charles Sanders Peirce. It was made popular through the work of William James and John Dewey, and was developed in social psychology by George Herbert Mead (an important influence on Habermas's account of self-identity and personal development). After a period of neglect after the second world war, pragmatism once more became a subject of respectable philosophical debate, with Richard Rorty being the prime exponent of a neo-pragmatism. Habermas finds in Peirce's work a core inspiration for his own account of the natural sciences. In Rorty he has more recently found an important opponent.

Peirce's pragmatism may in part be characterised by its fundamental opposition to the work of the seventeenth-century philosopher Descartes, and, as such, by its opposition to what Habermas calls the philosophy of **consciousness**. Descartes held that a belief could only count as knowledge if it was held to be certainly true. This certain truth was established by using reason. In practice, Descartes attempts to doubt everything he could doubt, until he comes to something that cannot be doubted and must therefore be certainly true. This point of certainty is the belief in his own existence (because he must exist in order to doubt it). From this solid foundation, Descartes attempts to rebuild knowledge with deductive certainty.

Peirce rejects this, point by point. To begin with, he questions this notion of belief. For Peirce a belief is something on which we are prepared to act. We do not need certainty, just enough confidence to be prepared to do something on the basis of the belief. So, I sit down on a chair. Whether I am conscious of it or not, I believe that the chair will take my weight. If I am right, and I sit comfortably, then why should I worry about the certainty of the belief? It works now, and that is all that matters. I might be wrong of course, and the chair gives way under me. This is the point at which science, or at least its everyday manifestation, begins. Now I have a real reason to doubt (rather than Descartes's forced doubt). I will want to work out what went wrong. Was the chair damaged? Am I putting on a little too much weight? I begin to refine my belief, but crucially not just by rationalising it. Rather, I test my new revised belief in practice. Perhaps I try to repair the chair; perhaps I gingerly sit on another one, to see if this one will take my weight, and so on.

By this means, Peirce has now redefined 'knowledge'. To know something is not to know it with certainty, but to trust that it works in practice. 'Truth' is then that which we believe to be true now. Peirce accepts that our present truths are in principle open to challenge. New tests and new experiences might come along that will prove them to be wrong, or at least inadequate. But, until then, I will worry about more pressing issues. When this is applied to science, it entails that science progresses through the use of experiments and the technological exploitation of scientific research. As technology grows more demanding, so the weaknesses of our existing scientific theories or beliefs will be found out. There is something Darwinian in all this. Just as Charles Darwin argued that species evolve by being tested by their environments, so that only those with appropriate adaptations will survive, so Peirce is suggesting that only those beliefs will survive which prove themselves effective in adapting to our technological and cultural environment. Ultimately, this entails testing our beliefs against a real world that exists independently of us.

There is one more important step in Peirce's account of science. Descartes reflected in isolation. Peirce, recognising that humans are fundamentally social beings, points out that science is done cooperatively. Science is not carried out solely by individuals, but by people who talk to each other, discuss their findings, criticise each other, and defend their results. Science is thus done by a community of scientists. Peirce can then begin to outline an ideal community in which everyone can contribute ideas, offer evidence, raise problems, and in which all can expect a reasonable reply. In fact, real scientific practice is not like this. Some ideas are repressed; some people will not be allowed to speak. But Peirce has begun to highlight not just why this is wrong, for it will lead to ineffective results, but also that science has a moral dimension.

For the early Habermas, Peirce is fundamental to his working out of the account of science given in the theory of **cognitive interests**. Peirce links science to Habermas's category of **labour**, which is to say

our everyday capacity to transform our environment through technological intervention. But, Peirce also begins to explore the role that
interaction, which is to say humanity's capacity to organise itself socially,
plays in science. In his later work, Peirce's image of an ideal community of scientists becomes an inspiration to Habermas's account of
the **ideal speech situation**, which is to say the counterfactual presupposition of open and truthful dialogue that people bring with them
to any conversation or social interaction (see Habermas 1992b: 88–112).

Rorty's neo-pragmatism is quite distinct from Peirce's original
inspiration. While Rorty takes up something of Peirce's anti-
foundationalism, which is to say the rejection of the equation of
knowledge and certainty found in Descartes, he takes this to radical
extremes. He is highly sceptical of Peirce's continuing commitment
to the notion of 'truth', and in particular of Peirce's argument that there
are rational processes through which truth claims can be justified. For
Rorty, justification cannot be confined to a narrow rational process,
not least because he embraces what he calls 'non-realism'. In effect, the
real world that Peirce presupposes as the ultimate test of a scientific
belief is abandoned by Rorty. For Rorty, that 'real' world is largely a
construction of human culture and language. For Habermas, this entails
a mere blurring of issues of truth and issues of artistic or rhetorical
expression. In effect Rorty is arguing that what matters in science is not
to test it against reality (for there is none), but rather to open up new
realities, new ways of imagining our world. For Habermas, what may
be acceptable in artistic expression is unacceptable in science, where the
task remains one of finding evidence and arguments to support the
relevance of a theory to Peirce's independently existing real world (see
validity claim). Thanks to its overwhelming emphasis on expression,
Rorty's neo-pragmatism degenerates, for Habermas, into a politically
impotent relativism (and thus into a form of **neo–conservativism**).
Rorty cannot rationally justify a moral position. He can at best give a
rhetorical defence that, he will acknowledge, can only appeal to other
people like him – which is to say, to other people with the same cultural background (see Habermas 1999a: 343–82).

Further reading: Arens 1994; Koczanowicz 1999; Aboulafia *et al.* 2001

PRINCIPLE OF ORGANISATION

The characterisation of stages in the evolution of human society, and
broadly equivalent to **Marx**'s concept of 'mode of production'.

Habermas uses this term in *Legitimation Crisis* (Habermas 1976b: 16–17) and in his development of the theory of **social evolution** (1979a: 130–77). Four stages are identified in the evolution of human society: the archaic; early civilisation; developed civilisation; and **capitalism**. Each stage is characterised in terms of its core institution, which is to say that part (or sub-**system**) of society that is dominant and that gives the society its character. In archaic societies the core institution is constituted by kinship relationships; in both early and developed civilisations, the state is dominant; and in capitalism the core institution is the economy. Core institutions therefore determine how individuals within the society relate to each other. In archaic society this is primarily in terms of membership of clans and lineages; in civilisations it is through the hierarchies of politics and status and through the legal system of the state; and in capitalism, people relate to each other primarily through the market, as economic producers and consumers. Further, such social relationships will be entwined with and supported by worldviews, or, put otherwise, by distinctive norms and values into which the members of the society are socialised.

With respect to Habermas's theory of social evolution, the principles of organisation are understood as a set of general and abstract rules that serve to characterise each stage of society in terms of its ability to learn and to adapt to internal and external challenges.

PSYCHOANALYSIS

An approach to the study of the mind, and to the treatment of psychiatric illness, most closely associated with Sigmund Freud. Psychoanalysis provides Habermas with an important model in articulating his early account of **critical theory** (Habermas 1971a: 246–300).

The psychoanalytic patient typically presents himself to the doctor as suffering from seemingly physical symptoms, such as paralysis, pain or blackouts. However, if no physical cause can be found for them, the assumption of the psychoanalyst is that the patient is generating the symptoms himself. In effect, the symptom is a product of the patient's free action, even though the patient does not recognise it as such. This is explained through appeal to the model of the mind as divided into the conscious and the unconscious mind, and the mechanism of repression. The patient experiences some traumatic event. He is unable to deal with that event consciously, so he represses it into his unconsciousness. While the idea associated with the experience may be repressed, Freud posits that energy associated with the idea continues to manifest itself. Hence the neurotic symptoms. However, the more subtle point to make is that symptoms are not arbitrary. Rather, they may be seen as symbolic expressions of the original trauma, albeit that the symbolism is typically that of a language that is private to the patient and not part of public language. This is part of what renders it incomprehensible to the patient's conscious mind.

This may be illustrated through one of Freud's early cases. Anna O. presented herself as suffering from impaired vision, paralysis on her right side and hydrophobia, with occasional periods of aberrant behaviour and delirium. Freud and his mentor Breuer were able to exploit these periods of aberrant behaviour for, during such periods, Anna O. uttered words that gave clues to the original source of her condition. Thus the hydrophobia was traced back to an occasion on which she had seen her female companion's dog drinking from a glass. She was disgusted by this, but crucially the disgust was motivated more by unacknowledged dislike of her companion than by the dog's action. Once that dislike could be acknowledged and consciously expressed, the symptom vanished. So the psychoanalytic cure is a talking cure, tracing the symptoms back to an original event, and frequently allowing conscious recognition of feelings (for example of sexual desire, jealousy or regret) that could not previously be expressed.

For Habermas, psychoanalysis is important in so far as it suggests a way of combining natural and social scientific methods within critical theory, and thereby bringing about an **emancipatory** science. The patient appears to be under the sway of natural forces, in so far as the symptoms seem to have physical causes. Natural science would treat them as such, and seek to intervene in that causal mechanism. In contrast, the psychoanalyst recognises the symptoms as a 'second nature', or as subjective actions that have come to present themselves as causally determined. The task of analysis is then to emancipate the patient from the symptoms, restoring to him his full autonomy. In effect, the patient is taking back conscious control of his actions. In order to do this, the analyst uses a hermeneutic, or interpretative technique, that attempts to restore meaning to the seemingly natural and meaningless symptoms. That meaning is the original traumatic experience and the complex of motivations and emotions that made it so traumatic. For Habermas, **ideology critique** uses a similar approach at the level of society, in order to restore political autonomy to a community.

Further reading: Freud 1962; Keat 1981

PUBLIC SPHERE

Those social institutions that allow for open and rational debate between citizens in order to form public opinion. The debate can be conducted face to face or through exchanges of letters and other written communications, and may be mediated by journals, newspapers and electronic forms of communication. Ideally the public sphere should be open to all, and agreement should be secured through the force of better argument, rather than through any exercise or threat of physical force. Habermas explores the history of the public sphere in his earliest sole-authored book, *The Structural Transformation of the Public Sphere* (1989a). This early concern with the public sphere highlights the fundamental place that notions of **democracy** and **communicative reason** occupy in his work.

The public sphere comes into existence with the maturation of **capitalism** in Europe in the eighteenth century. Crucially this is a bourgeois public sphere, which is to say that it is a space within which the members of rising commercial and professional classes may meet and communicate. The working class and the aristocracy are largely excluded. Within earlier feudal societies, the dominant aristocracy had more or less direct control over all aspects of social life, including the economy. While the feudal monarch might be presented in public, this personal presentation was a largely rhetorical show of the monarch's power. It did not invite any challenge or debate. As the bourgeoisie becomes increasingly powerful, not least in that it comes to control the economy, wresting control of the economy away from the state, it begins to seek an increasing say in government policy. Government policy, not least in international relations and internally through taxation, may have a major impact upon the economic interests of the bourgeoisie who in turn, therefore, seek to protect those interests. The issue here is less one of democracy, at least in the sense of a simple right to vote, and more one of making the state responsive to the bourgeoisie's expression of its needs and interests in public opinion (1989a: 14–26).

The public sphere is thus an intermediary between the public realm of the state and the private interests of individual members of the bourgeoisie. The public–private distinction is crucial at this stage. But the public sphere mediates between the public and private not merely as a way to bring together the voices of many private individuals, but also in so far as it facilitates the articulation of the individual bourgeois's sense of self. Bourgeois subjectivity is formed through the public sphere. Habermas here distinguishes between the literary public sphere and the political, and charts the early development of both in England.

The eighteenth century sees a fundamental development in art, and especially in literature. For the first time, in the form of the bourgeoisie, there existed a leisured and educated class that had the means to buy art and the time to enjoy it. While these conditions affected all the arts, commercialising them and freeing artists from the patronage of church or state, the most distinctive form of art to arise is the novel. This is the paradigm eighteenth-century art form, mass-produced, and perfectly suited to a newly literate market. However, Habermas makes the important point that the novel has its origins in the letter. The bourgeoisie was using its literacy and leisure to write letters. The first novels were, in effect, collections of model letters. The story is secondary to the possibility of teaching the bourgeoisie how to express itself in writing. This expression is not merely a matter of writing elegantly, but rather of articulating publicly one's inner emotions (1989a: 48–51). The letter thereby begins to bridge the realms of private and public.

The rise of the novel has a further implication. If people read at all prior to the eighteenth century, then they read the classics. There was no question about the classics' status as great art. The novel, precisely because it is new, poses a problem to its reader: is it actually worth reading (1992c: 423)? The literary public sphere thus begins to take shape in the requirement to debate and justify one's exercise of taste. Literature trains the bourgeois reader, not just in self-expression, but also in public argument. The literary sphere expands to encompass not merely fiction, but also essays, typically published in periodicals (such as the *Tatler* and the *Spectator*), that stimulate the discussion of a range of practical, scientific and social topics. These are complemented by institutions such as the salon, the coffee house and the learned societies, where in face-to-face meetings ideas can be exchanged, debated and defended.

The political public sphere thus comes into existence through this amalgam of diverse media and institutions. But it awaits one more crucial item. Political journalism, while on the one hand stimulated by the existence of periodicals with allegiances to particular political parties, on the other hand was still hampered by the exclusion of journalists from the British parliament. Political debate effectively occurred in private until space was provided for journalists in the House of Commons in 1803 (1989a: 62).

If this charts the rise of the public sphere, then Habermas is quick to point out its actual weaknesses and contradictions. While it articulates itself in terms of an ideal, such that all citizens may contribute to the debate, in practice that ideal is compromised. The working classes are excluded, and this entails that a number of fundamental issues are excluded from the debate. The contributors to the public sphere are homogeneous in terms of power and economic interests. Any individual differences between members of the bourgeoisie are typically economic interests, and are worked out in the market. The enormous conflict of economic interests that existed between the working classes and the bourgeoisie is not debated. In effect, it is not even politically recognised.

The expansion of the franchise in the nineteenth century, and the establishing of the welfare state in the early twentieth, begin to remedy this problem. However, Habermas suggests that this comes at the cost of the disintegration of an effective public sphere. Habermas's point here is not that the public sphere is incapable of rationally debating differences in class interest. It is rather that the development of capitalism is leading to a fundamental transformation in both working-class and bourgeois subjectivity, and that that transformation undermines debate. While the eighteenth-century bourgeois sense of self was grounded in the skills of self-articulation and argument, Habermas suggests that in the twentieth century both bourgeoisie and working class become increasingly privatised. That is to say that individuals can shrink away from the public defence of their tastes and opinions. In late capitalism, which is characterised by large-scale economic production, multi-national companies, and extensive bureaucracies both in the sphere of private economic production and in the state, the individual is increasingly understood in terms of a place within an economic or administrative system. Subsequently Habermas would develop this argument, in his analysis of the **colonisation of the lifeworld**, as people coming increasingly to relate to each other instrumentally and not communicatively. Complex social relationships, paradoxically, do not require complex communicative and self-reflective skills. They require instead the ability to respond to the situation as it is defined by the administrative economic structure, and that is highly simplified and schematic.

The atrophy of the communicative skills that are fundamental to the public sphere is reflected in both cultural consumption and politics. While the eighteenth-century member of the bourgeoisie was expected to be able to debate his tastes, the modern consumer of culture need do nothing more than exert them in an act of consumption. Taste is reduced to a purely subjective preference that is unsuitable for rational discussion (see **decisionism**). What is perhaps more problematic is that something similar happens to politics. Public debate is replaced by mass voting. Public opinion is reduced to a mere aggregate of individual, and subjective, preferences, rather than the open negotiation and debate of a common position. An election thereby becomes little more than a plebiscite on the respective manifestos of two or more political parties. Real issues are suppressed behind the simplified choice that is presented to the electorate. More subtly, Habermas suggests that modern public relations and advertising can further serve to erode the quality of any debate that does take place. Rhetoric replaces reasoning in the formation of 'non-public opinion' (1989a: 221).

While Habermas subsequently revised his views of the public sphere, and suggested that he was less pessimistic about the erosion of public debate (1992c), the concerns expressed in *Structural Transformation of the Public Sphere* are ones to which Habermas returns throughout his career.

Further reading: Holub 1991: 1–19; Cahoun 1992; Crossley and Michaels 2004

RATIONALISATION OF THE LIFEWORLD

The process of critically reviewing and justifying the everyday beliefs and skills that ordinary people typically take for granted. The rationalisation of the lifeworld may be seen as an integral part of **social evolution**, as members of society respond to challenges that either affect them personally, or affect the society as whole, and thereby stimulate a process of learning that increases their ability to solve problems. While something of this idea is beginning to emerge in *Legitimation Crisis* (Habermas 1976b), Habermas develops it fully in *The Theory of Communicative Action* (1984a: 143–271; 1987: 113–97).

The basic idea behind the rationalisation of the lifeworld may be understood through reference to **pragmatism**. In developing his pragmatist philosophy, Charles Peirce argued that human beings learn not through abstract reflection (as philosophers since René Descartes in the seventeenth century had tended to assume), but rather by responding to concrete problems. I am building a wooden fence. I hammer away, but the nails I use keep bending. I am confronted by a practical problem, and I must stop and reflect in order to solve it. Perhaps my hammer technique is at fault. Perhaps my hammer is too heavy, or the nails too weak or the wood too hard. A series of practical experiments with different techniques, hammers and nails will hopefully solve the problem. Once solved, I will have learnt something new. I will be that little bit better equipped to deal with problems in the future. But, crucially, this little example indicates that I typically learn new things because I need to. I learn in a particular situation, and in response to a pressing problem. Finally, I learn by questioning some of the beliefs (for example, about my skills as a hammerer, about hammers, nails and wood) that I had previously taken for granted. Up to now those taken-for-granted beliefs had served me pretty well, and so I did not have to worry about them. I reflect upon them only when they seem to be letting me down.

Taken-for-granted beliefs about building techniques are part of my **lifeworld**, along with a lot of other practical competences that allow me safely to navigate the social world (for example, how to open doors, obey traffic lights, pay my taxes); with my moral, political and aesthetic values; and with my personal beliefs, preferences and sense of self-identity. The rationalisation of the lifeworld occurs as these beliefs are subject to questioning, and although it will be individuals who do this questioning, the rationalisation of the lifeworld is manifest at the level of a culture (and thus at the level of the broad spectrum of beliefs and competences that are available to well-socialised and competent people in that particular society).

Habermas's core point is that the questioning of taken-for-granted beliefs is not a merely contingent or haphazard process. Rationalisation has a clear tendency to increased abstraction, and to the **differentiation** of separate types of problem and competence. In part, Habermas is here following, and heavily revising, the arguments of the German sociologist Max Weber concerning what he saw as global processes of rationalisation and 'disenchantment'. For Weber, the superiority of Western culture lay in the fact that it had greater rationality. In part this was expressed in greater and more consistent use of **instrumental reason**, not merely through highly efficient technology but also through effective administration and social organisation, rationally consistent legal and moral systems and even more rational art (Weber 1976: 13–23). As a process of 'disenchantment', this also entailed that modern Western societies were increasingly less reliant upon magical, religious and other traditional beliefs and values. While Habermas adopts from Weber something of this notion of disenchantment, at least in so far as rationalisation entails the questioning of the taken-for-granted contents of the lifeworld, he differs from Weber on two crucial points. First, the contents of the lifeworld can never be wholly eroded. While secular beliefs and values may predominate as societies become more rational, beliefs and values of all sorts remain vital in motivating people and giving their lives meaning. (Something of this is indeed recognised in Weber's notion of 'value rationality', where one's actions are made consistent with a set of fundamental values.) Second, Weber tends to concentrate on instrumental rationality. For Habermas, the all important development lies in the refinement of **communicative reason**, and in the recognition that the rational processes that are appropriate for reflecting on and challenging beliefs in science and technology are not the same as those that are appropriate for moral and legal issues, or for questions of self-understanding.

The rationalisation of the lifeworld may therefore be seen to entail the differentiation of the **validity claims**. That is to say that, as rationalisation takes place, people within a culture become increasingly aware of the difference between questions about the truth of their beliefs, questions about morality and rightfulness, and questions about their self-expression. Habermas asks us to imagine a small-scale society dominated by a single religious or magical worldview (1987: 87ff). He suggests that, in such a society, the worldview would answer all the questions that typically might trouble its believers. The cosmology would explain the origin and nature of the physical and social worlds (so resolving questions of truth); it would explain why the world was here and what roles people should play in it (and so resolve problems of morality); and finally it would tell these people who they are (as adherents to that belief system and possibly as descendents of those particular deities). As society grows more complex, and as it faces more demanding challenges, these answers are increasingly exposed as being inadequate. It will no longer be adequate to justify one's use of a particular technology by saying that that is how our ancestors taught it to us. To carrying on using inappropriate technology may lead to the starvation of the group. Similarly, as society grows in size and includes more and more diverse people, questions of morality and justice become more pressing. Traditional practices of judgement and punishment will again require justification, for example in terms of their consistency (are all people treated alike?) and effectiveness (and whether this really makes for a more peaceful and secure society). Appeals to increasingly general secular ideas or principles, such as those of human rights and the role of a political constitution consented to by all, gradually come to replace appeals to magical, religious or even nationalistic narratives in justifying law and morality. Finally, a complex society may in part be characterised by the diversity of the people who belong within it. As people become more aware of their individual differences, the justification of their opinions and preferences can no longer depend upon appeals to a common set of beliefs or narratives.

In summary, the rationalisation of the lifeworld is that process of social evolution through which a society increases its problem-solving capacity by reflecting upon existing beliefs and competences, and where necessary replacing them by beliefs and competences that can be justified in increasingly general, which is to say abstract, terms. In effect, it is a process by which both society and the individuals within it increase their scope for free and autonomous action. Habermas none the less complements this generally optimistic picture of social progress by entwining it with the more pessimistic account of the **colonisation of the lifeworld** that explains how social change also entails the compromising of freedom and the meaningfulness of human life.

Further readings: White 1987; Honneth and Joas 1991

RECONSTRUCTIVE SCIENCE

An approach to philosophical and social scientific inquiry, proposed by Habermas, that seeks to explicate the skills and knowledge that ordinary social agents must possess in order to act with competence (Habermas 1979a: 9).

This approach may be introduced through the example of linguistic competence. In order to be able to use language, and so to be able to communicate through well-formed sentences, the speaker must be able to follow and apply a complex set of grammatical rules. However, few speakers will be able to articulate exactly what these rules are. Their knowledge may thus be described as being 'unconscious' (1976a: 23) or 'intuitive' (1979a: 14). It is what the philosopher Gilbert Ryle called 'know-how', as distinct from 'know-that' (1979a: 12; Ryle 1963: 28–32). If we know *that* something is the case, we must be able to articulate that knowledge claim explicitly. Philosophical theories of knowledge traditionally took this to be the typical form of knowledge. Ryle's point was that much of our everyday competence relies upon our ability to follow and recognise complex rules – that is, we know *how* to go on – but we are unable to articulate this in explicit knowledge claims. A reconstructive science turns know-how into know-that, precisely in so far as it explicates our intuitive abilities to follow rules. So the reconstruction of the know-how of a competent Welsh-language speaker would entail explicating Welsh grammar.

This initial example is misleading, to the extent that it focuses on a particular language. Habermas's concern is rather with what he calls 'universal capacities', as opposed to the capacities of particular groups or individuals (1979a: 14). Thus a reconstructive science of linguistics will study not the competences of a particular linguistic community (such as the Welsh) or of a particular speaker, but the capacity to use human language *per se*. Its results therefore strive to be universal and anonymous (1976a: 22), which is to say that the rule systems that are explicated by a reconstructive science are the rules that make possible the general capacities of all human beings. The linguistics of Noam Chomsky serves as an important model for Habermas of a successful reconstructive science (Chomsky 1964). Chomsky sought to identify the 'deep structure' of Universal Grammar, which is to say a set of rules from which the grammars of all ordinary languages can be generated. This Universal Grammar may be understood as the set of rules that allows a human agent to become competent in at least one language, producing and understanding sentences in that language, and distinguishing well-formed from badly formed sentences (1979a: 14).

Yet, again, Chomsky provides only a partial model for Habermas's work. Crucially, Chomsky takes an essentialist approach to the problem of reconstruction, in the sense that the reconstructed 'deep structure' is understood as something that is hard-wired into the human brain at birth. It is the innate competence that allows the child to learn a language. In contrast, Habermas favours a model derived from the psychology of Jean Piaget and Lawrence Kohlberg. Here, competences are understood as developing as the child matures. The reconstruction is therefore not of a single structure, but rather of a series of stages, each of which must be completed before a higher stage can be built upon it. Thus, for example, Kohlberg identifies three broad stages in moral development, the pre-conventional (where the child obeys moral rules simply out of fear of punishment or desire for reward), the conventional (where the authority of the rule is recognised), and finally the **post-conventional** (where rational justification is sought for that authority). Kohlberg's work is influential upon Habermas's **discourse ethics**, itself an attempt to develop moral theory as a reconstructive science.

Reconstructive science becomes increasingly characteristic of Habermas's work from the early 1970s onwards, being fundamental to his understanding of **universal pragmatics** and his reconstruction of **historical materialism** as a theory of **social evolution**. This intellectual shift may be understood as a response to his dissatisfaction with the **transcendental arguments** that underpinned the theory of **cognitive interests**. The principle concern of *Knowledge and Human Interests* (1971a) was with the constitution of knowledge, which is to say with the conditions under which certain claims come to be understood as knowledge claims. So, in *Knowledge and Human Interests* Habermas was arguing that all knowledge claims are constituted in terms of certain basic interests: in our concern with transforming the natural world; with improving our communication with other human beings; and with bringing about political emancipation. These interests must be satisfied if humans are to flourish. The possibility of pure knowledge, independent of any such interest motivating and guiding its acquisition, is dismissed. Yet Habermas comes to recognise that a reconstructive science would be 'pure', for it would not be shaped by any of the cognitive interests. For example, knowledge of Universal Grammar does nothing to make one's communication or language use any more fluent than it already is (precisely because Universal Grammar merely explicates the grounds of the competence and fluency that one already has) (1976a: 23).

More problematic still, by focusing on the question of constitution Habermas sees himself as having failed to develop the question of how one establishes that a knowledge claim is valid or true. It is one thing to say that 'The earth revolves about the sun' is a knowledge claim, grounded in the interest in technological control of the natural environment, but it is quite another to say that this claim is true. In his self-critical comments, Habermas presents this problem as a failure to distinguish the two senses of 'reflection' that were at play in *Knowledge and Human Interests* (1971a: 377). The dominant sense of 'reflection' is that of self-reflection, and thus of the critical and emancipatory process through which the particular subject comes to understand itself better and in particular to free itself from the sort of mistakes and illusions that could be classified as **ideologies**. Here truth is secured through successful emancipatory action. A second sense is precisely that of reconstruction. There is already a suggestion of this in the account in *Knowledge and Human Interests* of both **psychoanalysis** and historical materialism. In order to reflect upon the neurotic and political distortions that assail particular individuals and societies, Freud and Marx began to construct general accounts of the normal development of the ego and of society respectively. Habermas's point is that such general accounts have a validity independently of their incorporation into therapy and political reflection, and thus independently of the emancipatory interest that otherwise motivated Freud and Marx. These general accounts are, then, Habermas's first models of reconstructive science, and it is these that find echoes in Habermas's later work.

REIFICATION

Literally, the transformation of something subjective or created by humans into an inanimate object. In social and cultural theory it therefore refers, most generally, to the process by which human society (that is ultimately the product of the largely conscious and intentional actions of ordinary people) comes to confront its members as an external, seemingly natural and constraining force. In a more precise or technical sense, the theory of reification was developed by the **Marxist** Georg Lukács (1971) from Marx's theory of commodity fetishism. Marx analysed the process in **capitalism** by which the meetings of humans in commercial exchange in the market place take on the appearance of relationships between things. Basically, in observing a market exchange, it seems as if the commodities that are being exchanged are communicating with each other. It is the commodities that seem to be involved in a social life, not the people who are doing the buying and selling. The relationships between humans come to be governed by properties – exchange values or prices – that appear to be inherent in the commodities exchanged. What is crucial about this is that human interaction has come to be governed by purely quantitative rules (that is, by the monetary values of the commodities they are dealing in), and not the qualitative rich meanings and emotions that should regulate human communication. For Lukács, this complex inversion (whereby commodities take on the social life of humans, and quantity replaces quality) is manifest in all social relations (and not merely economic ones). In an increasingly rationalised and bureaucratic society, that which is qualitative, unique and subjective in human relationships is lost, as such things are governed according to the purely quantitative concerns of the bureaucrat and the manager.

The concept of 'reification' is taken up by the **Frankfurt School** thinker Theodor Adorno. In his hands, it becomes a characterisation of the very way in which we think in late capitalist societies. For Adorno it becomes increasingly more difficult not to treat other people and objects instrumentally, quantifying them, and attempting to pin them down within neat categories. Something of this feeds into Habermas's early idea of **systematically distorted commu-nication** (1970a), where he suggests that deformations in language may prevent us from raising important issues and debating them. In his later work, reification becomes more closely linked to the idea of the **colonisation of the lifeworld**. While Habermas shares something of Adorno's concern over the role of **instrumental reason** in social life, he rejects Adorno's extreme view. For Haber-mas, instrumental reason can have an important and constructive role to play in the organisation of society. Complex societies are **sys-tematically integrated**, which is to say that they rely on human beings, in certain limited situations, relating to each other in highly simplified ways. Thus, for example, in a market I need to relate to the stallholder simply in terms of the prices of her goods. I treat her merely as a means to the end of my purchasing what I want. This simplification can allow highly complex social structures to be held together with relatively little effort. Habermas's point is that if we tried to sustain such structures through communicative action, in which we would try to come to a rich and meaningful agreement about the exchange with the stallholder, it would overwhelm us. Every exchange would have to start from scratch, negotiating the nature of a fair exchange, the meaning of money, and perhaps even discussing why I want to buy the goods and why she wants to sell them.

So, the instrumentalisation and quantification of social relations is not, in itself, a bad thing. It becomes a problem, and becomes reify-ing, as the complex social structures or **systems** that this instru-mentalism sustains begin to take on a life of their own. The systems will have their own, immanent way of working and developing, and they can thereby become inflexible and unresponsive to the true needs of human beings. Increasingly, in what Habermas terms the colonisation of the lifeworld, our everyday actions become con-strained by economic and bureaucratic systems. I do things, not because I want to or even because they make sense to me. Rather, I do them because the system demands them of me. Crucially, because a system is organised instrumentally and in terms of its quantitative efficiency, it becomes increasingly difficult to discuss and evaluate it using ordinary language. One can assess a system in terms of its instrumental efficiency, but once one starts to talk about the reason why it exists or the purposes that it serves, or indeed the humanity with which it treats its clients, one is in danger of using a language that is simply not understood within the system. Reification may therefore be seen as the process by which a system becomes resistant to the forms of critical challenge that are characteristic of **communicative reason** (see Habermas 1987: 367–73)

SCIENTISM

The conviction that the natural sciences represent not merely one source of knowledge, but are the only source of knowledge (Habermas 1971a: 4). This is to say that all valid knowledge claims must conform to the methods of inquiry found in the natural sciences. This conviction may be understood as an outcome of **positivism**, not least in so far as it seeks to demarcate science (as knowledge) from non-sense or metaphysics. Habermas's criticisms of scientism follow two lines. On the one hand, scientism is attacked as being inadequate as an account of how knowledge is acquired. On the other hand, scientism leads to a distortion of political decision-making processes in contemporary society (and thus to what Habermas calls **decisionism**).

The theory of **cognitive interests** may be understood as Habermas's fundamental assault on scientism as a theory of knowledge. While scientism recognises just one form of science, Habermas identifies three forms: the empirical–analytic (or natural) sciences; the historical–hermeneutic (or cultural) sciences; and the emancipatory sciences (1971a: 308–11; 1976a: 7–10). In each form of science, knowledge is acquired by a different method, and each responds to a different need that must be satisfied for human beings to survive and flourish. As such, each science is confined to a certain area of human experience and practice. The natural sciences serve a deep-seated human interest in the technological manipulation of their environment, through what Habermas calls 'purposive-rational' action (which is to say action oriented by the instrumental calculation of the most effective means to achieve a given end). Natural scientific knowledge is grounded in the possibility of identifying natural regularities (and hence laws of nature), and then using these regularities in order to predict and calculate technological interventions on the world. The hermeneutic sciences are concerned rather with intersubjective communication, and thus with the process of making sense of the meaning of texts and actions. Finally, emancipatory sciences are concerned with restoring human autonomy in the face of political and other forms of repression. For any one of these forms of science to overstep its legitimate remit is to invite at best nonsense (as, for example, in the hermeneutic interpretation of nature that formed a part of medieval and indeed Romantic approaches (Apel 1980: 49)), or at worst the perpetuation of political domination.

For earlier theorists in the **Frankfurt School** tradition, the entwining of natural science with the technological manipulation, or 'domination', of nature was *prima facie* suspect. Herbert Marcuse, for example, identified a 'fusion' of political domination and the technological domination of nature that entailed that the political emancipation of humanity from capitalism could only be achieved if the methods of the natural sciences themselves were radically changed (1971b: 85). Habermas's separation of the three forms of science allows him to reject this argument. On the one hand, a natural science that was removed from its grounding in manipulation and domination would deliver not knowledge but mystical nonsense. So, on the other hand, political domination cannot be explained in terms of the mere existence of the natural sciences, but rather in terms of the illegitimate extension of the natural sciences beyond their justifiable boundaries. This is precisely what scientism achieves by undermining the legitimacy of the hermeneutic and emancipatory sciences.

Habermas responds to this as the problem of the 'scientisation' of politics (1971b). On one level, he notes that contemporary technology has expanded, not just in the manipulation of nature, but also crucially in the manipulation of society. This is manifest in the obvious expansion of social administration or bureaucracy. If this entailed no more than the effective organisation of society, it would be unproblematic. Habermas's point, rather, is that scientism is not merely a philosophical position (or even the positivistic self-understanding of science itself), but rather feeds into the self-understanding of ordinary people (which is to say that it becomes part of the **lifeworld**). As part of everyday consciousness, scientism, accompanied by the expansion of technocratic or purposive–rational methods of problem solving into social life, fundamentally transforms the way in which social life is understood. Society becomes a 'nexus of behavioural modes', which is to say that people are seen as objects that can be manipulated, quite independently of their consent or active participation, just as the objects of natural science can be manipulated. The notion that society, especially as a political body, should be understood as a community, characterised and sustained by communication between its members, is lost (1976a: 255). Put otherwise, the expansion of technocratic methods of problem solving undermine the traditional contexts, such as mythologies, religions and other worldviews, through which human beings previously made sense of their lives and their relationships to others (1971b: 96). As life thus becomes increasingly meaningless (or, more precisely, as the hermeneutic knowledge that would give it meaning is marginalised), human needs are reduced to objects of technological control (1971b: 74). A consequence of scientism is that political decision making, both by professional politicians and the public that elects them, is reduced to a more or less arbitrary decisionism. As the conception of a political community is undermined, professional politicians are confined increasingly to frameworks articulated by their advisers, and the public is depoliticised, responding merely to the satisfaction of privatised and subjectively recognised needs (1971b: 112).

In his later works, Habermas takes up very similar themes in his analysis of the **colonisation of the lifeworld**.

SOCIAL EVOLUTION

The process by which societies change and grow in complexity. In the early 1970s Habermas sought to develop a theory of social evolution, in part as a response to the inadequacies that he identified in Marx's **historical materialism** and other earlier theories of social change (Habermas 1979b: 130–77). A theory of social evolution is strictly separated from the study of history. History entails the construction of particular narratives of contingent events. It is essentially a **hermeneutic** discipline, which is to say that it is concerned with understanding and recovering the meanings that historical figures attributed to their actions. In contrast, the theory of social evolution is a **reconstructive science**, which is to say that it is seeking the rules and structures that underpin and make possible all historical change. While history is concerned with the particular, social evolution is concerned with the general (see Habermas 1979b).

If a theory of social evolution is to be an account of social change that has general applicability, then for Habermas it must deal with the development of basic human capacities. This is to say that human history, taken as a whole (and thus once the process of natural evolution ceases, with the separation of modern humans or homo sapiens from other hominid species, such as the Neanderthals), is understood in terms of the growing intellectual, technical and social sophistication of humanity. Homo sapiens does not come on to the evolutionary scene fully developed. While the species may be full of potential, that potential is only going to be realised by living in, and indeed responding to the challenges of, historically changing societies.

The sophistication of a society is thus, in large measure, a result of the sophistication of the people within it.

It is the fundamental character of the relevant human capacities here that is all important. Habermas points out that he is not concerned with particular human achievements, however widespread their influence might be. So an account of the development of modern science, for example, is not yet social evolution. However, an account of the human capacity for rational thought and inquiry that underpins that science will be. Similarly, an account of the development of democracy as a form of government is not yet evolution, whereas an account of the interactive and communicative competences that underpin it will be. At this stage in his career, Habermas can still be seen to be appealing quite significantly back to the work of the 1960s, and especially to the theory of **cognitive interests**. What matters here is that the theory of cognitive interests itself postulated two fundamental (or 'anthropologically deep-lying' (1979b: 42)) competences: those of **labour** and of **interaction**, or in other words, the human ability to transform its environment (and thus to develop science and technology), and its ability to organise in social groups and communicate. Again, the theory of social evolution is not a mere narrative of the actual development of these capacities (so that the particular historical periods within which refinements occur are largely irrelevant to social evolution). Rather it is the account of how these capacities could develop, and thus of the underlying rules that their development obeys.

The crucial point that Habermas makes about social evolution is that it does not just happen. In part, Habermas's theory of social evolution is inspired by his engagement with Niklaus Luhmann's **systems theory** in the early 1970s (Habermas and Luhmann 1975). Luhmann offers an account of social evolution in terms of the **differentiation** of society, which is to say that evolution is seen as a process within which society develops more and more specialist institutions (or sub-**systems**), that allows it to deal with more complex and subtle challenges. One might loosely compare this to natural evolution. A primate is an evolutionary advance on, say, a horse, because it has developed specialist features (such as highly flexible fingers and toes, better vision, and a more developed brain) that allow it to cope in a more sophisticated way with its environment. One would not expect to see a horse manipulating a basic tool such as a stick to acquire its food. For a chimpanzee, however, such manipulation is quite possible. So, a modern society has a sophisticated economy, an educational system and a legal system. In a small-scale society, the family may be the primary unit of economic production, education and socialisation of children, and source of discipline.

While Habermas sees social evolution as differentiating societies, increasing the complexity of their social and **system integration**, he questions the explanation of change that systems theory seems to offer. At its worst, systems theory seems to present change as an automatic process, or as one that the society carries out for itself. For Habermas, in contrast, if societies change and develop, then they change because the human beings within them have brought about that change. Change thus requires at least two factors to be present before it can happen. One is a stimulus to change, and the other is the potential of those within the society to understand the challenge and to deal creatively with it (1979a: 122, 160). The stimuli are typically social **crises**, brought about either through external threats from the physical and social environment (such as long-term harvest failure or the exhaustion of natural resources, and threats of colonisation and plunder), or through internal tensions within the society (such as class conflict, or the manifest injustice of the political system). There is no guarantee that a crisis will be solved. An ecological crisis may destroy a society (as presumably happened to the original culture of Easter Island), and an invasion may destroy a culture or eliminate its members (as happened with the European conquest of the Caribbean). Simple societies do not automatically progress into complex ones. Social evolution is not inevitable, as systems theory might suggest, and it is not achieved by society as some sort of macrosubject (see **consciousness, philosophy of**), but by real people.

Habermas compares the capacity of a society to respond creatively to a crisis to the ability of an individual human being to learn. Here he makes a highly audacious and controversial move. He draws a parallel between the development of a species (phylogenesis) and the development of the individual (ontogenesis). The **genetic structuralism** of Jean Piaget provides Habermas with his model of ontogenesis. Piaget identifies a series of stages through which the individual human being must pass as she matures into adulthood. They represent the development of an individual's capacity to learn, to distinguish different types of entity within her environment (such as differentiating between herself and the external world, or between objects and people), and thus to respond to ever more complex challenges. However, a key point again is that this is not an automatic process. Individuals develop through their interaction with people around them, and much will depend upon the richness of the cultural resources (including **language**) that are available to that interaction (1979a: 98–9, 154). The comparison of phylogenesis and ontogenesis is, as Habermas himself acknowledges, problematic. There is for example the danger of suggesting that people within relatively simple or undeveloped societies remain in some sort of perpetual childhood. But Habermas does insist that there is an inherent plausibility to the comparison. If social change is brought about by the members of a society, then the capacity for change and evolution in a given society will depend ultimately upon the problem-solving capacities of its members.

The new-born child, in what Piaget calls the symbiotic stage, will not yet have distinguished between itself and its environment. Habermas suggests no social parallel to this stage. However, the next stage of egocentricism does have a social parallel (1979a: 104; 1974a: 92). The egocentric child has not yet separated the social from the natural environment (that is, persons from things). In the culture of simple or archaic societies, Habermas suggests, a continuity is established between the social and the natural world, not least in so far as systems of totemism link human family lineages to natural species. Nature is something to be understood, through narratives, and communicated with, rather than something to be explained scientifically. Piaget's next, sociocentric–objectivist, stage also has a parallel in human culture. The child comes to distinguish between the social and natural elements of its environment, and to imagine how that environment appears to other people. The culture of early civilisations entails the fusing of the many particularistic totemic narratives of the archaic culture into more systematic mythologies. Humans become separated from gods, and thus from a natural world controlled by the gods. A priesthood will emerge to regulate the relationships between the human and the divine. But, at this stage, the mythology remains polytheistic, which is to say that there are many gods, and that individuals will understand themselves in terms of their allegiance to a particular (local) deity.

Here we must pause. The crucial question for Habermas is how this social development has come about. His answer is to suggest that the archaic society will, of course, have to have faced some challenge (such as the threat of an invader). What Habermas calls the 'evolutionary promising' society will be able to respond, for example by a particular and far-sighted warrior taking organisational control of the society as a whole. Perhaps that very organisation requires a retelling of the basic narratives of the society's mythology, so that the unification of the mythology legitimates the unification of the society (and the warrior's control over it). If this organisation becomes permanent, rather than being abandoned once the crisis is over, the basic organisation of the society will have begun to shift from being grounded in the family to being grounded in the state (see **principle of organisation**). Crucially, individuals within the society have learnt how to deal with a problem, and in doing so they will have had to grow in the sophistication with which they understand their social and physical environment.

One other point can be noted. The move from archaic society to early civilisation is, for Habermas, indicative of a growth in rationality. On one level, this is a move from the particular to the general. Particular lineages are being brought together into a more unified and coherent structure. The mythology and the cosmology of the society is being made more coherent. On a second level, it is a growth in **instrumental rationality** (as more practical problems become soluble) and **communicative rationality** (as more complex social structures are sustained). Again, this may be understood as the development of the potential inherent in the deep-lying human capacities for labour and interaction.

Piaget's fourth stage is the universalistic stage. Here the adolescent develops the capacity to think hypothetically and to demand rational justifications for the beliefs that she is supposed to entertain about both the physical and social worlds. In terms of human society, Habermas traces the development of civilisations as they increase in size, and thus have to embrace ever more diverse cultures within a single body. The polytheism of early civilisations is thus gradually replaced (if the civilisation is thriving, responding creatively to the challenges of expansion) by monotheism. In effect, this serves to separate the self from society. The state treats its citizens increasingly as human beings, with increasingly formally defined legal rights, rather than as members of particular cultural groups, castes or classes. What is gradually developing here is a systematic legal system. What matters is not the will of the ruler, but the consistency with which the **law** is enacted. Here is a first hint of Piaget's universalistic stage, as citizens begin to expect a rational justification for the way in which they are treated. Appeal to the particular will of the emperor is no longer adequate.

In **capitalism**, society comes to be organised in terms of the economy rather than the state. Habermas suggests that this is symptomatic of a crisis in advanced civilisations, as it becomes increasingly difficult to legitimate the ruling aristocracy's monopoly of economic and political power in the face of challenges from other classes. The state thus relinquishes its overt control of the economy, thereby

separating (or, in Habermas's terminology, 'uncoupling') the economy from the state. Crises are not thereby wholly avoided, and
indeed *Legitimation Crisis* (1976b) may be read as an account of the
continuing potential for social evolution that is present in contemporary society (see **legitimation**).

Further reading: Schmid 1982; Rockmore 1989; Holub 1991: 106–32;
Roberts 1995; McCarthy 2001; Owen 2002

SOCIAL INTEGRATION

The organisation of a society, understood as if the society is the
creative and meaningful product of **communicative action**. Social
integration is contrasted by Habermas to **system integration**, as
representing two different theoretical approaches to the problem of
social order. While system integration treats society as a more or less
abstract structure with its own rules of internal organisation, the
concept of social integration is such that the existence of a society is
dependent upon the skills, knowledge and competences of its members if it is to retain stability and order. At the level of social integration, interaction between two or more people must make some
sense to them if it is to continue. For example, I wish to organise a
game of football. I round up various friends, explain to them why it
would be a good idea, and deal with any quibbles (okay, we'll finish
by three; it's only a friendly so it doesn't matter that you haven't got
your boots; Alan is getting the ball; we'll use our coats for goalposts;
and so on). In our negotiations, we come to share a view of the
world, complete with a recognition of certain possibilities and limitations, along with the purposes we want to achieve and why we
want to achieve them. If things begin to go wrong, and the social
interaction begins to break down, then we also typically have competences to deal with this (for example: we dispute the applicability
of the offside rule, and settle for disallowing the goal – but no offside
from now on; I foul Alan and he threatens to take his ball away, so I
apologise profusely, offer to buy him a drink, and we get on with the
game) (see **universal pragmatics**).

Habermas introduces the distinction between social integration and
system integration in *Legitmation Crisis* (Habermas 1976b: 28), and
there justifies the need for both approaches. While the notion of
social integration captures what ordinary people will understand
about their social skills – and even if they have never thought about it

before, they will at least recognise themselves in the descriptions that the social scientist offers – social integration is unable to explain the unintended consequences of actions. Habermas's contention is that, in complex societies such as those of modern **capitalism**, much of their organisation falls beyond the immediate understanding or intentions of ordinary people. However, their actions have consequences that are integrated at the more instrumental level of the system, that ensure large-scale stability. When I buy a cheap football from my local sports store, my prime intention is not to secure low-paid employment for somebody in the developing world; but because of the economic system that links my purchase to the person who made the ball, that is one consequence of my action. In Habermas's later works (1984a and 1987), the notion of social integration is more thoroughly linked to the idea of the **lifeworld**, as the sum of the social competences that help us to maintain social integration.

SPEECH ACT

The performance of a social **action**, such as making a promise, giving an order or asking a question, through the use of words. The theory of speech acts was originally proposed by the **analytic philosopher** J. L. Austin, and developed by John Searle. The theory is important in so far as it challenges the assumption, that had been dominant in philosophy, that the principle use of **language** was to state facts. Until this point, therefore, the philosopher was primarily concerned with sentences (or, in more technical language, statements or propositions) that make assertions about the world. On this assumption the philosophy of language was exclusively concerned with the conditions that make such sentences meaningful and truthful. Once the role of language in constructing and maintaining social relationships is recognised, however, the philosopher of language is concerned less with sentences than with utterances, which is to say with the particular way in which the sentence is used. The same sentence can be used in many different contexts and by many different speakers, and crucially therefore for different purposes. For example, the utterances 'Habermas is a German philosopher', and 'Is Habermas a German philosopher?' contain the same proposition, albeit in the first instance it is asserted as a fact, and in the second it is posed as a question. The philosophy of language can then separate the informational content of the utterance (which is termed its 'propositional content') from the specific action that it is performing (its '**illocutionary force**'). (See also **double structure of language**.) The concept of the 'speech act' is fundamental to Habermas's project of **universal pragmatics**, his theory of the skills and knowledge that socially competent people have to communicate with each other. Because it is through speech acts or utterances that people maintain the fabric of social life, it is these utterances that are the basic units of analysis in universal pragmatics (Habermas 1976e; 1979a: 1–68).

STRATEGIC ACTION

A type of social **action** where one or more of the participants treats the others as if they were objects, rather than as fellow human beings with whom agreement and mutual understanding should be achieved. Thus, if I use strategic action on you, I treat you instrumentally, as something that I can control and manipulate, possibly against your will. In the light of its instrumental aspect, Habermas defines strategic action as action oriented to success (Habermas 1982: 266). The concept is widely discussed by Habermas in his development of **universal pragmatics** (1979a: 41 and 209; 2001c: 12–13; 1999a: 224–6).

Habermas stresses that strategic action is a form of social action, and as such should not be confused with instrumental action (where a person manipulates the physical world around them). Strategic action is thus between two or more persons. However, it is contrasted with **communicative action** in so far as the person acting strategically does not attempt to established a shared understanding of the world with the other person. She does not attempt to share an understanding of the physical world, of the norms and customs that might govern or legitimate any actions, or even the intentions that might drive the person to act so. Instead, she cuts short all attempts at achieving agreement through various techniques. Rather, she coerces the other, so that he acts according to her intentions whether or not he understands them or agrees with them. Most blatantly, she might threaten violence, or resort to bribery or blackmail. Such action is openly strategic, as both parties can readily see that no attempt is being made to establish a genuine mutual understanding. More subtly, she might use rhetoric, so that the weaknesses of her argument are concealed in a flow of emotive language, exhorting the other to action. This is an example of latently strategic action. The hearer (and perhaps even the speaker) may be unaware of the strategic nature of the action. More insidiously still, at least in his earlier work on this topic,

Habermas suggested that there was a special form of strategic action which he called **systematically distorted communication**. Here the very language that the two people are using is distorted in such a way that certain issues cannot be coherently articulated in it, and so agreement cannot be secured.

Strategic action is not necessarily malevolent. In playing a game of chess, I may well treat my opponent strategically by planning my moves according to my instrumental predictions of her responses. I will be trying to force her to make moves against her will, as well as doing my best to conceal my own intentions. In Habermas's later works, this more benevolent and mundane aspect of strategic action becomes important in explaining how people interact with each other in social **systems**. In much everyday interaction, we relate to other human beings not through the meanings of their actions, but rather through their predictability. A consensus is established between us, not after discussion of our worldviews and motives, but through treating each other as beings who will react predictably to certain stimuli. Thus, for example, I can act strategically to a shop assistant because I know that when I give him the money for the goods, he will hand over the goods and the right change. I need know nothing about him, about his motivations or dreams, or his opinions of me. We need not even share a language. All we both need to know is that we will follow the rules that govern the behaviour of buyers and sellers, and thus play our part in the economic system of a complex modern society.

SUBJECT, PHILOSOPHY OF THE *see* **Consciousness, philosophy of**

SYSTEM

A structure of elements. Within a system the elements are selected and so ordered that only certain relationships between them are possible, and other relationships are prohibited or made impossible. Put otherwise, the selection and ordering of elements is strictly rule-governed. This makes the system clearly separable from its surrounding environment, not least because the environment is more complex (in that the environment allows for many more relationships between many more elements than can exist in the system).

Many different sorts of entity can be characterised as systems. For example, language is a system. Any ordinary language consists of relatively few different noises that can be combined in only a few different ways. So, for example, English does not include the noise that is written in Welsh as 'll'. Similarly, the sentence 'English include noise not' clearly breaks lots of grammatical and syntactical rules. Yet, whenever I say something, that sentence is clearly distinguishable as a highly organised structure in comparison to the seemingly chaotic noises of traffic, rain and the office photocopying machine that surround me.

An animal or plant organism can be understood as a system. The animal's skin or epidermis acts as a boundary between the system and its environment, but it also allows for an interchange between the two (as it takes in warmth and sunlight and releases moisture, for example). With the organism's death, this boundary collapses, the organisation within the system unravels, and it decays into the same degree of complexity as its environment. This example can be taken further, to begin to illustrate the general functions that a system must fulfil if it is to survive. These include adaptation to the environment (for example, an animal must feed and perhaps transform sections of the environment to provide shelter); the integration and organisation of the internal structure (so that blood keeps flowing, and food is digested); and the motivation of the system to achieve these and other specific goals (for example, an animal must reproduce; a language must convey information). The parts within a system may themselves be understood as (sub-)systems. Thus an organ such as a heart or a liver is itself an organised whole, interacting with the more complex environment that is composed of the rest of the animal body, and performing specific functions (pumping, or purifying blood).

The concept of a system can be applied to the explanation of societies. Initially what is known as functionalism or structural functionalism worked with an analogy between societies and organisms, and so developed a methodology for the social sciences that was modelled on biology. A more refined version of this approach was developed in the 1950s, not least by the American social theorist Talcott Parsons, who was by then more clearly influenced by the use of the concept of system in cybernetics. Habermas, in his mature works such as *The Theory of Communicative Action* (and especially the second volume (Habermas 1987)), engages both with Parsons's work and perhaps more importantly with that of the contemporary German social theorist Niklaus Luhmann (see **systems theory**).

Further reading: Luhmann 1987; Luhmann 1995

SYSTEMATICALLY DISTORTED COMMUNICATION

The failure to achieve the goal of communicative action, which is to say mutual understanding, because problems that are disrupting the social **interaction**, and that therefore need to be discussed in order to be resolved, exceed the communicative abilities of everyone involved. Habermas here makes a subtle distinction. On the one hand there are merely contingent failures that occur because one or more of the participants lacks a particular communicative skill. For example, one does not understand the idiom or the accent of the other. Such breakdowns in communication are typically repaired through **hermeneutic** skills, which is to say that, because all the participants will immediately recognise something has gone wrong, they will be able to use their more general interpretative skills to guess at possible solutions, and test them in further discussion. This is merely a contingent distortion – not a systematic one. Systematically distorted communication, on the other hand, is not amenable to repair by using the everyday skills that we have as competent communicators. Indeed, the breakdown may not even be recognised by those taking part in the conversation.

This idea may at first seem highly counter-intuitive: how can one not realise that something is wrong in one's relationships with others? Habermas is suggesting that people can go on talking to each other, thinking that they are making sense, and yet they are failing to communicate. He gives a simple and poignant example. A couple have been married for many years, and yet now have fallen out of love. The relationship is strained. Yet, they are so deeply fearful of the consequences of a possible break-up and of what it might mean for their emotional and personal security and self-esteem that they become unable to acknowledge the fact of their loveless relationship even to themselves, let alone each other. Being unable to acknowledge their own true emotions, they continue to express their love to each other in empty gestures (Habermas 2001c: 152). As Habermas puts this, the demands of the particular discussion 'overburden' the resources available to the participants. They simply do not know how to confront and resolve the problem, so they repress it.

Habermas develops this notion, initially, through the model of **psychoanalysis** (1970a). A psychoanalytic patient suffers symptoms that afflict her as if they were due to a natural cause. In fact, they are the result of the patient's own actions, albeit that the actions are unconscious. Further, the symptoms are symbolically linked to an earlier traumatic experience, with which the patient has been unable to cope consciously. The symptoms therefore form a private language (consisting of what Habermas calls symbols that are 'split-off' from public language) that even its creator cannot understand. The patient is only cured through the aid of a therapist, who is required to trace the symptoms back to the original trauma, and thus to facilitate the patient's ability to recall and so handle this experience rationally.

The notion of systematically distorted communication has important implications for political theory. In effect, it offers Habermas a way of developing a theory of **ideology critique**, which is to say a method for exploring and exposing the way in which political inequalities are maintained in a society through the manipulation of the ideas available in the dominant culture. Systematically distorted communication suggests that **ideology** works, not by simply offering a **legitimation** of the existing political structure, but rather by preventing people from perceiving, talking about and criticising that inequality. Systematic distortion blinds people to the inequalities and processes of repression within which they are entwined. The task of the **critical theorist** is therefore akin to that of the psychoanalyst, helping society become aware of its blind spots, of the actually meaningless gestures that clutter everyday communication.

While the concept of systematically distorted communication is important to Habermas's work of the early 1970s (1976b), and not least to his early engagements with **systems theory**, in practice the concept was soon abandoned. As his theory of **communicative action** develops in the late 1970s and 1980s, he discards his earlier commitment to ideology critique and a model of critical theory that is partially inspired by psychoanalysis, in order to turn to a theory that seeks to explore the way in which meaningful, everyday communication (grounded in what he calls the **lifeworld**) is disrupted by the intrusion of instrumental and largely meaningless mechanisms of social organisation (**systems**) into everyday life (see **colonisation of the lifeworld**).

SYSTEM INTEGRATION

The organisation of a society, understood as if the society was a **system**. The problem of social order is the problem, for social theory, of explaining how a society remains bound together in a stable and well-organised whole. To approach this problem from a **systems theory** perspective, which is what the concept of 'system integration' implies, entails that the relationships between people, and between institutions, within a society are seen as being governed by the sort of rules that govern a system. As elements within a system, people will relate to each other, not in terms of the meanings or motivations of their actions, but rather as if they were more or less automatic respondents to specific stimuli. Thus, if I do something, I can accurately predict how you will react, without my needing to know anything about you (beyond the social position or office that you are currently filling) or your needing to know anything about me. System integration is contrasted with social integration, as alternative approaches to the problem of social order. Habermas introduces the notions of system and social integration in *Legitimation Crisis* (1976b: 28).

SYSTEMS THEORY

Within sociology, an approach to explaining societies that proceeds by assuming that the society is a **system**, which is to say a self-maintaining, rule-governed structure. The systems theorist will assume that the society, as a system, has a series of highly abstract functions that it must fulfil in order to maintain itself. Concrete social institutions can be identified as carrying out these functions. Problems and instabilities within the society can be analysed in terms of the pressures placed upon the society by its environment, or by inconsistencies and tensions within the social system. Habermas begins to engage with systems theory, not least through a sustained dialogue with Niklaus Luhmann, from the early 1970s (Habermas and Luhmann 1975). Systems theory provides him with an important set of resources that allows him to offer explanations of the development of societies (or **social evolution**) (Habermas 1979a: 130–77; 1979b), and of **crisis** tendencies and instabilities within social formations (1976a).

If society is understood as a system, then the evolution of societies may be understood in terms of their growing complexity or system **differentiation**. That is to say that early human societies are likely to be simple systems, comprised of relatively few components and organised in terms of a few, relatively simple rules. Crucially, any component within the society is likely to have to contribute to the fulfilment of most or all of the necessary tasks that the society requires. Thus, for example, the family will be a unit of economic production, and thus serve the social system's adaptation to its physical environment; it will raise and educate children, and as such will bring about the internal organisation and motivation of the social system by socialising children into the cultural norms and values of the society. Similarly, because of the small population, relationships between individuals and families are likely to be governed by a few customs that, at least when viewed as the governing rules of a system, are quite simple. Such rules are likely to include not merely those governing personal interaction, but also rules of gift exchange that regulate the relationships between this community and other groups. As social systems expand, growing in complexity and finding the resources and organisational structures to fulfil ever more subtle and complex tasks, so specialist sub-systems will develop within the society. Economic production, for example, may be removed from the household and passed on to specialist economic sub-systems; the task of education may be passed on to schools; and so on. The relationships between individuals and groups become similarly more complex. Personal and face-to-face interactions are compounded by impersonal interactions, such as those governed by the market or by the exercise of political and administrative authority; people no longer just belong to families or tribes and lineages, but also to nations, companies, teams and parties; face-to-face interaction is complemented by forms of communication between people who are increasingly separated in time and space (and hence the conventions of letter-writing, journalism, telegrams and email).

If systems theory can provide a framework for explaining social change, linked to this is an account of social crises – crucially, crises that stimulate the need for change. Crises can be brought about either through challenges from the system's environment or through internal tensions. The environment poses both physical challenges, for example in the form of catastrophic changes in weather conditions or the exhaustion of resources, and socio-political challenges, such as threats of conquest or cultural influence from other social systems. The internal problems of the system come through its inability to sustain its internal integrity, perhaps through simple population growth, but more significantly through the consequences of responding to other challenges. For example, the technological innovations that may allow a creative and effective response to climate change or scarcity of resources may also give rise to a new group of experts within the system who begin to challenge the existing political hierarchy. A crisis in the economic sub-system may then become one in the political sub-system. The inability to resolve crises will lead to the disintegration and metaphorical death of the society.

Much of Habermas's argument in *Legitimation Crisis* is concerned with the movement of crisis tendencies from one sub-system to another within contemporary capitalism (1976a: 45–50).

Systems theory does provide Habermas with a powerful explanatory resource. Most significantly, systems theory is able to deal with the unintended consequences of human actions. It handles that aspect of society where it tends to confront its members as something thing-like and autonomous. Perhaps the most graphic example of this is the rise of modern bureaucracy, central to the German sociologist Max Weber's account of industrialised society. Weber's basic contention is that, as societies grow ever more complex, they require complex bureaucratic structures for their organisation. In effect, large numbers of people, involved in many different tasks, cannot be expected to coordinate their actions effectively through face-to-face interaction. So, bureaucracies serve to make large-scale coordination possible, in part by simplifying and schematising the activities in which people are involved, and linking them together in terms of easily manageable rules. This is all very well, but as sub-systems, the bureaucracies develop their own inherent ways of work – their own logic, as it were. Weber was aware that bureaucracies may then become problematic, not least in inhibiting individual freedom. The bureaucratic system thus confronts the individual as a faceless mechanism, living a life of its own and unresponsive to the demands and challenges of real human beings. This analysis was taken further by the Marxist Georg Lukács, in so far as he notes a similarity between the way in which bureaucracies work and the way in which the capitalist economy works. Again his argument is that the process of commodity exchange confronts the individual human being as something that has a life of its own, and that is following its own logic, indifferent to the needs and demands of real human beings. Lukács developed this insight as a theory of **reification**.

Systems theory therefore provides the social theorist with a model by which to account for these experiences, and to explore the autonomous workings of a social system (and its component sub-systems). But, importantly for Habermas, systems theory is inadequate if it stops at this point. Both Weber and Lukács are critical of the impact that autonomous bureaucracies and markets have upon social life. In contrast, Luhmann's systems theory accepts that that is the way things are. A crucial point of dispute between Habermas and Luhmann therefore focuses on the possibility of social theorists being critical of the society that they study, and thus the issue of **legitimation** (1976b: 98–9). Habermas's point is that, if society is just a system (as Luhmann suggests: see Habermas 1988a: 353), then it is a bad society, for such a society will have significantly eroded human freedom and indeed rendered life more or less meaningless. But, more significantly, Habermas does not believe that such a complete erosion is possible. The crucial theoretical weakness in systems theory lies in its failure to take account of the lived experience and social competence of ordinary people (1976b: 9). A systems theory approach suggests that ordinary human beings merely respond, more or less automatically, to the demands that the system places upon them. It credits them with no creativity or responsibility. While Luhmann does respond to this challenge, Habermas remains unhappy. For Habermas, society can only be fully understood if systems theory is placed in tension with those approaches to social theory that are grounded in **hermeneutics**. That is to say that the systems theory approach must be complemented by an approach that recognises the way in which ordinary people perceive society, make sense of it, and exercise their social skills.

Habermas places society as system in tension with society as **life-world**. His argument is again grounded in social evolution. In small-scale societies, a systems theory approach and a more interpretative approach will offer more or less the same analysis. Basically, a simple society, because it is simple, runs according to rules that the members of the society will recognise (at least once they are pointed out to them). So, for example, if a Triobriand Islander reads Marcel Mauss's classic study of gift exchange, he is likely to recognise what Mauss describes as something in which they take part. But, as society becomes more complex, then the systemic elements of it become more and more obscure to the ordinary member of society. As Habermas puts this, systems theory accounts of society are often counter-intuitive (1993b: 252). They do not obviously match up to the everyday experience of real people. The reason for this is that systems exist, as already suggested above, to make complex society workable. There is only so much that, using our everyday competences, we ordinary people can cope with. Systems reveal the burden placed upon these competences. What this entails is that there are in fact two ways in which ordinary people deal with social interaction. On the one level, I can engage in full-blown **communicative action** with you. We can treat each other as competent and responsible human beings, and we will coordinate our actions by negotiating a common view of the world and what ought to be done. We will come to understand each other. For example, we decide to go to the cinema. So, we find a movie we will both enjoy. We find a time when we are both free. We agree where to meet; and so on. On the other level, I respond much more **instrumentally**. For example, I hire a DVD from a shop. My interaction with the shopkeeper or assistant is extremely simple. I do not have to justify my choice of DVD. I simply hand over the DVD, the assistant tells me the rental price, I give him the money. The steps in our interaction are wholly predictable, and that is the point. I react to the shop assistant much in the same way that I would work a vending machine or an online shopping website. Actions on my part are means to produce predictable responses on the assistant's part (and vice versa). The meaning has been drained out of our interaction. But notice also that this particular interaction is the tip of an iceberg. Behind it lies a complex chain of similarly systematic actions and interactions that in concert serve to bring together all the economic resources necessary to provide me with my DVD. There is no way in which I could use my communicative skills to bring together all the people, raw materials, machines and technology that are required to produce and distribute a DVD. So I come to rely upon the economic system to do it for me.

Habermas is interested in systems precisely because of their ambiguous nature. On the one hand, precisely in so far as systematic organisation makes a complex society possible, it is necessary and a good thing – as the DVD example attempts to demonstrate. But, on the other hand, the more reliant that we become on systems, the more our freedom may be infringed (Habermas 1987: 318–31). While the economic sub-system may effectively deliver DVDs to my local shop, it necessarily restricts the DVDs that are available to me. This may not be particularly significant if it is a matter of my home entertainment, but it is far more significant if I am dealing with the local social services bureaucracy over the receipt of my pension. We noted how much simpler the interaction between a customer and a shopkeeper is than between two friends. The same simplicity will apply to the interaction between a social services officer and her client. The interaction must conform to the relative simple rules that have been formulated for the running and organisation of the administration. If I fail to comply, for example simply by having a lifestyle that cannot immediately be categorised in terms of the pre-existing classifications used by the bureaucracy, then it is not clear that the bureaucracy can cope, and my payments may be denied me. For example, my gay partner may recently have died. I claim that, because I was his long-term partner, then I am the legal beneficiary of his pension and life assurance. If the administration does not recognise gay partnerships, I am denied my claim. More insidiously, the administration tends towards a normalisation of social relationships, constraining them within predetermined patterns.

If the expansion of systems inhibits my freedom, then it also inhibits my capacity to give meaning to my life (Habermas 1984a: 346–50). Crucially, as more and more social interactions are conducted according to the rules of the system rather than according to the much richer and more complex rules of cultural life or the lifeworld, then again I appear to be obeying rules for their own sake – interacting in this way, because that is the only option given to me, and not because it makes any sense to me. It is precisely this erosion of freedom and meaning that Habermas addresses as the problem of the **colonisation of the lifeworld**.

In summary, Habermas uses systems theory as a resource to explain the manner in which society comes to confront human beings (who, after all, must create and sustain society through their actions) as an autonomous force. But systems theory alone is inadequate as a social theory, for it fails adequately to take account of the creativity and meaningfulness of human action. The tension between these two perspectives also begins to explain the problems of contemporary society, as the dominance of political and economic sub-systems infringes upon the freedom and meaningfulness of everyday life.

Further reading: Luhmann 1987; Holub 1991: 106–32; Luhmann 1995; Roberts 1995

TRANSCENDENTAL ARGUMENT

A form of philosophical argument developed by the German philosopher Immanuel Kant as a response to the problems that he identified in orthodox approaches to the theory of knowledge (or epistemology). Habermas uses what he calls 'quasi-transcendental' argument in developing his theory of **cognitive interests**.

Transcendental argument can be briefly characterised in terms of the basic question it poses: How is knowledge possible? A transcendental argument begins from the assumption that we do indeed have knowledge. (Newtonian physics is of particular importance to Kant, and his core work in epistemology, the *Critique of Pure Reason*, may be read as a defence of the basic foundation of that physics from sceptical criticism.) From this assumption of the possession of knowledge, the transcendental philosopher asks after the conditions that must be in place for such knowledge to be acquired. For Kant, these conditions are to be found through an examination of the way in which the human mind processes the information that it receives through the senses, and so constitutes the sort of objects of which it can have knowledge.

Transcendental inquiry may be approached by considering one of Kant's own metaphors. He described his approach as bringing about a 'Copernican Revolution' in philosophy (Kant 1933, Bxvi). It was the astronomer Copernicus who challenged the ancient notion that the sun moved round the earth. The analogy to Kant may be understood so: we have knowledge of the movement of the stars – they appear to us in a certain order and move in a certain way – and the problem is to explain why they appear to us as they do. The old Ptolemaic system (with the Earth at the centre of the universe) may be seen to take the position of the human observer for granted, and inquire only into the nature of the stars that are observed. Copernicus's moment of genius is to suggest that the way in which the stars appear to us may have as much to do with our position (and thus how we move relative to the stars) as it does with the movement of the stars themselves. Similarly, Kant is arguing that, if we wish to understand how objects appear to us, and thus how we can know them, it is insufficient to focus on the object alone. Prior to Kant, philosophers had sought to remove the illusions that might have distorted our perception of the object, in effect attempting to turn the observer into a passive, unprejudiced vessel for knowledge (sitting, like the Ptolemaic astronomer, motionless at the centre of the universe). Kant, in contrast, is arguing that we can only have knowledge if the human subject actively constitutes the objects that it knows.

Kant argues that the human senses deliver, to the mind, a 'chaos of manifold sensations', which is to say an unordered flood of sounds, sights, smells and tactile feelings. Faculties in the human mind then process or synthesise this 'manifold' into a structured and unified whole. The faculties of sensibility and imagination shape the chaos in time and space, before the faculty of understanding stabilises it through the imposition of general concepts (or categories) such as causality, substance and negation. The radical implication of this argument is that such seemingly familiar entities as space, time and causality are not 'out there' in an object that exists independently of the observing subject. Rather, they are part of the complex framework that exists in the human mind prior to any experience, and precisely because they shape and make sense of our experience, they make knowledge possible. Beings other than humans, be they animals or angels, may not experience the world in the same way that we human beings do if they lack our mental structures. Human knowledge can therefore only be knowledge of how the world appears to humans – what Kant calls the 'phenomenal' world.

Habermas takes up transcendental argument in order to criticise contemporary arguments (associated with **positivism**) that present 'pure theory' as a precondition of valid knowledge. A defence of pure theory would suggest that knowledge claims can only be valid if they are untainted by any contribution on the part of the knowing subject. Knowledge claims thus aspire to be free of all contaminating values or interests. In opposition to this, Habermas argues that the acquisition of knowledge by humans will be motivated by one of three fundamental cognitive interests. These are interests in the technical manipulation of the world, in communication and interaction with other human beings, and in being free from oppression (leading to natural science, **hermeneutics** and **critical theory** respectively).

While these three interests play a transcendental role, making knowledge possible, Habermas's argument differs from Kant's in a number of respects. First, while Kant unifies all knowledge in terms of a single structure of the mind, Habermas identifies three distinct forms of knowledge. Indeed, Habermas's primary concern may be understood as a response to the epistemological and political problems that occur when different forms of knowledge are confused (and, most significantly, when social processes are subjected to the methods of the natural sciences: see **scientism**). Second, Habermas is critical of Kant for failing to reflect upon the emergence of the human mind, either in human evolution or in terms of the development of the ego (Habermas 1971a: 7–24). This leads to the third, crucial difference. Habermas's enquiry is quasi-transcendental. This is to say that is it grounded, not in a philosophically construed model of the mind, but rather in empirically identifiable interests that, Habermas notes, are 'anthropologically deep seated' (1976a: 8). That is to say that the cognitive interests are grounded in human nature, as the contingent product of natural and subsequently **social evolution** (1971a: 312).

Habermas gradually abandons transcendental argument in the early 1970s, as he begins to develop the theory of **communicative action**. While he occasionally refers to the transcendental, he becomes increasingly dissatisfied with the term 'quasi-transcendental' (1976a: 14–15). There is an undeniable tension within an approach that appeals both to transcendental argument (that seeks the conditions that make knowledge of nature in science possible) and to empirical argument (that appeals to the very nature that science has constituted). **Reconstructive science** takes the place of quasi-transcendental argument in Habermas's later work.

Further reading: Körner 1955; Copleston 1960; Apel 1980

TRUTH

Habermas has approached the philosophical problem of truth repeatedly throughout his career (Habermas 1971a; 1979a; 1984a; 1987; 1999; 2001c; 2003a). His concern with truth takes different forms according to the wider overarching theories that characterise his work during different periods, and in particular with respect to the theory of **cognitive interests** of the 1960s, and the later theory of **communicative action**. The main outlines of these arguments will be reviewed here, beginning with the later period of Habermas's career.

The philosophical problem of truth may be understood in terms of two questions. First, we might ask what it means to describe a proposition or sentence as true. Put otherwise, what conditions have to be satisfied in order for the sentence, 'Habermas is a philosopher', for example, to be true? Second, we may inquire into how we establish that a proposition is true. How do we find out that those desired conditions have indeed been satisfied? Or, to use a term frequently used by Habermas himself, how do we *justify* the truth that is claimed of a proposition? **Analytic philosophy** and **pragmatism** have explored these questions extensively, and Habermas draws upon both in his own arguments.

In his mature theory, as developed in *The Theory of Communicative Action* (1984a; 1987), truth is understood as one of four '**validity claims**'. This is to say that, whenever I say anything, what I say will contain certain assumptions about the external world. Even if I ask a question, such as 'Can you pass me today's paper?', I am assuming that what I see really is today's newspaper, that you are capable of reaching it and passing it to me, and so on. If you were to challenge any of these assumptions (for example, by observing that it isn't today's paper, but yesterday's), then you are challenging the truth of my assumption. This entails that a statement is true if the assumptions that it makes actually correspond to the way the world is (that is, the assumption in my question would have been true if that really had been today's newspaper). In philosophy, this is known as a correspondence theory of truth – the statement corresponds to the way the world is. Recently Habermas has come to stress the importance of this argument, feeling that it was underplayed or neglected in his earlier reflections on the problem of truth. He summarises that by noting that we should ultimately accept a statement to be true because it is true in this sense (2003a: 8).

This still leaves open the second problem, however, of how one finds out that the world really is as my statement assumes, and thus how one justifies one's claim. Habermas's important point here is that establishing the truth of a statement typically poses a complex problem, not least because we do not obviously have direct access to that reality. Reality does not speak for itself. Our experience is shaped by our **language**, by our culture and values, and by our practical concerns, and so we must make sense of our raw experience, clarifying its relevance to us. The problem of the newspaper is relatively simple. If I doubt your word, perhaps you pass the newspaper to me, and I see yesterday's date on it. Here I have empirical evidence that my assumption was actually false. But notice that even here there has been a debate, however rudimentary, between two people to establish the truth of the matter. Establishing the truth of a proposition cannot be left to a single person, for that one person can be mistaken. For example, I look at the date on the newspaper, but mistakenly believe that today is the 25th when it is really the 26th. I need you to correct or confirm my belief. So, the truth of a proposition is established through discussion, the presentation of appropriate evidence, and justifications of why that evidence is indeed appropriate. The process of discussion stops, ideally, when everyone who is involved is happy.

The example of the newspaper is excessively simple, but consider this claim: there are nine planets in the solar system. The empirical evidence is now much more elusive, and I cannot simply push nine planets under the nose of the person who doubts me. A debate may ensue within the community of scientists about what counts as evidence for, say, a tenth planet – or even the status of Pluto as a planet at all. It is at this point that we should see how problematic evidence might be. I will not show you a planet, but perhaps a rather vague image provided by the Hubble telescope, or even more elusively a series of measurements of the irregularities in the movements of Neptune and Uranus. I must then justify that this is evidence of Pluto's size or the existence of a tenth planet, and not the image of a comet, an error in the design of the telescope, or an irregularity in movement that is explicable in terms of Jupiter's orbit (and so on).

Even if all the world's astronomers came to an agreement that Pluto was indeed worthy of being called a planet, and that there was no tenth planet lurking deeper in the solar system, there is still a problem. While 'the solar system contains nine planets' may be regarded as true now, it is still in principle capable of being made false. In the future, better measurements, or more subtle interpretation of the data that we have, may reopen the debate. What Habermas has done here is to answer the second problem by evoking what is known as the consensus theory of truth. Such a theory argues that a proposition is true if all (or most) of those appropriately informed at a given time believe that is it true. Such a theory is problematic because it seems to make truth relative to a particular community of believers (so that, for example, 'there are seven heavenly bodies' was true in Ancient Greece, but not today). Habermas avoids this relativism by arguing that the process of falsification, and the subsequent replacement of one belief by another, is no arbitrary process, but rather one that is disciplined by rational debate. He is, in effect, making a distinction between what in practice we accept to be true today, and what we would accept to be true under ideal circumstances. What is accepted as truth today is a step on the way to an unconditional truth. At one stage Habermas articulated that unconditional truth in terms of what he called the **ideal speech situation**, which is to say a projection of perfect conditions for debate (where all relevant parties have all the evidence they need to make a judgement on the grounds of good reason alone, with no coercion or other distortions interfering with the conclusions reached) (2001c: 97–9). Later Habermas comes to be dissatisfied with such a seemingly utopian projection, and turns rather to focus on the process of rational argument through which truth claims are challenged and justified (1999a: 367–8). The notion of the ideal speech situation thereby becomes more clearly a critical tool, through which we can identify the possible and actual failings and irrationalities that characterise and distort the current debate. Habermas can therefore formulate his 'discourse theory of truth', so 'a proposition is true if it withstands all attempts to refute it under the demanding conditions of rational discourse' (1999a: 367).

Earlier in his career, Habermas approached the problem of truth somewhat differently. His concern in *Knowledge and Human Interests*, and in much of his other work at that time, was to challenge the **positivist** account of science and the acquisition of knowledge. For the positivist, the only knowledge claims that have a good foundation, and thus can confidently or even meaningfully be asserted to be true, are those that are justified by the types of inquiry used in the natural sciences. Habermas was concerned to show that there were in fact three different ways of justifying the truth of propositions, corresponding to the methods of the natural sciences and the cultural or historical sciences, and to critical theory. It is here, however, that in considering the methods of the natural sciences Habermas comes to consider pragmatism, and this forms the basis for much of what we have already looked at in the later work.

The American philosopher Charles Peirce argued, on the one hand, that the natural sciences discover more and better knowledge of the natural world by using empirical experiments. Crucially, a hypothesis must be tested against reality, and a false hypothesis will be found out, because the experiment will not turn out as the scientist predicted. Only good scientific theories will work in practice, and so the truth of a theory is being tested every time it is being used to guide technology (and as our technology gets more demanding, so the tests of our scientific theories become more rigorous, and old theories that may have been accepted may be found wanting). Here, then, is the correspondence theory of truth. Ultimately, a scientific theory is true if it corresponds to reality that exists independently of the scientists and their theories. On the other hand, Peirce's concern with experimentation is also a concern with the justification of the truth of theories. Here he argues that it is not experimentation by isolated scientists that matters, but rather the work of the scientific community. Experimental evidence must be debated as to its relevance; new theories must be scrutinised for their coherence and relevance, and so we have the consensus theory of truth again. But Peirce is keen to separate the actual consensus today from an ideal consensus at the end of the process of scientific inquiry. It is thus from Peirce that Habermas derives much of his notion of an ideal speech situation, albeit that Peirce imagines an ideal community of scientists, where scientists are unhampered by lack of evidence, irrationalities, personal animosities, or hierarchies that prevent individuals from making relevant contributions, and may thus finally uncover the nature of reality.

The social sciences are seen by Habermas to rely, similarly, on discussion and rational justification, albeit that, because the object of study is another human being, or the meaningful actions and artefacts produced by human beings, that debate also embraces them. Cultural or **hermeneutic** science is a process of dialogue between the living community of scientists and the dead or absent subjects being studied. The truth of a proposition in the cultural sciences may then be understood in terms of a putative agreement between the scientist and the subject studies as to what the latter's actions meant. This is taken further in the case of critical theory.

An important model here is **psychoanalysis** and the dialogue initiated between the patient and the therapist. While the social scientist assumes that the meanings of the actions of historical or social agents are readily comprehensible to those agents, the psychoanalyst assumes that the patient does not understand his or her own actions. Consider the following examples. A Serbian nationalist student, Gavilo Princip, shoots the Archduke of Austria on 28 June 1914, in Sarajevo. This is a meaningful action, and the historian can reflect upon the student's intentions, just as I might reflect upon your intentions a while ago in not passing me my newspaper. Implicitly, the historian is asking, 'Why did you do this?' But, the historian inevitably has a broader view of the student's action and its consequences, and can interpret the action as 'starting the first world war'. While this was not the student's overt intention, he would still be able to understand that this was indeed the consequence of his act.

The problem for psychoanalysis is different. A patient presents himself with, let us say, a paralysis. The patient will not recognise this paralysis as his own action (while the student can readily acknowledge his own action and its consequences, even if unintended). The paralysis seems to be inflicted upon the patient. The psychoanalyst, however, approaches the paralysis as an unconscious action on the part of the patient, and as such as a determinate and meaningful response to an earlier traumatic experience. The task of the analysis is then not simply to make sense of the paralysis, but to restore to the patient the capacity to appreciate that meaning – which is to say to recognise the link between the paralysis and the original trauma, and thus to accept the paralysis as his own active response to that trauma. The justification of the truth of a proposition in psychoanalysis, and thus in critical theory in general, lies not simply in dialogue and rational justification but in the impact that that dialogue has upon the actions of the person or people involved. The therapist's diagnosis is true if the patient accepts it, and has his or her memory and autonomy restored. This conception of the justification of a truth claim is made all the more problematic (but also subtle and interesting) by the fact that, at least on Freud's account, the patient may resist a true interpretation of their symptoms, so that the failure to restore autonomy is not necessarily an indication of the falsehood of the diagnosis, while the failure of a scientific experiment is an indication of the falsehood of the hypothesis being tested.

While Habermas was subsequently to abandon the research programme of *Knowledge and Human Interests*, in part because he felt that it confused the question of the justification of a truth claim with the problem of the way in which the different sciences conceived of and thus constituted the objects that they were studying, it remains a rich source of ideas about the nature of truth and its justification.

TRUTHFULNESS

The commitment that a speaker makes, in principle, to justify his or her sincerity to anyone who should challenge them. As such, it is one of the four **validity claims**.

Habermas's understanding of truthfulness shifts as his theory of **communicative action** develops. Initially, Habermas is influenced by his study of psychoanalysis. Truthfulness is thus understood in terms of the freedom of individual agents to present themselves to others. The neurotic or hysterical patient is unable to do this, because he lacks full conscious control of his body (where, for example, paralysis, speech impediments, fainting fits and pains may all be self-induced, albeit unconsciously, so that these symptoms confront the patient as purely physical maladies), and have distortions in his memory (because he is unable to consciously recall the traumatic events that lie behind his symptoms). This lack of freedom or autonomy will inhibit the individual's ability to participate in free and open communication. In particular, if challenged about the discrepancy between his bodily movements or gestures and his verbal accounts of what he is doing, he will be incapable of responding (Habermas 1970a; 1970b).

Subsequently, as psychoanalysis becomes increasingly less influential to Habermas's theorising, so the notion of truthfulness shifts, to focus on a person's deliberate evasions and ironies. The liar and the ironist are both unable to justify the truthfulness of their speeches, albeit they are well aware of this, and at least in the case of the liar are likely to take steps to maintain the illusion created by the lie. However, as was the case with the earlier notion, truthfulness is recognised as a problem because of a discrepancy between what the speaker says and what the speaker does. The ironist lauds President Bush's initiative against terror, while voting Democrat. The liar says he was in the library at nine, whereas I saw him in the bar at that time. This makes truthfulness a special case amongst validity claims, as the truthfulness of the speaker cannot be justified through rational discussion (for they might still be lying or being ironic), but must appeal to the observation of the speaker's previous and subsequent behaviour.

In more recent writings, Habermas has begun to link truthfulness to self-expression, and in particular to the role that art can play in articulating the self-understanding of groups and individuals. In effect, this serves to acknowledge the expressive function that language can serve. As such, truthfulness becomes, perhaps rather awkwardly, associated with the capacity of art to create and articulate a view of the world, and concern shifts from simple examples of liars and ironists, to more subtle examples that raise the question of the adequacy of a particular art form to express the inner life and cultural frameworks of the individual (1992b: 205–27).

UNIVERSAL PRAGMATICS

The theory of the skills and competences that human beings need in order to be able to communicate. For Habermas, a reconstruction of such competences also provides an explanation of how human beings produce and maintain the fabric of everyday life. He proposed the programme of universal pragmatics in the early 1970s (Habermas 1976e; 1979a: 1–68; 2001c), and under the revised name of 'formal pragmatics' it continues to ground his work in social theory (1984a; 1987), ethics (1990) and political and legal philosophy (1996).

Universal pragmatics is an example of what Habermas calls a **reconstructive science**. That is to say that he seeks to reconstruct the rules that competent agents must follow in order to communicate with each other, although the agent herself need not be aware of the rules or that she is following them. A model for Habermas's inquiry is provided by the linguist Noam Chomsky (Habermas 2001c: 68). Chomsky was interested in the rules that agents must follow in being able to use language competently, as for example in formulating well-formed and meaningful sentences. Chomsky is not interested in the grammatical rules of a particular language, such as German or Welsh, but rather in a deeper set of rules that are common to all languages. This 'deep grammar' is a set of rules that, Chomsky argues, all competent speakers are born with the ability to follow. It is precisely this competence that allows individuals to learn and use any particular language.

Habermas is not concerned with Chomsky's linguistic competence, but rather with a broader communicative competence. While Chomsky is interested in sentence formation, and may therefore be seen to focus on sentences that make assertions about the way the world is, Habermas is interested in utterances. That is to say that

Habermas recognises that language is used for more than just conveying facts or opinions about the world. Rather, language is used to establish social relationships with others, for example by asking questions or giving orders (see **speech acts**). In an utterance, a speaker uses a sentence in a particular context, to particular listeners, to achieve a particular outcome. Therefore the concern of universal pragmatics is the ability, not just to formulate meaningful sentences, but rather to engage others in interaction, drawing on an awareness of the cultural and physical environment within which they act in order to begin communication and to repair breakdowns in communication.

Communication can be understood as a process in which two or more people come to share a view of the world, or at the very least to recognise aspects of a common world about which they disagree. This can be a difficult and time-consuming activity. Habermas identifies four conditions that everyone involved in communication must try to secure, if that communication is to succeed and continue. First, everyone must be able to share their understanding of the world about them. They must therefore be able to discuss the facts of the physical and cultural world. So, if I tell you that the weather is fine, you must be able to understand what it is that I am referring to, and be able to understand the evaluation I am making (even if you happen to disagree with me). Next, precisely because in making an utterance I am initiating a social relationship, everybody needs to agree that I have a right to say what I am saying. It is one thing to tell my friend that it is a nice day, or even to chat to a shopkeeper as I await my change, but to stop a stranger in the street and impart this information may raise suspicions. This illustrates the fact that communication is not just about using the right words, or even saying something that is in itself coherent and meaningful. When and where you say it matters. Sometimes certain utterances are inappropriate or simply culturally prohibited (for example, trying to start a conversation with another member of the audience at a classical music concert). Third, Habermas recognises that not every utterance is necessarily made sincerely. Sometimes I will be joking, being ironic or just lying. If this is not recognised by my audience, sustained communication becomes highly problematic, and possibly embarrassing. Finally, what is said must be meaningful. Everyone must share the same language, and recognise enough common idioms to sustain communication. At the very least, if I say something that you do not understand, in order to keep communication going I need to be able to rephrase it in a way that you do understand.

Habermas summarises all this in terms of what he calls **validity claims**. When I say anything, I am making more or less implicit assumptions about the nature of the world around me, my right to speak, my subjective state, and the coherence of what I am saying. Similarly, those listening to me assume, unless there is evidence to the contrary, that I am correct in my assumptions about the world, that I have a right to speak, that I am sincere, and that what I have said is meaningful. If these assumptions were not made, communication and interaction could not continue. I could not interact with someone if I assumed that she was an habitual liar, for example. Such rigorous scepticism about the motives of this other person would simply render me unable to make sense of anything that she said, because I could not trust it. We thus enter into communication with a rather studied naivety. The people with whom we communicate are given the benefit of the doubt, until we have good reason for that doubt.

The subject-matter of four validity claims are, in summary, **truth**, rightness, **truthfulness** and **meaning**, and in speaking I am at least implicitly promising to be able to justify what I say and do, if challenged, on any of these four themes. My promise to respond, reasonably and convincingly, to a challenge is precisely what keeps communication, and this particular interaction, going. (Again, if I suspect someone of being an habitual liar, I am not going to acknowledge any such promise.)

Consider the following scenario. I promise to meet you at the library café at five. Although this is a promise, and not an overt statement about the world, I am still making a whole series of assumptions about how the world is, and I am further assuming that you share them. I am, for example, assuming that the library café is still open at five, and you might challenge me on this fact. Here my promise would have failed as an attempt to sustain social interaction. We did not share quite the same view of the world after all. However, communication and the attendant interaction could readily be repaired by agreeing to meet somewhere else. There may be more problems though. You might challenge my right to make such a promise. Perhaps I am not free at that time. I had forgotten that I had already promised to meet somebody else at five, or I will still be at work at five. I might here be able to reply that my other engagement has been cancelled, or that I leave work early on Fridays. This would be a reasonable reply, justifying the promise that I am offering and my right to make it. Perhaps the worst situation occurs if you reply that I never keep my promises, and that last week you waited thirty minutes for me and I still didn't turn up. I am accused of being insincere.

While I might protest my innocence (something unforeseen came up; the train broke down; I had a puncture; and so on), I might still be lying. Ultimately, my sincerity or truthfulness is established only if my future behaviour is seen to be consistent with my utterances (so that I do keep my promises, and what I said about the train breakdown is demonstrated to be true). Finally, you might just mishear me; what I say may be ambiguous; or I might slur and confuse my words. You can then reasonably ask me to repeat myself, to rephrase or clarify what I am saying. In practice, as his work on universal pragmatics continues, Habermas loses interest in meaning as a validity claim, and a shared language is very much taken for granted.

Habermas is arguing that the competent communicator has the ability to challenge and justify (or 'redeem') each of the four validity claims. This is the general or formal skill that I must possess in order to be a competent social agent. In addition, as the example above begins to suggest, in order to exercise this skill, I must also be able to draw upon the cultural assumptions that are common between myself and the people with whom I am interacting (so that we mutually draw on what Habermas calls the **lifeworld**). At worst, we must be able to recognise when we do not share common assumptions, and so begin to share them, bringing our assumptions into harmony with each other. Habermas himself offers the vivid example of a new worker on a building site being asked to get beer for the morning break. The request from an older worker draws on a series of assumptions about the local geography (for example, that there is an off-licence open near by), the hierarchy of the building site (for example, that he has the right to order the young worker to undertake menial tasks), as well as his sincerity (how many novices have been sent to ask for left-handed screwdrivers?), and that they speak the same language (for the young man may be a guestworker who knows only limited German) (Habermas 1987: 121ff). Breakdowns in communication expose specific assumptions that we do not share. There may be many other things that we could disagree about, and that might disrupt future interactions, but in practice we will only worry about those things that matter to this particular interaction. We can use the skills and items of knowledge that we do share to heal specific breakdowns in communication. Rarely if ever could everything we take for granted be thrown into doubt in a single interaction, however profound our disagreements and confusions.

Further reading: Thompson 1981; Cooke 1994; Nussbaum 1998; Zinkin 1998; Swindal 1999

VALIDITY CLAIM

The commitments that speakers make, often unwittingly, to justify what they have said and what they are doing. In his theory of **universal pragmatics**, Habermas identifies four validity claims: to **truth**, to rightness; to sincerity or **truthfulness**; and to **meaning**. In practice, this means that when I say something I am more or less implicitly making a series of assumptions: about how the world around me is; my right to say what I am saying; that I am being sincere or otherwise in what I say; and that what I say is coherent and comprehensible. Any listener can, in principle, challenge me on any of these points. So, if I ask you to lend me your pen, I am assuming that you have a pen, and you might respond by saying that you do not have one, or that you left it in the library. I am assuming that it is acceptable for me to borrow things from you, and you might reply that you never got the last pen back, so no, you are not lending me another. I might just be teasing you, being well aware of my record of not giving back borrowed pens, and you might indeed reply 'You must be joking!' Finally, I might have stumbled over my words, so that I actually said 'Can I porrow your ben?', and you might ask me to repeat myself, perhaps more carefully, loudly or in different words (see Habermas 1976e; 1979a: 1–67).

BIBLIOGRAPHY

(Dates of original publication, where significant, are in brackets after the date of the cited edition.)

Aboulafia, Mitchell, Bookman, Myra and Kemp, Catherine (eds) 2001. *Habermas and Pragmatism*. London: Routledge.

Adorno, Theodor W. 1973 *(1966)*. *Negative Dialectics*, E. B. Ashton (trans.). London: Routledge and Kegan Paul.

—1974 *(1951)*. *Minima Moralia: Reflections on a Damaged Life*, E. F. N. Jephcott (trans.). London: Verso.

Adorno, Theodor W. *et al.* 1976 *(1969)*. *The Positivist Dispute in German Sociology*. London: Heinemann.

Ahler, Rolf 1970. 'Is Technology Intrinsically Repressive?', *Continuum* 8(1), 111–22.

Alford, C. Fred 1985. *Science and the Revenge of Nature: Marcuse and Habermas*. Gainesville: University Presses of Florida.

Alway, Joan 1995. *Critical Theory and Political Possibilities: Conceptions of Emancipatory Politics in the Works of Horkheimer, Adorno, Marcuse, and Habermas*. Westport, CT: Greenwood Press.

Apel, Karl-Otto 1980 *(1972/1973)*. *Towards a Transformation of Philosophy*, Glyn Adey and David Frisby (trans). London: Routledge and Kegan Paul.

—1981. *Charles S. Peirce: From Pragmatism to Pragmaticism*, John Michael Krois (trans.). Amherst: University of Massachusetts Press.

—1998. 'Openly Strategic Uses of Language: A Transcendental-Pragmatic Perspective (A second attempt to think with Habermas against Habermas)'. In Peter Dews (ed.), *Habermas: A Critical Reader*. Oxford: Blackwell.

Arato A. and Gebhardt E. (eds) 1978. *The Essential Frankfurt School Reader*. Oxford: Blackwell.

Arens, Edmund 1994. *The Logic of Pragmatic Thinking: From Peirce to Habermas*. Atlantic Highlands, NJ: Humanities Press International.

Ashenden, Samantha and Owen, David (eds) 1999. *Foucault contra Habermas*. London: Sage.

Austin, J. L. 1975 *(1960)*. *How to Do Things with Words*, J. O. Urmson and Marina Sbisá (eds). Oxford: Clarendon Press.

Babich, Babette E. (ed.) 2004. *Habermas, Nietzsche, and Critical Theory*. Amherst, MA: Humanity Books.

Baxter, Hugh 1987. 'System and Life-world in Habermas's *Theory of Communicative Action*', *Theory and Society* 16(1), 39–86.

Benhabib, Seyla 1986. *Critique, Norm, and Utopia: A Study of the Foundations of Critical Theory.* New York: Columbia University Press.

Benhabib, Seyla and Dallmayr, Fred (eds) 1990. *The Communicative Ethics Controversy.* Cambridge, MA: MIT Press.

Benjamin, Walter 1970 *(1936)*. 'The Work of Art in the Age of Mechanical Reproduction'. In his *Illuminations*, Hannah Arendt (ed.). London: Fontana.

Bernstein, J. M. 1995. *Recovering Ethical Life: Jürgen Habermas and the Future of Critical Theory.* London: Routledge.

Bernstein, Richard J. (ed.) 1985. *Habermas and Modernity.* Cambridge: Polity Press.

Best, Steven 1995. *The Politics of Historical Vision: Marx, Foucault, Habermas.* New York and London: Guilford Press.

Bowring, Finn 1996. 'A Lifeworld without a Subject: Habermas and the Pathologies of Modernity', *Telos 106*, 77–104

Brand, Arie 1990. *The Force of Reason: An Introduction to Habermas' Theory of Communicative Action.* Sydney: Allen & Unwin.

Bronner S. E. and Kellner D. M. (eds) 1989. *Critical Theory and Society: A Reader.* London: Routledge.

Browning, Don S. and Fiorenza, Francis Schüssler (eds) 1992. *Habermas, Modernity, and Public Theology.* New York: Crossroad.

Cahoun, Craig (ed.) 1992. *Habermas and the Public Sphere.* Cambridge, MA: MIT Press.

Campbell, Margaret M. 1999. *Critical Theory and Liberation Theology: A Comparison of the Initial Work of Jürgen Habermas and Gustavo Gutierrez.* New York: Peter Lang.

Chambers, Simone 1996. *Reasonable Democracy: Jürgen Habermas and the Politics of Discourse.* Ithaca, NY and London: Cornell University Press.

Connerton, P. (ed.) 1976. *Critical Sociology.* Harmondsworth: Penguin.

Cook, Deborah 2004. *Adorno, Habermas and the Search for a Rational Society.* London: Routledge.

Cooke, Maeve 1994. *Language and Reason: A Study of Habermas's Pragmatics.* Cambridge, MA and London: MIT Press.

—1997. 'Authenticity and Autonomy: Taylor, Habermas, and the Politics of Recognition', *Political Theory 25*(2), 258–88.

Copleston, F. C. 1960. *A History of Philosophy*, vol. 6. London: Burns and Oates.

Crossley, Nick and Roberts, John Michael (eds) 2004. *After Habermas: New Perspectives on the Public Sphere.* Oxford: Blackwell.

Dallmayr, Fred 1972a. 'Reason and Emancipation: Notes on Habermas', *Man and World 5*, 79–109.

—1972b. 'Critical Theory Criticized: Habermas's *Knowledge and Human Interests* and Its Aftermath', *Philosophy of the Social Sciences 2*, 211–29

Deflem, Mathieu (ed.) 1996. *Habermas, Modernity and Law.* London: Sage.

Derrida, Jacques 1977. 'Limited, Inc.', *Glyph 2*, 162–254.

—1982 *(1972)*. 'Signature Event Context'. In his *Margins of Philosophy*, Alan Bass (trans.). Brighton: Harvester Press.

Dews, Peter (ed.) 1998. *Habermas: A Critical Reader*. Oxford: Blackwell.

Durkheim, Emile 1984 *(1902)*. *The Division of Labour in Society*, W. D. Halls (trans.). Basingstoke: Macmillan.

Duvenage, Pieter 2003. *Habermas and Aesthetics: Limits of Communicative Action*. Oxford: Polity Press.

Edgar, Andrew 1995. 'Discourse Ethics and Paternalism'. In *The Social Power of Ideas*, Yeager Hudson and W. Creighton Peden (eds). Lewiston: Edwin Mellen Press.

—2005. *The Philosophy of Habermas*. Chesham: Acumen.

Elster, Jon 1986. 'The Market and the Forum: Three Varieties of Political Theory'. In Jon Elster and Aanund Hylland (eds). *Foundations of Social Choice Theory*. Cambridge: Cambridge University Press.

Eriksen, Erik Oddvar 2003. *Understanding Habermas: Communicative Action and Deliberative Democracy*. London: Continuum.

Fairfield, Paul 1994. 'Habermas, Lyotard and Political Discourse', *Reason Papers 19*, 58–80.

Finlayson, J. G. 1998. 'Does Hegel's Critique of Kant's Moral Theory Apply to Discourse Ethics?'. In *Habermas: A Critical Reader*, P. Dews (ed.), 29–52. Oxford: Blackwell.

Fleming, Marie 1997. *Emancipation and Illusion: Rationality and Gender in Habermas's Theory of Modernity*. University Park, PA: Pennsylvania State University Press.

Flyvbjerg, Bent 1998. 'Habermas and Foucault: Thinkers for Civil Society?', *British Journal of Sociology 49*(2), 210–33.

Foster, Roger S. 1999. 'Strategies of Justice: The Project of Philosophy in Lyotard and Habermas', *Philosophy and Social Criticism 25*(2), 87–113.

Foucault, Michel 1970 *(1966)*. *The Order of Things: An Archaeology of the Human Sciences*. London: Tavistock.

—1971 *(1961)*. *Madness and Civilization: A History of Insanity in the Age of Reason*. London: Tavistock.

—1976 *(1963)*. *The Birth of the Clinic*. London: Tavistock.

—1977 *(1975)*. *Discipline and Punish: The Birth and the Prison*. Harmondsworth: Penguin

Freud, Sigmund 1962 *(1910/1926)*. *Two Short Accounts of Psycho-Analysis*, Harmondsworth: Penguin.

Freundlieb, Dieter 2003. *Dieter Henrich and Contemporary Philosophy: The Return to Subjectivity*. Aldershot: Ashgate.

Fukuyama, Francis 1992. *The End of History and the Last Man*. London: Hamish Hamilton.

Garrigan, Siobhán 2004. *Beyond Ritual: Sacramental Theology after Habermas*. Aldershot: Ashgate.

Geuss, Raymond 1981. *The Idea of a Critical Theory: Habermas and the Frankfurt School*. Cambridge: Cambridge University Press.

Giddens, Anthony 1982. 'Labour and Interaction'. In *Habermas: Critical Debates,* John B. Thompson and David Held (eds). London: Macmillan.

Habermas, Jürgen 1954. 'Die Dialektic der Rationalisierung: Vom Pauper-
ismus in Produktion und Kunsum', *Merker 8*, 701–24.

—1970a. 'On Systematically Distorted Communication', *Inquiry 13*, 205–
18.

—1970b. 'Towards a Theory of Communicative Competence', *Inquiry 13*,
360–75.

—1970c. 'Summation and Response', *Continuum 8*(1), 123–33.

—1971a *(1968)*. *Knowledge and Human Interests*, Jeremy J. Shapiro (trans.).
Boston, MA: Beacon Press

—1971b *(1968–69)*. *Toward a Rational Society: Student Protest, Science and
Politics*, Jeremy J. Shapiro (trans.). London: Heinemann.

—1974a. 'On Social Identity', *Telos 19*, 91–103.

—1974b. 'The Public Sphere: An Encyclopaedia Article', *New German Critique 3*, 49–55.

—1975. 'The Place of Philosophy in Marxism', *Insurgent Sociologist 5*, 41–8.

—1976a *(1971)*. *Theory and Practice*, John Viertel (trans.). Boston, MA:
Beacon Press.

—1976b *(1973)*. *Legitimation Crisis*, Thomas McCarthy (trans.). London:
Heinemann.

—1976c *(1969)*. 'The Analytical Theory of Science and Dialectics'. In *The
Positivist Dispute in German Sociology*, Theodor W. Adorno *et al.*, London:
Heinemann.

—1976d *(1969)*. 'A Positivistically Bisected Rationalism'. In *The Positivist
Dispute in German Sociology*, Theodor W. Adorno *et al.*, London: Heinemann.

—1976e. 'Some Distinctions in Universal Pragmatics', *Theory and Society 1*
(3), 155–67.

—1979a *(1976)*. *Communication and the Evolution of Society*, Thomas McCarthy (trans). Boston, MA: Beacon Press.

—1979b. 'History and Evolution', *Telos 38*, 5–44.

—1980 *(1970)*. 'The Hermeneutic Claim to University'. In *Contemporary
Hermeneutics: Hermeneutics as Method, Philosophy and Critique*, Josef Blei-
cher, London: Routledge and Kegan Paul.

—1981a. *Kleine Politische Schriften 1–4*. Frankfurt am Main: Suhrkamp.

—1981b. *Philosophisch-Politische Profile*. Frankfurt am Main: Suhrkamp.

—1982. 'A Reply to My Critics'. In *Habermas: Critical Debates*, John B.
Thompson and David Held (eds). London: Macmillan.

—1983a. *Philosophical-Political Profiles*, F. G. Lawrence (trans.). London: Heinemann.

—1983b *(1980)*. 'Modernity – An Incomplete Project'. In *Postmodern Culture*, Hal Foster (ed.). London: Pluto Press.

—1984a *(1981)*. *The Theory of Communicative Action* vol. 1: *Reason and the
Rationalisation of Society*, Thomas McCarthy (trans.). Cambridge: Polity
Press.

—1984b. *Vorstudien und Ergänzungen zur Theorie des Kommunikativen Han-
delns*, Frankfurt am Main: Suhrkamp.

—1987 *(1981)*. *The Theory of Communicative Action* vol. 2: *Lifeworld and System: A Critique of Functionalist Reason*, Thomas McCarthy (trans.). Cambridge: Polity Press.

—1988a *(1985)*. *The Philosophical Discourse of Modernity: Twelve Lectures*, F. G. Lawrence (trans.). Cambridge, MA: MIT Press.

—1988b *(1967)*. *On the Logic of the Social Sciences*, S. Weber Nicholsen and J. A. Stark (eds). Cambridge: Polity Press.

—1989a *(1962)*. *The Structural Transformation of the Public Sphere: An Inquiry into a Category of Bourgeois Society*, Thomas Burger and Frederick Lawrence (trans). Cambridge: Polity Press.

—1989b *(1985)*. *The New Conservatism: Cultural Criticism and the Historians' Debate*, Shierry Weber Nicholsen (trans.). Cambridge, MA: MIT Press.

—1990 *(1983)*. *Moral Consciousness and Communicative Action*, Christian Lenhardt and Shierry Weber Nicholsen (trans). Cambridge, MA: MIT Press.

—1992a. *Autonomy and Solidarity: Interviews with Jürgen Habermas*, Peter Dews (ed.). London: Verso.

—1992b *(1988)*. *Postmetaphysical Thinking: Philosophical Essays*, W. M. Hohengarten (trans.). Cambridge, MA: MIT Press.

—1992c. 'Further Reflections on the Public Sphere', Thomas Burger (trans.). In *Habermas and the Public Sphere*, Craig Cahoun (ed.), Cambridge, MA: MIT Press.

—1993a. *Justification and Application: Remarks on Discourse Ethics*, C. Cronin (trans.). Cambridge: Polity Press.

—1993b. 'A Reply'. In *Communicative Action: Essays in Jürgen Habermas's* The Theory of Communicative Action, Alex Honneth and Hans Joas (eds),. Cambridge: Polity Press.

—1994 *(1990)*. *The Past as Future*, Max Pensk (trans.). Cambridge: Polity Press.

—1996 *(1993)*. *Between Facts and Norms: Contributions to a Discourse Theory of Law and Democracy*, W. Rehg (trans.). Cambridge: Polity Press.

—1997 *(1995)*. *A Berlin Republic: Writings on Germany*, S. Rendall (trans.). Lincoln: University of Nebraska Press.

—1998a *(1996)*. *The Inclusion of the Other: Studies in Political Theory*, C. Cronin and P. de Greiff (eds). Cambridge, MA: MIT Press.

—1998b. 'Law and Morality'. In *The Tanner Lectures on Human Values*, vol. VIII, S. M. McMurrin (ed.). Salt Lake City: University of Utah Press.

—1999a. *On the Pragmatics of Communication*, M. Cooke (ed.). Cambridge: Polity Press.

—1999b. 'Introduction', *Ratio Juris* 12(4), 329–35.

—1999c. 'A Short Reply', *Ratio Juris* 12(4), 445–53.

—2001a *(1997)*. *The Liberating Power of Symbols: Philosophical Essays*, Peter Dews (trans.). Cambridge: Polity Press.

—2001b *(1989)*. *The Postnational Constellation: Political Essays*, Max Pensky (trans.). Cambridge, MA.: MIT Press.

—2001c. *On the Pragmatics of Social Interaction: Preliminary Studies in the Theory of Communicative Action*, Barbara Fultner (trans.). Cambridge: Polity Press.

—2001d. 'Constitutional Democracy: A Paradoxical Union of Contradictory Principles?', *Political Theory 29*(6), 766–81.

—2002. *Religion and Rationality*, Eduardo Mendieta (ed.). Cambridge: Polity Press.

—2003a *(1999)*. *Truth and Justification*, Barbara Fultner (trans.). Cambridge, MA: MIT Press.

—2003b *(2001)*. *The Future of Human Nature*, Hella Beister (trans.). Cambridge: Polity Press.

—2003c. 'On Law and Disagreement. Some Comments of "Interpretative Pluralism"', *Ratio Juris 16*(2), 187–94.

—2005. *Time of Transitions*. Cambridge: Polity Press.

Habermas, Jürgen and Luhmann, Niklaus 1975. *Theorie der Gesellschaft oder Sozialtechnologie: was leistet die Systemforschung?* Frankfurt am Main: Suhrkamp.

Habermas, Jürgen, von Friedeburg, Ludwig, Oehler, Christoph and Weltz, Friedrich 1961. *Student und Politik: Eine Soziologische Untersuchung zum politischen Bewußtsein Frankfurter Studenten*. Neuwied: Hermann Luchterhand.

Hahn, Lewis Edwin (ed.) 2000. *Perspectives on Habermas*. Chicago, IL: Open Court.

Hanks, J. Craig 2002. *Refiguring Critical Theory: Jürgen Habermas and the Possibilities of Political Change*. Lanham, MD: University Press of America.

Harrington, Austin 2001. *Hermeneutic Dialogue and Social Science: A Critique of Gadamer and Habermas*. London: Routledge.

Healy, Paul 1997. 'Between Habermas and Foucault: On the Limits and Possibilities of Critical and Emancipatory Reason', *South African Journal of Philosophy 16*(4), 140–9.

Heath, Joseph 2001. *Communicative Action and Rational Choice*. Cambridge, MA and London: MIT Press.

Hegel, G. W. F. 1931 *(1807)*. *The Phenomenology of Mind*, J. B. Bailley (trans.). London: Allen and Unwin.

—1970 *(1817)*. *Philosophy of Nature*, A. V. Miller (trans.). Oxford: Clarendon Press.

—1971 *(1817)*. *Philosophy of Mind*, W. Wallace and A. V. Miller (trans). Oxford: Clarendon Press.

—1975a *(1817)*. *Hegel's Logic*, W. Wallace (trans.). Oxford: Clarendon Press.

Heidegger, Martin 1962 *(1927)*. *Being and Time*, John Macquarrie and Edward Robinson (trans). Oxford: Blackwell.

Held, David 1980. *Introduction to Critical Theory: Horkheimer to Habermas*. London: Hutchinson.

—1982. 'Crisis Tendencies, Legitimation and the State'. In *Habermas: Critical Debates*, John B. Thompson and David Held (eds). London: Macmillan.

Hesse, Mary 1982. 'Science and Objectivity'. In *Habermas: Critical Debates*, John B. Thompson and David Held (eds). London: Macmillan.

Holub, Robert C. 1991. *Jürgen Habermas: Critic in the Public Sphere*. London: Routledge.

Honneth, Axel 1991. *The Critique of Power: Reflective Stages in a Critical Social Theory*, Kenneth Bayes (trans.). Cambridge, MA: MIT Press.

—1995. 'The Other of Justice: Habermas and the Ethical Challenge of Postmodernism'. In *The Cambridge Companion to Habermas*, Stephen K. White (ed.). Cambridge: Cambridge University Press.

Honneth, Axel and Joas, Hans (eds) 1991. *Communicative Action: Essays on Jürgen Habermas's The Theory of Communicative Action*. Cambridge, MA: MIT Press.

Horkheimer, Max 1972. *Critical Theory: Selected Essays*, Matthew J. O'Connell (trans.). New York: Herder and Herder.

Horkheimer, Max and Adorno, Theodor W. 1972 *(1947)*. *The Dialectic of Enlightenment*, John Cumming (trans.). New York: Seabury Press.

How, Alan 1995. *The Habermas–Gadamer Debate and the Nature of the Social: Back to Bedrock*. Aldershot: Avebury.

Huch, Kurt Jürgen 1970. 'Interest in Emancipation', *Continuum* 8(1), 27–39.

Ingram, David 1987. *Habermas and the Dialectic of Reason*. New Haven, CT and London: Yale University Press.

Jay, Martin 1973. *The Dialectical Imagination. A History of the Frankfurt School and the Institute of Social Research, 1923–1950*. London: Heinemann Educational Books.

—1984. *Marxism and Totality: The Adventures of a Concept from Lukacs to Habermas*. Berkeley: University of California Press.

Kant, Immanuel 1933 *(1781/1787)*. *Critique of Pure Reason*, N. Kemp-Smith (trans.). Basingstoke: Macmillan.

—1952 *(1790)*. *Critique of Judgement*, James Creed Meredith (trans.). Oxford: Clarendon Press.

Keat, Russell 1981. *The Politics of Social Theory: Habermas, Freud and the Critique of Positivism*. Oxford: Blackwell.

Kelly, Michael (ed.) 1994. *Critique and Power: Recasting the Foucault/Habermas Debate*. Cambridge, MA and London: MIT Press.

Kitchen, Gary 1997. 'Habermas's Moral Cognitivism', *Proceedings of the Aristotelian Society* 97, 317–24.

Koczanowicz, Leszek 1999. 'The Choice of Tradition and the Tradition of Choice: Habermas' and Rorty's Interpretation of Pragmatism', *Philosophy and Social Criticism* 25(1), 55–70.

Kohlberg, Lawrence 1981. *Essays on Moral Development:* Vol. 1, *The Philosophy of Moral Development: Moral Stages and the Idea of Justice*. San Francisco, CA: Harper & Row.

Kompridis, Nikolas 1988. 'Heidegger's Challenge and the Future of Critical Theory'. In *Habermas: A Critical Reader*, Peter Dews (ed.). Oxford: Blackwell.

Körner, Stephan 1955. *Kant*. Harmondsworth: Penguin.

Kortian, Garbis 1980. *Metacritique: The Philosophical Argument of Jürgen Habermas*. Cambridge: Cambridge University Press.

Larrian, J. 1979. *The Concept of Ideology*. London: Hutchinson.

Lévi-Strauss, Claude 1969 *(1949)*. *The Elementary Structures of Kinship*, James Harle Bell, John Richard von Sturmer and Rodney Needham (trans). Boston, MA: Beacon Press.

Li, Kit-Man 1999. *Western Civilization and Its Problems: A Dialogue between Weber, Elias and Habermas*. Aldershot: Ashgate.

Locke, John 1980 *(1690)*. *Second Treatise of Government*, C. B. Macpherson (ed.). Indianapolis: Hackett.

Luhmann, Niklaus 1982. *The Differentiation of Society*, Stephen Holmes and Charles Larmore (trans). New York: Columbia University Press.

—1987. 'Modern Systems Theory and the Theory of Society'. In *Modern German Sociology*, Volker Meja, Dieter Misgeld and Nico Stehr (eds), New York: Columbia University Press.

—1995. *Social Systems*. Stanford, CA: Stanford University Press.

Lukács, Georg 1971. *History and Class Consciousness: Studies in Marxist Dialectics, Rodney Livingstone (trans.). London: Merlin.*

Lyotard, Jean François 1984 *(1979)*. *The Postmodern Condition: A Report on Knowledge*, Geoff Bennington and Brian Massumi (trans). Minneapolis: University of Minnesota Press.

—1985 *(1979)*. *Just Gaming*, Wlad Godzich and Brian Massumi (trans). Minneapolis: University of Minnesota Press.

Marsh, James L. 2001. *Unjust Legality: A Critique of Habermas's Philosophy of Law.* Lanham, MD: Rowman & Littlefield.

Martinich, A. P. and Sosa, D. (eds) (2001) *A Companion to Analytic Philosophy*. Oxford: Blackwell.

Marx, Karl 1975a *(1859)*. 'Preface to *A Contribution to the Critique of Political Economy*'. In his *Early Writings*, Lucio Colletti (intro.), Rodney Livingstone and Gregor Benton (trans.). Harmondsworth: Penguin.

—1975b *(1859)*. 'Introduction to A Contribution to the Critique of Hegel's Philosophy of Right'. In his *Early Writings*, Lucio Colletti (intro.), Rodney Livingstone and Gregor Benton (trans.). Harmondsworth: Penguin.

—1975c *(1845)*. 'Theses on Feuerbach'. In his *Early Writings*, Lucio Colletti (intro.), Rodney Livingstone and Gregor Benton (trans.). Harmondsworth: Penguin.

—1976 *(1867)*. *Capital: A Critique of Political Economy*, vol. 1, Ben Fowkes (trans.). Harmondsworth: Penguin.

Marx, Karl and Engels, Frederick 1975 *(1847)*. 'The Manifesto of the Communist Party'. In *The Revolutions of 1848*, David Fernbach (ed.). Harmondsworth: Penguin.

—1977 *(1845–6)*. *The German Ideology*, C. J. Arthur (ed.). London: Lawrence & Wishart.

Matustik, Martin J. 1993. *Postnational Identity: Critical Theory and Existential Philosophy in Habermas, Kierkegaard, and Havel*. New York: Guilford Press.

—2001. *Jürgen Habermas: A Philosophical–Political Profile*. Lanham, MD: Rowman & Littlefield.

Mauss, Marcel 1966 *(1925)*. *The Gift: Forms and Functions of Exchange in Archaic Societies*. London: Routledge and Kegan Paul.

McCarthy, George E. 2001. *Objectivity and the Silence of Reason: Weber, Habermas, and the Methodological Disputes in German Sociology*. New Brunswick, NJ: Transaction.

McCarthy, Thomas 1978. *The Critical Theory of Jürgen Habermas*. London: Hutchinson.

—1982. 'Rationality and Relativism: Habermas's "Overcoming" of Hermeneutics'. In *Habermas: Critical Debates,* John B. Thompson and David Held (eds). London: Macmillan.

Meehan, Johanna (ed.) 1995. *Feminists Read Habermas: Gendering the Subject of Discourse.* London: Routledge.

Morris, Martin 2001. *Rethinking the Communicative Turn: Adorno, Habermas, and the Problem of Communicative Freedom.* Albany: State University of New York Press.

Negt, Oskar and Kluge, Alexander 1993 *(1972)*. *Public Sphere and Experience: Toward an Analysis of the Bourgeois and Proletarian Public Sphere,* Peter Labanyi, Jamie Owen Daniel and Assenka Oksiloff (trans). Minneapolis: University of Minnesota Press.

Nietzsche, Friedrich 1979 *(1873)*. 'On Truth and Lies in a Nonmoral Sense'. In his *Philosophy and Truth: Selections from Nietzsche's Notebooks of the Early 1870s,* Daniel Breazeale (ed.). Brighton: Harvester.

—1993 *(1872)*. *Birth of Tragedy: Out of the Spirit of Music,* Shaun Whiteside (trans.). London: Penguin.

Nussbaum, Charles 1998. 'Habermas on Speech Acts: A Naturalistic Critique', *Philosophy Today* 42(2), 126–45.

Offe, Claus 1984. *Contradictions of the Welfare State,* John Keane (ed.). London: Hutchinson.

—1985. *Disorganized Capitalism: Contemporary Transformations of Work and Politics,* John Keane (ed.). Cambridge: Polity Press.

—1987. 'Towards a Theory of Late Capitalism'. In *Modern German Sociology,* Volker Meja, Dieter Misgeld and Nico Stehr (eds). New York: Columbia University Press.

—1992. 'Bindings, Shackles, Brakes: On Self-limitation Strategies'. In Axel Honneth *et al.* (eds). *Cultural-Political Interventions in the Unifinished Project of the Enlightenment.* Cambridge, MA: MIT Press.

Ottmann, Henning 1982. 'Cognitive Interests and Self-reflection'. In *Habermas: Critical Debates*, John B. Thompson and David Held (eds). London: Macmillan.

Outhwaite, William 1994. *Habermas: A Critical Introduction.* Cambridge: Polity Press.

—(ed.) 1996. *The Habermas Reader.* Cambridge: Polity Press.

Owen, David S. 2002. *Between Reason and History: Habermas and the Idea of Progress.* Albany: State University of New York Press.

Passerin d'Entréves, Maurizio and Benhabib, Seyla (eds) 1996. *Habermas and the Unfinished Project of Modernity: Critical Essays on* The Philosophical Discourse of Modernity. Cambridge: Polity Press.

Peirce, Charles S. 1960. *Collected Papers of Charles Sanders Peirce* (8 volumes), Charles Hartshorne and Paul Weiss (eds). Cambridge, MA: Belknap Press.

Pleasants, Nigel 1999. *Wittgenstein and the Idea of a Critical Social Theory: A Critique of Giddens, Habermas and Bhaskar.* London: Routledge.

Powers, Michael 1993. 'Habermas and Transcendental Arguments: A Reappraisal', *Philosophy of the Social Sciences* 23(1), 26–49.

Pusey, Michael 1987. *Jürgen Habermas.* Chichester: Ellis Horwood.

Raffel, Stanley 1992. *Habermas, Lyotard and the Concept of Justice*. London: Macmillan.

Rasmussen, David M. 1990. *Reading Habermas*. Oxford: Basil Blackwell.

Rasmussen, David M. and Swindal, James (eds) 2002. *Jürgen Habermas*. London: Sage.

Rawls, John 1972. *A Theory of Justice*. Oxford: Clarendon Press.

—1985. 'Justice as Fairness: Political not Metaphysical', *Philosophy and Public Affairs 14*(3), 223–51.

Rehg, William 1994. *Insight and Solidarity: A Study in the Discourse Ethics of Jürgen Habermas*. Berkeley and London: University of California Press.

Ricoeur, Paul 1970. *Freud and Philosophy: An Essay on Interpretation*, Denis Savage (trans.). New Haven, CT: Yale University Press.

Roberts, David (ed.) 1995. *Reconstructing Theory: Gadamer, Habermas, Luhmann*. Melbourne: Melbourne University Press.

Roblin, Robert (ed.) 1990. *The Aesthetics of the Critical Theorists: Studies on Benjamin, Adorno, Marcuse, and Habermas*. Lampeter: Edwin Mellen Press.

Rockmore, Tom 1989. *Habermas on Historical Materialism*. Bloomington: Indiana University Press.

Roderick, Rick 1986. *Habermas and the Foundations of Critical Theory*. Basingstoke: Macmillan.

Rosenfeld, Michel and Arato, Andrew (eds) 1998. *Habermas on Law and Democracy: Critical Exchanges*. Berkeley: University of California Press.

Ryle, Gilbert 1963 *(1949)*. *The Concept of Mind*. Harmondsworth: Penguin.

Schmid, Michael 1982. 'Habermas's Theory of Social Evolution'. In *Habermas: Critical Debates*, John B. Thompson and David Held (eds). London: Macmillan.

Schomberg, René von and Baynes, Kenneth (eds) 2002. *Discourse and Democracy: Essays on Habermas's* Between Facts and Norms. Albany: State University of New York Press.

Searle, John 1977. 'Reiterating the Differences: A Reply to Derrida', *Glyph 1*, 198–208.

Siebert, Rudolf J. 1985. *The Critical Theory of Religion: The Frankfurt School: From Universal Pragmatic to Political Theology*. Berlin: Mouton.

Swindal, James 1999. *Reflection Revisited: Jürgen Habermas's Discursive Theory of Truth*. New York: Fordham University Press.

Teigas, Demetrius 1995. *Knowledge and Hermeneutic Understanding: A Study of the Habermas–Gadamer Debate*. Cranbury, NJ: Associated University Presses.

Thompson, John B. 1981. *Critical Hermeneutics: A Study in the Thought of Paul Ricoeur and Jürgen Habermas*. Cambridge: Cambridge University Press.

Thompson, John B. and Held, David (eds) 1982. *Habermas: Critical Debates*. London: Macmillan.

Trey, George 1998. *Solidarity and Difference: The Politics of Enlightenment in the Aftermath of Modernity*. Albany: State University of New York Press.

Villa, Dana R. 1992. 'Postmodernism and the Public Sphere', *The American Political Science Review 86*(3), 712–21.

Weber, M. 1946a. *From Max Weber: Essays in Sociology*, H. H. Gerth and C. W. Mills (eds). London: Routledge and Kegan Paul.

177

—1946b *(1921)*. 'Bureaucracy'. In his *From Max Weber: Essays in Sociology*. London: Routledge and Kegan Paul.

—1946c *(1919)*. 'Science as a Vocation'. In his *From Max Weber: Essays in Sociology*, London: Routledge and Kegan Paul.

—1946d *(1915)*. 'Religious Rejections of the World and Their Directions'. In his *From Max Weber: Essays in Sociology*. London: Routledge and Kegan Paul.

—1968 *(1921)*. *Economy and Society*, Guenther Roth and Claus Wittich (eds). New York: Bedminster Press.

—1976 *(1904–5)*. *The Protestant Ethic and the Spirit of Capitalism*, Talcott Parsons (trans.). London: George Allen and Unwin.

Wellmer, Albrecht 1970. 'Empirico-analytical and Critical Social Science', *Continuum 8*(1), 12–26.

White, Stephen K. 1987. *The Recent Work of Jürgen Habermas: Reason, Justice and Modernity*. Cambridge: Cambridge University Press.

—(ed.) 1995. *Cambridge Companion to Habermas*. Cambridge: Cambridge University Press.

Wiggershaus, Rolf 1994. *The Frankfurt School: Its History, Theories and Political Significance*. Cambridge: Polity Press.

Wittgenstein, Ludwig 1958. *Philosophical Investigations*, G.E.M. Anscombe (trans.). Oxford: Blackwell.

Zinkin, Melissa 1998. 'Habermas on Intelligibility', *Southern Journal of Philosophy 36*(3), 453–72.

INDEX

action 3, 10, 13, 18, 19, 29, 78, 103, 130, 132, 143, 161; and behaviour 3, 9, 18, 78,
Adorno, T. W. 9, 44, 48, 49, 50, 89, 91, 92, 106, 133, 134
administrative power 3–4, 23, 85
advertising 38, 127
aesthetics 37, 102, 106
Apel, K.–O. 44, 65, 66,
art and literature 13, 36, 37, 49, 58, 70, 93, 102, 115, 121, 125, 128, 163
Austin, J. L. 5, 6, 26, 72, 111, 143
autonomy 41, 57, 77, 118, 135, 162; and morality 56, 57, 76; personal 54, 69–70, 92, 116, 123, 161, 162; and political emancipation 15, 135; social 48, 92, 116, 123; and truth 161

base and superstructure 29, 63, 64, 92
Bataille, G. 102
Benjamin, W. 48, 49
Bloch, E. 67, 68
bourgeoisie 69–71, 124–6
bureaucracy 9, 49, 91, 118, 136, 151, 153

capitalism 6–9, 30, 33, 48, 49, 50, 51, 53, 63, 68, 74, 87, 88, 89, 92, 98, 102, 117, 122, 124, 126, 133, 136, 141, 143, 151
Chomsky, N. 113, 131, 163
citizen 3, 4, 7, 23, 38–40, 82–5, 88, 124, 126, 141; citizenship 83

civil society 98
class 6, 16, 62, 63, 67, 68, 69, 70, 87, 117, 124, 125, 126, 139, 141
cognitive interests 10–7, 34, 47, 59, 75, 76, 77, 116, 120, 132, 135, 138, 154, 156, 157
colonisation of the lifeworld 3, 9, 17–21, 35, 50, 53, 56, 58, 62, 69, 81, 82, 85, 88, 91, 98, 99, 101, 103, 116, 118, 126, 134, 137, 148, 154
commodity fetishism 68, 117, 133, 151
communication 14, 22, 23–6, 28, 33, 44, 47, 49, 64–7, 69, 78, 99, 104, 107, 132, 133, 134, 136, 147, 162, 163–6; break down in 14, 16, 42–4, 104, 164; cognitive interest in 10, 12, 34, 59, 132, 135, 156; impact of genetic on 54–6, 58; and systems 18, 19, 36, 118, 148; unrestricted communication community 65
communicative action 3, 18, 19, 20, 21–3, 28, 42, 55, 65, 66, 69, 75, 79, 93, 105, 115, 118, 134, 142, 147, 152, 156, 157, 162
communicative power 23
communicative reason 23–6, 35, 36, 50, 75, 86, 88, 99–100, 102, 107, 109, 114, 118, 124
competence 17, 39, 51, 58, 89, 90, 105, 128, 130, 138, 142, 143, 152, 163; communicative 17–8, 24, 79, 138, 152, 163; linguistic 130–2, 163; moral 45,

consciousness, philosophy of 26–9, 59, 102, 110–12, 113–16, 119, 139, 145

consensus 43, 45, 46, 145, 160

constitution 10, 39–40, 57, 89, 93, 129

constitutional patriotism 39

crisis 7, 29–31, 64, 139, 141, 149, 150

critique 69

critical theory 10, 24, 30, 31–6, 44, 47, 48–51, 69, 71–2, 92, 117, 122, 123, 148, 156, 160–1

culture 9, 30, 31, 41, 42, 49, 62, 67–8, 69, 71, 74, 96, 109, 113, 126, 128, 129, 140–1, 148, 158

decisionism 26, 36–8, 46, 74–75, 126, 135, 137

democracy 6, 38–40, 51, 57, 93, 124, 138

Derrida, J. 26, 102, 113, 115–16

Descartes, R. 4, 26, 97, 104, 119–20, 121, 127

differentiation 40–2, 51–2, 128, 129, 138, 149

discourse 20, 25, 42–4, 55, 83, 84, 159

discourse iethics 28, 35, 44–6, 52–3, 57, 61, 83, 84, 104, 112, 117, 131

double structure of language 46–7, 72, 144

Durkheim, E. 92

emancipation 8, 10, 14, 16, 30, 34, 47–8, 76, 93, 98, 114, 132, 136

Enlightenment 30, 96–100, 112

epistemology 10, 154

evolution, natural 120, 156

family 41, 62, 63, 64, 91, 139, 141, 149

Foucault, M. 102, 113–14, 116

Frankfurt School 4, 9, 31, 44, 48–51, 67, 68, 73, 89, 91, 106, 117, 136,

freedom 17, 53, 57, 84, 97, 99; bourgeois 70; loss of 8, 9, 74, 81, 88,

89, 91, 92, 101, 130, 151–154; and rights 81; and truthfulness 162

Freud, S. 49, 50, 71, 108, 122–3, 132–3, 161

functionalism 146

Gadamer, H.–G. 59, 60, 61

Garfinkel, H. 92

genetics 32, 46, 52–8

Hegel, G. W. F. 5, 29, 48, 49, 67, 71, 75, 76, 77, 91, 98, 110, 111

Heidegger, M. 4, 26

hermeneutics 12–3, 14, 15, 16, 24, 25, 33–5, 50, 58–62, 77, 79, 93, 94, 107–8, 123, 135–7, 147, 152, 156, 160

historical materialism 62–4, 87, 92, 132, 137

history 29, 39, 59, 78, 96–7, 108, 111; iend of human history 65; and scientific inquiry 13, 59; and social evolution 137

Horkheimer, M. 31–4, 48–50, 90–1, 92

Husserl, E. 26, 89, 115

ideal speech situation 45, 64–7, 121, 159, 160; and unrestricted communicative community 66

ideology 14, 61, 67–8, 69, 76; of intimacy 69–70

ideology critique 16, 30, 34, 35, 49, 69–72, 123, 148

illocutionary component 47, 72

illocutionary force 72–3, 144

instrumental action 18, 73, 135, 144

instrumental reason 21, 24, 25, 26, 36, 50, 73, 74–5, 76, 88, 99–100, 102, 118, 128, 134

interaction 9, 45, 75–6, 90, 111, 121, 142, 164–5, 166; cognitive interest in 46, 77, 78; and communication 21, 25, 26, 78, 89, 107, 147, 156, 165; and genetics 55–6; and philosophy of consciousness 27–9, 64; and social evolution 138–41, 150; and systems 19–21, 80, 91, 99, 100, 103, 105, 118, 133, 145, 151, 152–4

journalism 125, 150
justice 27–8, 68, 129

Kant, I. 4–5, 27, 49, 71, 98; and ethics 27, 29, 45, 52; and transcendental philosophy 11, 97, 154–6
Kohlberg, L. 109, 131
Knowledge and Human Interests 10, 14, 24, 31, 33, 38, 49, 69, 71, 73, 92, 108, 132, 159, 161

labour 12, 19, 30, 41, 63–4, 68, 75, 77, 141; and knowledge 12, 73, 76–7, 120–1, 138; and social change 64
language 3, 33, 54, 60–1, 77–9, 85, 94, 95, 112, 117, 134, 140, 145, 158, 166; and cognitive interests 12, 14, 16, 75–7; philosophy of 4–6, 22, 26, 36, 37, 50, 105, 106, 111, 115, 121; private 34, 123, 148; as system 146; use of 6, 21–2, 46–7, 51, 72, 75, 89, 111, 115–6, 130–2, 143, 144, 163–4
language–game 95
law 3–4, 10, 23, 35, 39, 40, 52, 57, 79–85, 87, 89, 107, 108–9, 117, 129, 141
learning 52, 58, 127
legitimation 7, 15, 17, 19, 24, 25, 35, 40, 67–8, 69, 76, 86–9, 117, 141, 148, 151; and law 79–82, 84–5, 109
Legitimation Crisis 7, 8, 17, 31, 44, 79, 87, 89, 122, 127, 142, 149, 151
legitimation crisis 30, 69, 87, 88
Levi–Strauss, C. 113
liberalism 27, 92–3; and genetics 53, 57
lifeworld 17–21, 25, 39, 89–91, 103, 127–30, 89–91, 103, 136, 143, 148, 166; colonisation of 3, 9, 17–21,

35, 50, 53, 56, 58, 62, 69, 81, 82, 85, 88, 91, 98, 99, 101, 103, 116, 118, 126, 134, 137, 148, 154; and genetics 53, 54, 56, 57, 154; rationalisation of 42, 90, 110, 115, 127–30; and system 3, 8–9, 35, 46, 54, 82, 89, 90, 108, 152
linguistics 112, 113, 131, 163
Locke, J. 4, 81,
Luhmann, N. 7, 80, 86, 108, 138, 146, 149, 151–2
Lukács, G. 48, 67, 91–2, 117, 133, 151

Marcuse, H. 5, 48, 49, 73, 136
Marx, K. 12, 16, 49, 62, 67, 68, 76, 77, 91, 98, 99, 117, 121, 132, 133
Marxism 8, 14, 30, 32, 33, 48–50, 62–4, 67, 69, 71, 91–3, 99; Hegelian 29, 48, 67, 91; neo–4, 7, 68, 117; structural 113; Western 91
mass media 23, 67
Mead, G. H. 92, 119
meaning 7, 19, 21, 53, 75, 88, 90, 93–6; and action 3, 21–23, 29, 33–6, 55, 76, 77–8, 107, 134, 142, 161; and hermeneutics 13, 24, 33, 61, 79, 93, 94, 135, 160; and linguistics 112–3, 163–4; loss of 8–9, 20, 74, 81, 82, 91, 101, 103, 108, 130, 133, 137, 145, 148, 149, 152–4; and philosophy 5, 36, 93–5, 105–6, 115–6, 143, 159; and psychoanalysis 16, 108, 123, 161; as validity claim 22, 44, 165–6, 167
metaphysics 5, 39, 91, 110, 111, 112, 135; of presence 115–16
methodological individualism 29
Mill, J. S. 71
modernity 39, 96–100; unfinished project of 97–8, 101, 113, 116
money 18–9, 100–101, 103–4, 118, 134
morality 57, 97, 129; and law 80, 83, 129; post–conventional 109–10
motivation crisis 30

nature 10, 15, 30, 33, 59, 73, 77, 105, 135, 136, 140, 156; second nature 16, 47, 76, 123

Nietzsche, F. 99, 113–14

ontogenesis 139–40

Parson, T. 92, 146
pathologies 9, 36, 101, 102, 113, 114
performative contradiction 66, 104–5
Peirce, C. S. 12, 27, 33, 65, 108, 119–21, 127, 160
phenomenology 50
Philosophical Discourse of Modernity 50, 96–100
philosophy 10, 91, 97, 104, 105–9, 110–12, 113–16, 119–21, 143, 155; analytic 4–6, 50, 79, 93, 94, 111, 157; legal 39, 79, 80, 82, 84, 163; and literature 116; political 37, 112
Piaget, J. 51–2, 113, 139–41
Popper, K. 106, 107
positivism 5, 11, 14, 16, 27, 33, 36–7, 59, 69, 70, 91, 102, 105–9, 111, 113, 135, 136, 156, 159; legal 80–4
post–modernism 96, 98
post–structuralism 112–6
power 3, 35, 43, 67, 69, 89, 90, 96, 116–19, 124, 126, 141; administrative 3, 85; and authority 86–7; and cognitive interests 10, 14–17, 76, 78, 116–17; and communication 49, 51, 56, 65, 85; communicative 23, 85; as steering medium 4, 18, 19, 20, 101, 103, 117–18; will to power 99, 114
pragmatism 33, 44, 50, 108, 119–21
principle of discourse ethics (D) 45, 83
principle of organisation 63, 121–2, 141
principle of universalisation (U) 45, 83
progress 30, 64, 91, 97–8, 100, 130, 139
proletariat 91–2

psychoanalysis 15–6, 30, 33, 48, 49, 50, 68, 71, 108, 113, 122–3, 132, 147, 148, 161, 162
public opinion 3, 4, 23, 38, 124, 127
public relations 127
public sphere 23, 24, 49, 86, 124–7; bourgeois 69, 124–6; literary 125

rationalisation 87
rationalisation of the lifeworld 42, 90, 110, 115, 127–30
Rawls, J. 27–8, 93
reason 20, 25, 26, 40, 43, 45, 50, 74, 75, 85, 96, 97, 99, 100, 101–2, 109, 113, 114, 115, 117, 118, 119, 127, 165; communicative 23–6, 35, 36, 50, 75, 86, 88, 99–100, 102, 107, 109, 114, 118, 124; force of reason alone 66, 159; instrumental 21, 24, 25, 26, 36, 50, 73, 74–5, 76, 88, 99–100, 102, 118, 128, 134
reconstructive science 113, 130–3, 137, 157, 163
reflection, two senses of in *Knowledge and Human Interests* 132
reification 34, 35, 61, 68, 76, 91, 108, 117, 133–5, 151
relativism 61, 62, 112, 121, 159
religion 30, 67, 87, 136
rhetoric 8, 102, 115, 121, 127, 144
rights, human 87, 117, 129; and genetic modification 57; legal 40, 83–5, 141; natural 81–2
rightfulness 44, 129, 165, 167
Rorty, R. 93, 119, 121
Ryle, G. 111, 130

Schutz, A. 89
science 7, 24, 32, 52–3, 58, 65, 70–1, 96, 99, 102, 111, 116, 119–21, 129; cultural and social 7, 10, 13–14, 33–6, 47, 49, 58–62, 77–8, 105–9, 135, 146, 156, 160; emancipatory 10, 14–17, 33–6, 38, 47–8, 61, 123, 135–6, 156, 160; natural 5, 10–14,

16, 24, 33–6, 47, 73, 74–5, 77–8, 105–9, 119, 123, 135–6, 156, 160; philosophy of 10–11, 36, 105–9, 111, 119–21; 135, 159; reconstructive 113, 130–3, 137, 157, 163

scientism 7, 14, 24, 59, 106, 116, 135–7, 156

Searle, J. 6, 72, 115, 143

social action 3, 29, 73, 143, 144

social evolution 6, 31, 40, 52, 63, 64, 106, 109, 113, 121, 122, 127, 130, 132, 137–42, 149, 152, 156; and historical narratives 137

social integration 18, 41, 142–3, 149

society, in the 'narrow sense' 41

sociology 3, 29, 34, 50, 89, 108, 149

speech act 6, 22, 28, 47, 51, 72, 79, 95, 115, 143–4, 164

spirit (*Geist*) 110–11

state 3–4, 23, 63, 99; ancient Greek 38; in ancient civilisations and feudalism 63, 96, 122, 141; in capitalism 6–8, 21, 51, 85, 86, 88, 91, 122, 124, 126, 141–2; and law 23, 39, 84, 122, 141; welfare 51, 88, 93, 126

steering media, non–symbolic 18, 100, 103–4, 116, 117–18

strategic action 3, 18, 23, 73, 144–5

structuralism 112–13, 115, genetic 51–2, 139; post–100, 102, 112–16

Structural Transformation of the Public Sphere 7, 24, 39, 60–71, 79, 86, 124–7

system 3, 4, 7, 9, 36, 40–2, 53–4, 56, 69, 100–101, 103–4, 122, 134, 138–9, 143, 145–6; crisis 30–1; law as 79–82, 84–5, 122, 148–9, 149–54; and lifeworld 3, 8, 17, 17–21, 35, 54, 89–91, 108, 126, 148, 154

systematically distorted communication 43, 49, 56, 65, 69, 134, 145, 147–8,

system integration 18, 139, 142, 148–9

systems theory 7, 29–31, 40–2, 69, 80, 86–7, 89, 103, 108, 116, 138, 146, 148, 149–54

technology 7, 10, 24, 33, 47, 62, 74–5, 76–7, 99, 128, 129, 136, 138; genetic 52–5, 58

Theory of Communicative Action 8, 17, 21, 24, 38, 50, 79, 81, 82, 92, 108, 116, 127, 146, 157

traditional theory 32–4

transcendental argument 11, 27, 97, 132, 154–7

truth 23, 32, 42 157–62, 112, 119; consensus theory 159, 160; correspondence theory 32, 116, 157, 160; discourse theory 43, 110, 115, 158–9; and emancipatory science 132, 159, 161; and pragmatism 120–1; as validity claim 27, 35, 44, 94, 104, 129, 157, 165, 167; and the will to power 114

truthfulness 42, 44, 66, 118–9, 162–3, 165, 166, 167

universal pragmatics 6, 17, 22, 27, 28, 35, 42, 44, 47, 61, 65, 79, 89, 93, 95, 131, 142, 144, 163–6, 167

validity claim 27, 28, 35, 42, 44, 73, 90, 121, 129, 157, 162, 165–6, 167

Weber, M. 3, 8, 9, 29, 49, 74, 86, 92, 128–9, 151

welfare state 51, 88, 93, 126

Wittgenstein, L. 5, 26, 95, 111

Young Hegelians 5, 77, 98